The CREATIVE Echo Chamber

The CREATIVE Echo Chamber

Contemporary Music Production in Kingston, Jamaica

Dennis O. Howard

IAN RANDLE PUBLISHERS
Kingston • Miami

First published in Jamaica, 2016 by
Ian Randle Publishers
16 Herb McKenley Drive
Box 686
Kingston 6
www.ianrandlepublishers.com

© Dennis O. Howard

ISBN 978-976-637-894-3

National Library of Jamaica Cataloguing-In-Publication Data

Howard, Dennis

The creative echo chamber : contemporary music production in Kingston, Jamaica / Dennis Howard.

pages ; cm.

ISBN 978-976-637-894-3 (pbk)

1. Sound recording industry – Jamaica   2. Music trade – Jamaica

I.   Title

780   dc 23

All rights reserved. No part of this publication may be reproduced, stored in a retrieval system or transmitted in any form or by any means electronic, photocopying, recording or otherwise, without the prior permission of the publisher and author.

Cover and Book Design by Ian Randle Publishers

Printed and Bound in the United States of America

Contents

List of Figures /viii

List of Tables /ix

Foreword /xi

Acknowledgements /xiii

Introduction /xv

Acronyms and Abbreviations /xxxv

1. **Background to the Business in Jamaica** /1
    Weak Framework
    The Issue of Copyright
    The Role of Technology
    Central Questions
    Cultural Production
    Organisational Structure

2. **Surveying the Soundscapes:**
   Writing on the Jamaican Music Scene /14
    Biographies
    Intraorganisational Research
    Value Chain Dynamics
    The Popular Music Industry Model
    Traditional Music Industry Value Chain
    Musical Networks Value Chain
    Michael Witter's Circular Income Flow
    Interorganisational Research
       Jamaican Music Industry
       The Structure of the Recording Industry
       Technology and Popular Music
       Economic and Cultural Geography
       Copyright: A Cultural Perspective
    Cultural Studies Perspective
    Dub Version

3. **Making Popular Music in the Creative Echo Chamber** /37
    Periods of Cultural Production
    Folk Culture (Pre 1950s–56)
    Period of Appropriation (1957–60)
    Innovation (1961–69)
    Internationalisation (1970–80)
    Neoinnovation (1981–2000)
    Crossing over by Collaboration
    Global Interaction: 2001–Present
    Concluding Thoughts

4. **Value Chain Dynamics in the Creative Echo Chamber** /72
    Kingston: Beat City, the Creative Echo Chamber
    Value Chain Dynamics in the Recorded Music Industry
        Primary Activities
        Support Activities
    Kingston Value Chain
    Voicing/Sound System Income Stream
    Recording /Distribution Income Stream
    Live Performance Income Stream
    Organisational Structure
    Sound Systems in the Value Chain
    Musicians and their role in the Value Chain
    Dub Plate Culture in the Value Chain
    Manufacturing and Distribution in the Value Chain
    The Multiple-Simultaneity Modes of Production Model
    Conclusion

5. **Too Much Mix Up Mix Up: Copyrighting Culture** /110
    What is Copyright?
    Copyright within Kingston's Creative Echo Chamber
    Who Owns the Music?
    The Performing Rights Society
    Copyright Dynamics in The Creative Echo Chamber
    Creative Commune
    The Open Domain
    Multiple Simultaneity Production Model (Copyrighting Culture)

      A Call to Action on the 1993 Copyright Act
      Home-grown Societies
      National Consolidation or International Coercion?
      In the Interest of 'Babylon System'
      Copyright Extension 2015 – Legislative Overreach
      Literary Property and the Author
      The Internet and Copyright
      Conclusion

6. Tek-no-li-gy Processing: Reshaping the Soundscape /147

      Punching for Recognition of the Jukebox Culture in Jamaica
      Sociocultural Hybridity and Imperial Hegemony
      From Ghetto Laboratories in the Creative Echo Chamber
          to the Technosphere
      Version Galore
      The King at the Control
      A Likkle a Dis an a Likkle a Dat (The Remix Culture)
      The Tom Tom Club Mash up: A Case Study
      Outro

7. Mastering our Fate: Jah Jah Children Them a Moving Up /176

      Music for Days and Extra Days
      Cultural Production Periods
      Value Chain
      Future Research Initiatives
      Recommendations
      Las Lick

References /185

Index /199

List of Figures

Fig. 2.1	Organisation of the Pop Music Industry	/19
Fig. 2.2	The Traditional Music Value Chain	/21
Fig. 2.3	Musical Networks	/24
Fig. 2.4	Circular Flow of income in the Jamaican Music Industry	/25
Fig. 3.1	The famous Forrester's Hall, North Street, Kingston	/45
Fig. 3.2	Shang-Hi Solophonic Sound System at the Jazz Hut, West Kingston	/46
Fig. 3.3	Treasure Isle Studio, Bond Street, western Kingston	/49
Fig. 4.1	'Beat Street' Orange Street, downtown Kingston	/72
Fig. 4.2	Value Chain Analysis by Michael Porter	/78
Fig. 4.3	Kingston Music Industry Value Chain	/80
Fig. 4.4	Kingston's Music Industry Organisational Chart	/86
Fig 6.1	Jukeboxes at a bar in east Kingston	/152

List of Tables

Table 4.1 Feeder Sound Systems   /101

Table 5.1 Jamaican R&B/Pop Cover Classics   /115

Table 5.2 Jamaican Originals and Their Local Covers   /125

Table 5.3 National Collecting Agencies   /131

Table 5.4 Featured Artist – Digital Performance Royalties, 2012–15   /135

Foreword

The name of the book – *The Creative Echo Chamber* – is a good one because the echo produces good vibrations. In the early days of musicians like Tubby, we began creating the music of the creative echo chamber. We used to take pieces from TV like the theme song of the movie Kojak and work it into a rhythm. That was where some of my music came from, and we called it 'Lee Scratch Perry Presents'. It was like doing a movie, an international movie presentation of the music. Even then I was doing dancehall things with Tubby. It's a different dancehall going on now.

The music of that time was more spiritual and not just for dancing… teaching, meditation, godliness…it was like a map people can follow… grow up the children to follow and usually included something that involved Garvey, Rastafari and things like that. A part of it was to teach the culture of Rastafari. We the people wanted to get away from government and really didn't want to mix up with them…it was our philosophy that we live our lives and they live theirs. We used to talk about ganja as we believed ganja should release a long time before.

Songs from that creative period included 'Jah Live', 'Man to Man', and 'Small Axe' – these are the songs I write for Bob Marley when he asked me to lend him a hand. That was how we used to help each other.

That's how the music started. We started to build a musical nation to represent the spiritual vibration in Jamaica. We put it together and then we build Jamaica with a special rhythm and blessing to make the thing that was impossible, possible. That's what we were trying to do. We were given that energy and power to lead a certain number of people in the community to make the force of unity stronger. The important combination that we have here is the music – some can play it and some can sing it.

We have the key – a master key which must be from the master who made the lock. The master who made the master lock gave us a master key and showed us how to summon the master so we could make music representing God…my music must be representing God.

In terms of the business side of the music, from dem [artists] come into your studio, you have to make sure that you have some money, because they would not be coming to you unless you have some money

From the moment those artists come to meet you, you start to pay them because of problems at home, problems in the pocket. So, all those money that you give them is free money? So you shouldn't take it back or try to get back any of it? When you try to get it back dem say is rip you rip dem off.

The book – *The Creative Echo Chamber* – is a good idea. Tell the people the truth, tell the people what you know. Don't put it in your pocket…you share with other people, you don't put it [your knowledge] in your pocket and hide it. Once you are sharing the truth, it will reach everywhere because then the people will hear about it and another one will say, 'you want to hear something, I was reading a book and I know exactly how the Jamaican music started and developed'. And, finally, the word go out and the world know and the book come out of the dark to say something that no other book says.

The final word about the book is that it's a very good idea for you to search in the dark and find the truth and when you find the truth in the dark you bring the truth into the light and expose it to the people. That makes you a like marvel or a genius. History – you find the real history, the Black Ark Miracle – not even me did think about it – and it appear just like dat. That's why the word come like that – a it dat – it was somewhere in your head.

You were there from long time to see the truth, so now you are here to write a book about it. That's how God's work appear and talk to the people and you hear the word and say 'it's the living truth': that's the way God operates.

Lee "Scratch" Perry

Acknowledgements

This project could not have been a reality without the support, assistance and encouragement of so many people. Professor Mike Alleyne your contribution has been tremendous; along our journey I have discovered a colleague, a kindred sprit and a friend for life. To James Howard and Cynthia Thompson thanks for life and making my childhood such an amazing experience. To Markeits Laing, you always believed in me; I thank you for that endorsement. Your support and encouragement was invaluable. To the indefatigable Professor Carolyn Cooper, your guidance, academic brilliance and support will never be forgotten. Your trailblazing efforts in the Institute of Caribbean Studies are a remarkable achievement.

Professor Claudette Williams, thanks for caring and massive support. Clinton Hutton, special thanks for your invaluable input and guidance and for being a friend and colleague. Special thanks to my extended academic circle of brilliant scholars who together made such an important contribution to the project through encouragement, sending of relevant material and/or direct feedback: Jason Toynbee, Sonjah Stanley Niaah, Karen Carpenter, Patrik, Wikstrom, Christopher Charles, Louis Chude-Sokei, Christopher "the Balla" Jones and Bennie Watson. To the many musicians, producers and industry folks who have mentored and supported my forays into the entertainment business – Sly Dunbar, Michael Bennett, Paul Henton, Ralston Barrett, Ossie Harvey, Errol Wonder, Alvin Campbell, Winston "Niney" Holness, Bunny Lee, Lee "Scratch" Perry, Alton Ellis, Steven Stanley, Joel Chin, Sangie Davis, Denroy Morgan, Elaine Valentine, Ken Boothe, Stranger Cole, John Marshall, Trevor Elliott, John Wakeling, Morgan Heritage, Donovan Germaine, Roy Francis, Jason Lee and Clyde Mckenzie – you were instrumental in many ways. To my extended family of men who nurtured me from day one – Winston "Merrow" Merricks, Dorian "Nut" Grey, Tony Laing, Raymond Sharpe, Rex, Wycliffe Bennett, Dermott Hussey, Herbie Miller, Hope Howard, Charles Lewin, Newton James, Tomlin Ellis, Winston Williams and Donat Bucknor – and the women in my life – Pauline Scott Blair, Denise Dennis, Kaye Mundle, Athlene Howard, Chloe Webb, Novlette Howard, Leonie Edwards, Marjorie Campbell, Novia Howard, Nicola Howard, Janice Howard, Tashan Hendricks, Simone Guy, Dr. Maxine Hamilton and Barbara Johnson – I am truly indebted. A special thanks and love for Maxine McDonough who was a pillar of strength and helped to shape this project and my dissertation.

Introduction

The primary focus of this book is to examine the Jamaican music business from its inception in the early 1950s to ascertain the economic, social, legal and international structures which affected its development. This is critical to an understanding of why the recorded music business in Kingston, Jamaica, is unique, with no parallel anywhere else in the world. Jamaican popular music, through its various genres of ska, rocksteady, reggae, dub and dancehall, is not equalled in terms of output per capita. When one considers the size of the island and its geopolitical reality, it is amazing that it has created so much music and has had such an impressive influence on world popular culture.

The importance of the Jamaican music business is well documented in terms of its economic value and its influence in creating genres that have been globally accepted and appropriated by many cultures. Bob Marley is one of the biggest global stars, a fact that is never addressed sufficiently due to the myopic North Atlantic perspective that the world revolves around North America, Europe and its white, postcolonial outposts, including Australia and New Zealand. The fact is Marley and his music is known on virtually every continent, yet, the dominant canons of popular music epistemology have placed Marley at the periphery,[1] while placing white American and British popular artists at the pinnacle of pop superstardom.

Kingston, the creative city of Jamaica, has been recognized as a major production centre for popular music (Power and Hallencruetz 2002). Yet, Jamaica has not sufficiently benefited economically from its impressive creative output. Several reasons have been proposed for this situation, including the lack of effective copyright legislation and intellectual property management regime (Power and Hallencruetz 2002; Hebdige 2000). The fragmented nature of the production firms, which supplied the bulk of the music, is another factor that has retarded the economic growth of the business. This is an area of critical research that needs some attention as comparatively little work has been completed in this regard.

The literature on Jamaican music is devoid, for the most part, of material that deals with sound systems, venues, producers, musicians, media retailers and audiences in an integrated fashion. Disciplines such as economic geography, political economy and cultural studies, which look at the structure of the music business, are critical to an understanding of the structure of the recording industry in Jamaica. The majority of research on Jamaican music production has centred on personalities, analyses of lyrical content, sexuality, gender and historiographies.

What accounts for the dynamic nature of popular music production in Kingston, despite its deviation from the North Atlantic model of cultural production and distribution? To my mind, it can only be explained by the social, legal and economic milieu which existed in the colonial and postcolonial periods during which it was produced and which led to the creation of modes of production that were counter to the models in the developed world while simultaneously employing Anglo-American modes of production to enter and engage in the international music industry. While the deficiencies of the model have had a debilitating effect on the development of the domestic industry, Jamaican music industry personnel have also managed to create new business models and modes of creativity based on the creative imagination centred on non-Western cosmology, hybrid construction and hegemonic and counterhegemonic ripples that have had significant impact on the global recording industry.

Methodology: A Personal Journey

What, then, are my credentials? What gives me the right to declare myself an insider? My journey in the music industry started at an early age. I remember being carried to dances by my father, a popular dance promoter and part-time sound system selector. Some of the legendary dances my father promoted used foundation sound systems such as Coxsone Downbeat, Duke Reid the Mighty Trojan and the Voice of the People Prince Buster. I first saw Count Ossie and the Mystic Revelation of Rastafari perform in 1972 at a dance that my father promoted in Montego Bay at the Intercontinental Beach. The featured sound systems were Fox Hi Fi and Tipper Tone with Big Youth, pioneer deejay, as the selector.

My father, James 'Jimmy Solo' Howard, ran a betting shop and bar in western Kingston on Charles Street between Pink Lane and Oxford Street. Just one street away to the west was Bond Street, where the legendary Treasure Isles was located at the corner of Charles Street. I have vivid memories of many potential singers waiting for an audition with Duke Reid.

During the sometimes long wait, these singers, mainly groups, practised their harmonies and melodies. It was a very strenuous experience for many of the aspirants, as Reid did not accept many people on any given day. Many had to come innumerable times before being accepted by Reid, and many, after years of trying, never gained acceptance.

Many of these 'talents' came to my father's bar, after being rejected, to drown their sorrows. I remember the vocal group, the Paragons with John Holt, as regulars on the corner of Bond Street and Charles Street on the side adjacent to the studio. Pioneer and father of toasting, Hugh Roy, was also a regular on the corner. The imposing figure of Duke Reid, armed with his shotgun and his revolver strapped to his leg in a gun belt western style, would be invariably positioned in front of his liquor store, which was at the front of the building that housed the studio.

By the '70s, my father's business had been moved to Rose Lane and was renamed the Jazz Hut. By 1972, he had collaborated with his boyhood friend to form a sound system called Shanghai Solophonic and this is where my life as a selector began. On weekends, while still in high school, I became one of the resident selectors at the Jazz Hut. The main selectors would not allow me to play at engagements outside of the Jazz Hut. My study of popular music had begun in earnest. By reading linear notes, record and album credits, I learnt more about some of the people whom I had seen in the area; people like Ken Boothe, Stranger Cole and Brent Dowe who visited the Jazz Hut on a regular basis to drink and smoke weed.

I was playing music on weekends and occasionally hanging out in various record shops in downtown Kingston, tagging along with my father while he bought records for the sound system. I recall passing the likes of Prince Buster and Lee 'Scratch' Perry while on my way to my father's bar on Charles Street. I also saw, on a regular basis, Derrick Harriott, the Wailers and Gregory Isaacs; I heard their music on the radio, jukeboxes and sound systems and was soon able to identify them with their music. This was the beginning of a lifelong career which would be built on the marvel that is Jamaican music.

My introduction to radio was at the Jamaica Broadcasting Corporation (JBC), now Television Jamaica (TVJ) where I worked as a technical operator for five years. I worked with some of the top radio deejays including Errol

Thompson, Charles Lewin, Winston Williams and Barry Gordon. I interfaced with many artists and was instrumental in breaking many of the top names in reggae and early dancehall, including Jr. Reid, Half Pint, Robert Ffrench, Eek-a-Mouse and Yellowman. During this period, I also frequented Dynamic Studio, Channel One and King Jammy, learning as much as I could about production and studio engineering. And, I was constantly at sessions and dances all over Kingston playing sound system or attending with my father.

While working on radio and playing the sound system, I came up with the idea of establishing a publicity company targeted at the music industry. An idea ahead of its time, in Jamaica. It was resisted by industry personnel, some of whom did not know what a bio was or that you could get airplay by other means than payola. My first clients were Lassana Bandele, Mixing Lab and Tappa records. Following that, in 1990, when Irie FM, the first 24-hour reggae station was formed, I became programme manager and was the deejay for the afternoon slot. This was a history-making period. Irie FM took the number one slot in Jamaican radio just a few months after its inception, with my afternoon show beating veterans like Barry Gordon and Winston Williams who had ruled the airwaves before Irie FM.

My life as a record producer began during this period and I recorded many of the top artists of that time including Beenie Man, Luciano, Garnet Silk, Tony Rebel, Bounty Killer and Tanya Stevens. In addition to producing, I began to manage artists including Anthony Red Rose, Tanya Stevens, Goofy and Peter Lloyd. My publicity and artist development work unearthed Morgan Heritage, Stevie Face, Abijah and Natty King. I have also worked as an entertainment analyst on radio and television and was a columnist on entertainment at the *Jamaica Observer* for over six years. My work continues in the recording industry as a consultant and an adjunct lecturer, at various tertiary level institutions. I have experienced, first hand, many of the cultural periods of production and have contributed to the development of the industry.

By engaging in a self-narrative utilizing the auto-ethnography methodology, I was able to bring to light data and information from an insider's perspective. Collecting data through this method was essential to the 'the auto ethno continuum' focus of the study. While working in the different fields of entertainment and broadcasting, I had engaged in participant observation at various points especially when I wrote for a local newspaper and various magazines. Participant observation, again, was used in data collection in the study both for reinforcement of prior knowledge, due to my insider status, and also to glean new information and insight into the phenomenon under study. Richard Johnson et al. (2004) argue, 'an explicit ethics of participation should be embedded in ethnographic research because all ethnography involves some participation by those whom we study' (215).

Other sources of information included trade and music magazines, artist biographies, and dance and concert posters, album liner notes, jukebox playlists and album credits. Recordings of Jamaican music of all genres and periods were a very important source of data; so, too, were several album covers and photographs. Listening to the music that I was writing about was very stimulating, taking me back in time to many events that were stored in the recesses of my memory. The music, as a data source, made the research come alive in unimaginable ways which would not have been possible for a researcher with no insider status or who was not a part of the group being studied.

Heewon Chang (2008) notes, 'auto-ethnography values your personal memory, whereas ethnography relies on informants' personal memory and ethnographers' recent memory of what they observed and heard in the field.' While most ethnographers avoid including their personal memories with those collected in the field, the auto-ethnographer acknowledges personal memories as primary data (71) so the playing of records, audio and videocassettes provided an avenue through which to explore and revisit events, personnel and personal memories of my involvement in the Jamaican music industry. In this sense, the audio-visual material represents a sort of cultural artefact. Chang, again, notes that cultural artefacts are 'objects produced by members of the society that explicitly or implicitly manifest societal norms and values.' Cultural artefacts, such as long-playing vinyl records (LP), eight tracks and audiocassettes, all have emotional, ceremonial and utility value in the lives of people, 'by identifying artefacts important to your life, you will be able to examine what constitutes your primary cultures' (80).

The exercise of playing records from my vast collection, which represents all genres of Jamaican music, cassettes of my radio shows on JBC, Irie FM, KLAS FM and sound system play outs, provided not only recall of events, people and music but also energised the research process in a way that made it feel like a living organism. It also helped to stimulate theoretical insights through the unique aesthetic of the music, which did not seem to happen without the presence of a cultural insider as myself, who has been immersed in the art form on so many levels. It seems I had what Peter Tosh described as *Reggaemylitis*:

> Reggaemylitis, I say
> It's reggaemylitis, I say
> You only catch it one way
> It's reggaemylitis, what I say
> Sometimes your temperature
> It really gets higher
> And the music
> Sets your soul on fire[2]

The listening process was not only as important as the other methods of data collection; it added another dimension, which, while not as easily measureable as the other methods, certainly gave potency and authenticity to the research initiative.

The use of photographs, music videos and VHS cassettes of dances and concerts were also very significant in bringing forth the many narratives, which constitute this research project. Heewon Chang (2008) observes, 'power of visualisation as a communication tool is enhanced by the simplicity and succinctness of a visual image into which complex texts are condensed and captured' (81). One can add to this important observation the fact that these visual cues are open to many semiotic interpretations which depends on the position of the interpreters in terms of social orientation, insider/outsider status, interest and agenda. This allows these texts to be interrogated and analysed in new and interesting ways not open to more quantitative inquiries.

My interpretations were influenced by my own experience in the music business, as record producer, publicist, artist-manager and radio personality. This was accentuated by the established literature in the area and the circuit of culture conceptual framework that informed the writing of the book. In many instances, the analysis deviated radically from the established canons of Jamaican music production and history but it reinforced established historiographies, theoretical notions and perspectives. My own position, experience and the use of a new theoretical lens brought to the analysis a fresh perspective, albeit coloured by my own biases, perceptions, cultural background and influences. An insider's perspective of the major players in the Jamaican music business, past and present, including many of the pioneers of the business embracing categories such as recording artists, engineers, producers, sound system owners, selectors/live deejays, lawyer-managers, booking agents, radio deejays, radio programme managers, musicians and representatives, label bosses and production house owners provided important insights into the evolution of the industry.

Theoretical Considerations

For the purpose of this inquiry, I have taken a multidisciplinary approach and have drawn from areas such as cultural studies, popular music studies, soundscape studies and ethnomusicology. Disparate disciplines find a comfortable fit within this initiative, including political economy, postcolonial theory, hegemony, technological culture, which are just some of the framework that this work draws on. This facilitates the proposal on my part of offering a model to augment the established theoretical lens utilized in this book. Let's now look at this perspective that to my mind is most significant to this inquiry. This theoretical device is the model I call the *creative echo chamber*. Rooted in ethnomusicology and cultural studies, the *creative echo chamber*, in essence, is an Ethno-model that elucidates and theorizes on the mechanisms which are responsible for the unique, creative process of the Jamaican recording industry, which is embedded in an Afro-Caribbean aesthetic. It explains the motivations, the methods, devices and techniques employed by 'symbol creators'[3] within the creative space of Kingston – the creative cauldron. The *creative echo chamber* is, simultaneously, physical space, discrete methodologies, mythologies and intangible mechanisms, which are responsible for the 'cross rhythms'[4] of Caribbean culture. This has created a 'diaspora-centric' reality that the African diaspora represents a 'global space', an international network that accounts for the primary role of Africa but also the indispensible work of the diaspora and its people who were transported to 'New Worlds' by force.

The *creative echo chamber* can be articulated through three distinctive dimensions; these are *Geospatiality*, *Repetition* and *Communality*.

Geospatiality

Geospatiality explains the notion of the Jamaican music process as a creature of the Black Atlantic. Jamaican sonic, visual and literary culture take place in what can be called the *creative cauldron*, this is the physical space locating the studios, rehearsal rooms, dub plate studios, sound systems, the art studio, the canvas of street walls, within certain geographical creative clusters, where the business deals were played out and ideas are transformed to art. Creative spaces such as Orange Street, Maxfield Town, Trench Town, Warika Hill, Big Yard and Robert Crescent,[5] and the Eastwood cluster which served and continues to serve as incubators for symbol creators. In the decades of the 1960s and 1970s, Kingston's *creative cauldron* was the cradle for hybridity, syncretism, 'decentring orthodoxies', creolisation and the destabilisation of the status quo of European melodies trumping African rhythms and the search for that 'viable organic third dimension'.[6] But, there are also the spatiotemporally located diaspora communities of London, Toronto and New York, which in turn, had their own creative clusters, studios, dubplate studios,[7] sound systems and rehearsal rooms. At the foundation of this model is the African continent from which sprung the Black Atlantic movement of forced removal, diaspora movements and repatriation invocations. We then move to the Caribbean and mainland cities such as New York and Miami where again the influence on Kingston is significant in influencing the creative process and cultural production. Musical styles coming out of Trinidad and Tobago, Haiti and Cuba have helped shaped the Jamaican music scene. This syncretic movement between the various islands 'suspended in a soup of signs'[8] have served the region well as Antonio Benitez-Rojo (1996) submits:

> ...within the sociocultural fluidity that the Caribbean archipelago presents, within its historiographic turbulence and its ethnological and linguistic clamour, within its generalized instability of vertigo and hurricane, one can sense the features of an island that 'repeats' itself, unfolding and bifurcating until it reaches all the seas and lands of the earth, while at the same time it inspires multidisciplinary maps of unexpected designs (3).

There are many examples of this phenomenon in action. One can easily note the influence of calypso on Jamaican mento. Cuban son, bolero and Haitian rara and merengue have all played a significant role in the formation of Jamaican genres such as ska and even reggae. Similarly, Jamaican dancehall gave rise to soca and reggaeton and reggae-influenced Barbadian spouge. The cross-fertilisation in the exchanges between metropolises such as New York, London, Birmingham and Miami has resulted in some amazing musical bonding resulting in hip hop, grime, reggae, ska, garage, drum and bass, lovers rock, dub step and rocksteady, and the development of a cultural mosaic whose paternity is sometimes difficult to unravel. In essence, *Geospatiality* operates within a borderless creative cauldron which stretches across the Black Atlantic and electronic. It has facilitated what Orlando Patterson (1994, 6) describes as 'the development of regional cosmos' a direct consequence of the complex global cultural interaction that presents itself within the geospatial dimension of the *creative echo chamber*. According to Patterson, a regional cosmos:

> ...is best conceived of a system of flows between a metropolitan centre and a set of politically independent satellite countries within what the urban sociologist Saskia Sassen calls a 'transnational space'. People, wealth, ideas and cultural patterns move in both direction influencing both the metropolitan centre as well as the peripheral areas, although asymmetrically (6).

Patterson identifies the interaction of the Caribbean and the eastern seaboard of the United States as the *West Atlantic regional cosmos*. This regional cosmos has played a significant role in the germination/development of a Jamaican musical aesthetic and as a distinctive transnational society that operates freely within the West Atlantic cosmos and the Black Atlantic region of Europe. Patterson notes that a critical facet of the exchange between what he calls the cosmopolis and the West Atlantic periphery is in the intellectual realm. He makes a powerful observation when he states:

> The special contribution of West Indian intellectualism in the cosmopolitan context will be a transference of its distinctive strategy of aggressive engagement with the dominant tradition of neo-European civilisation – a strategy that at its worst, generates enormous identity crises and self-destructive emotional and physical violence, but at the same time, and at its best, is the crucible for the explosively competitive syncretism that finds expression in Rastafarianism and *voudon*, reggae and merengue, and negritude, magical realism, *omeros*, and the self-loathing genius of V.S. Naipaul (9).

Repetition

James Snead (1981) notes that:

> Culture as a reservoir of inexhaustible novelty is unthinkable. Therefore, repetition, first of all, would have to creep into the dimension of culture just as it would have to creep into that of language and signification because of the finite supply of elementary units and the need for recognition in human understanding (146).

However, Richard Middleton (1996, 1) observes that 'repetition without renewal is also a kind of death', so in music 'the art of iteration', regeneration and replenishment which ultimately leads to new manifestations and interpretations are critical. As methodology, the *creative echo chamber* represents the cyclical and repetitive devices of the creative project within the borderless *creative cauldrons*. Echoes reverberate to create new forms and also to reinforce old forms. It is through *repetition* that musical styles, idioms and practices are reinforced and passed on to succeeding generations through echoes from Africa, reverberating across the Black Atlantic continuum to the Caribbean, all the way to the North Atlantic and back to the African continent. More than anywhere else, Kingston, through the *creative echo chamber*, has been able to create a significant number of genres, each one feeding off the one before it to create new forms. This is more than methodology; it is a philosophical and epistemological understanding of creation and a reinterpretation of aural text composition within a Black Atlantic continuum. The echoes of the creative chamber sustain, create, recreate, reinforce and preserve the traditions, practices and innovations of the Kingston creative collectives. These are achieved through various practices and devices, in the music making production techniques developed within the *creative cauldron*. A critical example of the process is the creation of versioning and the studio techniques that created dub and the trademark ostinatos of reggae. Julian Henriques (2011) states that these innovations 'provide striking examples of both the creative and intensifying powers of repeating, reiterating and recursive practices' (165).

The *creative echo chamber* model has facilitated the destabilisation of orthodox Western creative processes to create texts, musical practices and idioms which in turn through the process of repetition, copying and intensification, create new text, musical practices and idioms, always drawing on the past, present and future for styles, practice, traditions, stories and performativity. Intensification is the process of replication that results in the development of new styles and idioms, over time, as a by-product of the practice. Through *repetition* and the trope of *intensification* within the creative cauldron, the important process of *hyper-creativity* becomes a phenomenon of the *creative echo chamber*. According to Henriques (2011), 'this creative technique of making something different, allowing a becoming of difference, or simply to 'try a ting', as would be said, is at the heart of the Jamaican sensibility' (167). Circularity is an essential component of Jamaican cosmology; as Mervyn Alleyne (1988) suggests, 'the circle is central to the conceptual framework of the Jamaican worldview…the corpus of dancers move in a circle (as we have seen) and the gyrating hips of the individual dancer carve a circular pattern' (160–61).

Hypercreativity is a phenomenon that presents itself in the form of periods of intense and prolonged cultural production which is incongruent with the natural capacity of the music ecosystem in a particular music scene. In the 1960s and '70s, Kingston had the record for producing, recoding and manufacturing the most records per capita than anywhere else. Lyric compositions, singles and albums were being produced at an unbelievable rate not matched in any other recording industry.

Dick Hebdige (1987) sees repetition as an important aspect of Afro-Caribbean music. Disagreeing with Western Eurocentric notions, he sees repetition as 'the basis of all rhythm and rhythm is at the core of life' (15). The *creative echo chamber* is based on a democratic principle of what Hebdige calls invoking to evoke, he continues:

> …just like a rhythm or a melody which is brought in from another source in a record or in a live performance of a piece of music…it implies that no one has the final say. Everyone has a chance to make a contribution. And no one's version is treated as holy writ (14).

The process of 'circular causality' becomes the critical component of this iterative and recursive model. It facilitates the development of a pop aesthetic and production modality within the creative cauldron of Kingston through repetition, inversion, pastiche, synthesis and genericism. As Keith Negus (1996) notes:

Musical genres do not fill eras, nor do they continue neatly along the path of progressive development – being born, maturing and then dying. They arise out of and are actively made through dialogic – or perhaps polylogical movements through time but also space (163).

Julian Henriques (2011) also sheds light on the importance of repetition in the Jamaican music production ecosystem when he states that:

It offers an analysis based on movement and process, that is, the intensities, energies and dynamics, as well as the static structures. Another is that it allows for an emphasis on auditory phenomena, characterised by their particularities and relationships, as well as on visual phenomena. Furthermore, it allows for an understanding of identity, continuity and the construction of phenomena in terms of difference variation and propagation, as well as similitude, consistency and being (140).

Repetition is not a device for continuity for the sake of continuity; it is, as we have said before, for the regeneration and creation of something new but something that has its genesis rooted in the repeated patterns of the African musical traditions of the never ending movements. Peter Van Der Merwe (1989) reminds us that as it relates to musical traditions, 'the matrix of pre-ordained end seems to be a fairly recent and sophisticated development. The natural musical form is the repeated cycle' (107). However, through repetition new forms are created, which is central to the idea of the *creative echo chamber*. Again, Van Der Merwe suggests:

African repetition is in fact, virtually always subtle variation…they consist only of a slightly changed rhythm, an altered note, a discrete ornament, and so on. It is not the boldness of the variations that is admired, but their *rightness* (107).

Variation in the cycle is critical as it facilitates one aspect of the continuing development of the matrix; the cycle is adjusted, edited, compared and extended. These result in *hypercreativity*; as Van der Merwe declares, 'the cycle was made to come to a stop. It no longer repeated itself. The independent movement had been born' (108).

Communality

Communality is the final facet of the *creative echo chamber* continuum, it is one that runs counter to Western philosophical tradition of the individual creative genius and favours an Afrocentric modality based on community, the free flow of ideas and expression devoid of individual notions of ownership. It is this communal ethos that provides the systems of mentorship, apprenticeship, personal development and knowledge transfer that facilitated the *hypercreativity* that is the hallmark of the Kingston *creative cauldron* through devices such as genericism, pastiche and synthesis which were at the foundation of genre development in the Kingston music scene. The creative process of the Jamaican music scene was an entirely communal phenomenon. Olive Lewin (1974) reminds us:

> in all phases of life in the traditional community, there is a oneness, not only with the whole universe because we are all linked by the same creative sprit; not only in the community where each person's problem become the problem of the whole community with every member contributing to the solution through music, through cooking through helping to prepare the setting…but also through the 'oneness' of the individual.

Kingston's music scene has always been and continues to be a community of likeminded participants freely sharing ideas, styles, 'riddims', records, lyrics, and production techniques with no notions of individual ownership through intellectual property or any other forms of individual ownership. This however, has created numerous problems and obstacles for music stakeholders when interface with the Anglo American recorded music and copyright industries is initiated. I contend that the music scene in Jamaica benefited from the communal nature of the creative music-making processes within the *creative cauldron*. Alleyne (1968) and Erna Brodber (1975) both emphasised the concept of collectivity as a central component of the social organisation of Jamaican society. According to Alleyne (1968), 'this notion of collectivity is at the basis of the kinship, respect shown to elders, and the ready acceptance of destitute children into the home of relatives or other members of the community' (158). This observation is critical in understanding how the music community operated from the inception to the present. In recent decades, that community spirit has been eroded due to the adoption of Anglo American music business practices, such as copyright, rights management and notions of individualism surrounding stardom and ambitions of individual financial success. Kinship and respect have guided the music scene with musicians, vocalists, engineers and producers working within a community framework to facilitate the amazing creative output that the scene has achieved. Young artists are adopted by established stars and are nurtured until they, too, get their break. This in the absence of established structures for the organised development of new talent due to the lack of record companies, collective management right organisation, and established linkages with media to expose talent.

This apprenticeship structure was critical and was extended through the sound system organisational structure which also had apprentices in their personnel; up-and-coming artists and selectors/deejays were a staple on all the top sound systems for a very long period. This provided a vehicle for artist development and mentorship 'learning the ropes and paying your dues', the honing of skills in anticipation of the 'big buss'. The conceptual framework of *Communality* reinforces notions of Kingston being an organic creative city where creativity is not encouraged through local and national official intervention but a movement that develops out of the belly of a particular Jamaican citizen. These are poor, mainly black and some Chinese, urban dwellers who find themselves at the periphery of the society, unrecognised and having no future in a society that made no provision for upward mobility into a middle-class status or even some semblance of modest living within an working class structure. Rex Nettelford (1995) observes that:

> Centuries of marginalisation will have placed him on the periphery of existence, taunting him to great expense of energy in a bid to enter a 'mainstream" not of his making, rather than attributing to him, as human being, the capacity for participating in the determination of that mainstream (80).

This organic creative city is not predicated on economic success and aggrandisement but is rooted in a deeper process of liberation, mental slavery distraction, a 'battle for space' and a process of becoming. This achieved through what Nettleford (1995) calls the power of the creative imagination and intellect:

> In the Caribbean, mind and imagination – creative intellect and artistic creation – have been major ingredients in the Caribbean's battle for

space in the first place and in the other, in the region's effort to 're-integrate' self and society into an organic totality by the harmonisation of inner and outer space. We in the Caribbean have not built pyramids, pillars, cathedrals, amphitheatres, opera houses etc. that are the wonders of the world, but we have more creative artists per square inch than probably good for us, in addition we have created and are creating mental structures which are intended to be the basis of that self confidence, that sense of place, purpose and power without which there can be no integration of inner and outer space. Music, dance, religious expression, language, literature, appropriate designs for social living are the structural products of the Caribbean creative impulse (83).

The Political Economy of Black Music: A Structure of Stealing

Jamaican music production has to be positioned within the context of the international exploitation of culture which is twofold; on the one hand, there is race; on the other, the realities of a small nation state with a history of institutionalised slavery, colonialism, economic abandonment and neocolonialism. The racial trajectory has to be looked at from the historical fact that black music, especially in North America and the Caribbean, has been exploited by the white capitalist class to the detriment of black people who are the originators of most popular forms of blues, jazz, rhythm and blues, rock and roll, ska, rocksteady, reggae, hip hop, and dancehall. Norman Kelly (2005) notes:

> Through various modes of production and avenues of exchange, the relationship between the two races has historically rested on whites' ability to exploit and dominate blacks' bodies, images, and cultures. In the case of music, black artistes have rarely received the just benefits of their work, especially in comparison to their white counterparts and those who control the music industry (6).

Black music, for the purpose of this book, refers to cultural creations by, and expressions of the experiences of, people of Africa and of African descent.[9] Kelly elucidates on the assertion that black music has operated within a 'structure of stealing' from as far back as the days of slavery when black people were commoditized and their heritage and culture treated with disregard or ridicule. Blackface minstrel music performed by whites in the nineteenth century is an example of this phenomenon (Kelly 2005, 7).

Production of Culture Perspective

Sociologists such as Richard Peterson, Paul Hirsch and Howard Becker challenge the argument that cultural products are exclusively the work of individual creativity and suggest that cultural production is determined by complex division of labour and the social, political, legal and economic milieu within which it is produced. Richard Peterson (1982) suggests six constraints, which affect the method in which cultural goods are produced:

- Law – This dictates and shapes the conditions of the development of any art form, 'statute law and government regulation shape the financial and aesthetic conditions within which popular culture develops' (144). The issue of copyright legislation – its enforcement and nonenforcement – is critical to the development of Jamaican popular music and has impacted the method of music production on the Kingston music scene.

- Market – This refers to the audience, the fan base, the consumer of cultural goods, the market is identified and conceptualised mainly by financial decision makers within the cultural industry. The market is determined by the notion of the profitability of any cultural good which would justify the production, distribution and promotion of that good (146). Another critical issue for the market in this context is its ability to 'interact with creators in shaping cultural products' (Ryan and Peterson, cited in Peterson 146).

- Technology – This has been the engine for growth of all sectors within the cultural industries. Technological advances have created new forms of cultural products that have affected the commercial value of these products. Technological innovation has changed the way in which music is produced, recorded, stored, played and consumed. Hence, technology has played a big part in the way cultural products are created, reproduced and circulated.

- Organisational Structure – Refers to the 'structures within the boundaries of the firm, coordinating the activities which generate the cultural products' (Wikström 2006, 24).

- Occupational Career – An area which has 'received relatively little attention'; this concerns 'the routine ways people coordinate their efforts in actualizing a symbolic product or service' (Peterson 1982, 147). This is critical to the way individuals on the Kingston music scene function simultaneously at many levels.

- Industry Structure – This speaks to issues of size and number of firms involved in the production of cultural products. Richard Peterson and David Berger (1990, 150) found that the greater the number of firms operating within a market, the greater the diversity and innovation in the music. The size and scope of firms on the Kingston music scene is directly related to creativity and diversity and accounts for the rapid development of genres in Kingston.

The Structure

Chapter one provides a comprehensive background of the area of study, identifying the gaps and problems. Jamaica's involvement in the North American music industry is traced back to the 1940s when Jamaican mento music was marketed in the United States as calypso through the likes of Lord Flea and Harry Belafonte. The chapter also sets up the scenario of Jamaican music influence of the international front despite the lack of traditional institutional structures typical in any established music industry to support it. This raises the question of what accounts for the sporadic success and tremendous influence that Jamaican music has enjoyed globally ever since the first attempts at recording popular music occurred in the 1940s in Kingston.

Chapter two reviews the existing body of work to establish any gaps and to critique the work of researchers in the field. The chapter extends the theoretical body of work already positioned by the leading academics in the various disciplines examined. Consequently, a review of the current body of work was critical as it provided a vehicle for honing the precision with which questions were formulated to address a particular area of empirical inquiry (Yin 2003, 9). Utilising a model developed by Patrik Wikström (2006), the literature is divided in four distinctive areas. They include research on individuals in the music industry; on intraorganisational issues; or on interorganisational issues and works from a cultural studies perspective.

Chapter three outlines the evolution of the Jamaican system of popular music production through several periods of cultural production. Additionally, the development of several distinctive musical genres in Kingston will be established. Periods of cultural production are defined as those periods, which are marked by distinctive codes, practices, styles, sociopolitical and sociocultural developments that have impacted the way cultural artefacts are produced. Jamaican music production is then viewed through the prism of a series of distinctive and complex periods of production including folk culture, appropriation, innovation, internationalisation, neoinnovation, and global-interaction. This is necessary to view the creative process of music-making through a process of signposting that gives the narrative some contextual exigency.

In chapter four, the notion of a *creative echo chamber*, an extension of the creative city concept, is discussed by looking at the organisational structure that developed in Kingston and how it impacted on the techniques of making popular music. Value chain analysis is used to interrogate the recorded music industry in Kingston to highlight its deviation from the Anglo-American model.

Chapter five interrogates the effects of copyright and intellectual property rights management on the recording industry. The chapter looks at the development of the popular music in Kingston within the absence of a strong copyright regime and examines how it affected the making of popular music. The lack of copyright enforcement prior to 1993 played an important role in the development of Jamaican music and business processes. The validity of a copyright philosophy is also questioned and alternative measures are suggested. The chapter also positions copyright as a legal monopoly which favours the major entertainment conglomerates that control the majority of the world copyright while leaving creators of intellectual property at the lower levels of the economic totem pole. It is argued that the Jamaican reality runs counter to Western philosophical notions of copyright and its efficacy and that the economic motivation, which according to the copyright industry, is a critical incentive for creation.

Chapter six addresses the role of technology as a major contributor to popular music formulation. The role of the once ubiquitous jukebox is examined to establish its importance to the development of popular music production and utilization. The development of distinctive studio practices that evolved into production techniques giving birth to dub is explored.

This is juxtaposed with celebrated Anglo American landmark albums noted for their huge influence in shaping studio practice, for example, the Beach Boys' *Pet Sounds* with the seminal work of King Tubby and Lee 'Scratch' Perry, *King Tubby Meets the Upsetter*. It is argued that the techniques of Osbourne and Perry are as important to popular music production as their North American and British counterparts. In addition, I examine the process of appropriation without adequate recognition which was at play with the significant role that dub and its techniques played in reshaping the sonic architecture of popular music globally.

Chapter seven focuses on the assertions that were developed as a consequence of the findings within the theoretical framework of the study. The chapter articulates the way forward, establishing a new paradigm for the analysis of popular music production in the Caribbean. Recommendations are outlined which enunciate how the music industry can benefit from new alignment within the social, cultural, legal and economic milieu within which popular music is made.

NOTES

1. This is changing with the number of academic works on Marley steadily increasing.
2. Peter Tosh, 'Reggaemylitis', in *Wanted Dread and Alive*, Rolling Stones Record, EMI Records, 1981.
3. A term developed by David Hesmondhalgh. See David Hesmondhalgh, *The Cultural Industries*, 2nd ed. (London: Sage Publications Ltd., 2007), 4.
4. Antonio Benítez-Rojo in his book, *Repeating Island*, quotes Janheinz Jahn that 'the principle of crossed rhythms is a common feature of African Cultures.'
5. Trench Town was the domicile ghetto where many performers emerged including The Wailers, Toots Hibbert and Alton Ellis. Warika Hill was the area where most of the members of the Skatalites, the most famous band from Kingston, lived. Big yard on Orange St, in downtown Kingston was where Dennis Brown and dub specialist Augustus Pablo lived. Robert Crescent was the base for Sugar Minott and his Youthman promotion crew and was the first incubator for the dancehall genre.
6. See Rex Nettelford, *Mirror Mirror: Identity Race and Protest in Jamaica* (New York: William Marrow & Company Inc, 1972).
7. Dub plate studios are facilities where acetate is used in the mastering process of vinyl production to make sample records which are used by sound systems to differentiate in the competitive space of the dancehalls.

8. See Antonio Benítez-Rojo, *The Repeating Island: The Caribbean and the Postmodern Perspective*, 2nd ed., trans. James E. Maraniss (Durham and London: Duke University Press, 1996).
9. Black music is used by Kelly primarily to denote African American music. However, I am extending the definition to include the music of the Caribbean, and Jamaica in particular.

Acronyms and Abbreviations

A & M	Alpert and Moss
ADAMI	The Civil Society for the administration of the Rights of Artists and Musicians
A & R	Artist and Repertoire
AM	Amplitude Modulation
ASCAP	American Society of Composers, Authors and Publishers
BET	Black Entertainment Television
BMI	Broadcast Music Incorporated
CBS	Columbia Broadcasting System
CD	Compact Disc
CIA	Central Intelligence Agency
COTT	Copyright Office of Trinidad and Tobago
DJ	Disc Jockey
DVD	Digital Versatile Disc
EMI	Electric and Musical Industries
GATT	General Agreement on Tariffs and Trade
GLADD	Gay and Lesbian Alliance Against Defamation
GDP	Gross Domestic Product
Hi Fi	High Fidelity
ICS	Institute of Caribbean Studies
IFPI	International Federation of the Phonographic Industry
IIPA	International Intellectual Property Alliance
IIPI	International Intellectual Property Institute
IMF	International Monetary Fund
ISER	Institute of Social and Economic Research
IT	Information Technology
JACAP	Jamaica Association of Composers, Authors and Publishers
JAMCOPY	Jamaican Copyright Licensing Agency
JAMMS	Jamaican Music Society
JAMREC	Jamaica Recording and Publishing Company
JBC	Jamaica Broadcasting Corporation

JIPO	Jamaica Intellectual Property Office
JFM	Jamaica Federation of Musicians
JAMRAS	Jamaican Musical Rights Administration
JAPAS	Jamaica Performers Administration Society
LDC	Lesser Developed Country
LP	Long Playing
Lt.	Lieutenant
MCA	Music Corporation of America
MCPS	Mechanical Copyright Protection Society
MPAA	Motion Picture Association of America
MP3	Moving Picture Experts Group layer3
MTV	Music Television
NMPA	National Music Publishers Association
PRS	Performing Rights Society
R & B	Rhythm and Blues
RJR	Radio Jamaica Rediffusion
RIAA	Recording Industry Association of America
RPM	Revolutions Per Minute
BMG	Bertelsmann Music Group
SPEDIDAM	Society for the Collection and Distribution of the Artist-Performers Rights
TCC	The Conservative Connoisseur
TRIPS	Trade Related Intellectual Property
TV	Television
TVJ	Television Jamaica
UNESCO	United Nations Educational, Scientific and Cultural
UNCTAD	United Nations Conference on Trade and Development
UK	United Kingdom
UNIA	Universal Negro Improvement Association
USA	United States of America
USTR	United States Trade Representative
UWI	University of the West Indies
VHS	Video Home System
WIPO	World Intellectual Property Organization
WTO	World Trade Organization

Background to the Business in Jamaica

Introduction

> *Too often only half the story is told. And the background, the upheavals and changes the island of Jamaica went through just before and since independence, gets forgotten in the face of so much music.*
>
> **Prince Buster**

Jamaica has been recognised, internationally, as a major centre for the arts and entertainment for many decades. By the beginning of the rock and roll era in the early 1950s, Jamaican mento star Lord Flea was already internationally renowned. In fact, during the American 'calypso craze' of the late '50s, Lord Flea and his band toured the major North American cities of New York, Las Vegas and Hollywood. In 1957, Flea released an album, *Swingin' Calypso*, on the Capitol label and appeared in two Hollywood calypso movies: *Bop Girl Goes Calypso* and *Calypso Joe* (Barrow and Dalton 2004, 9). With the change in the sound of Jamaican music to ska in the 1960s, the music gained some international exposure and limited success with the seminal ska band, the Skatalites, travelling to Britain and Europe.[1]

Although Jamaican music, through its stages of ska, rocksteady, reggae and dancehall, has made significant contributions to international pop culture and Jamaica's gross domestic product (Witter 2006, 25; Lehman 2002, 9), the nation is yet to realise the full economic potential of its music industry. This is due, first, to the inadequacy of existing structures within the Jamaican music business, and second, to the weak and inadequate legal framework which existed for the greater part of the most productive and creative years of Jamaican music and other cultural productions.

Considering our small size, our accomplishments in global popular music are remarkable. The works of Bob Marley, Jimmy Cliff, Frederick 'Toots' Hibbert, Peter Tosh, Keith 'Bob Andy' Anderson and Don Drummond have generated significant revenues for the international copyright industry (Lehman 2002, 3). We have developed markets for the export of copyrighted material in the form of vinyl records, and later CDs, to the Jamaican Diaspora and international markets. Our Jamaican performers have toured extensively and have headlined some major festivals and concerts globally. In fact, we developed the reggae festival concept with the world famous *Reggae Sunsplash* and *One Love* concerts which have been replicated on almost every continent.

Despite these laudable achievements, Jamaica's music business is assessed by some music sector and cultural studies scholars as being disorganised and fragmented (Power and Hallencreutz 2002, vol. 34; Kozul-Wright and Stanbury 1998, vol. 138). And, while the revenues generated by reggae worldwide are in 'excess of US$1 billion globally' (Ibid), only a very small percentage returns to the domestic economy. Bruce Lehman's (2002) observations on Jamaica's intellectual property capacity are telling:

> Jamaica has obvious knowledge-based assets that are well known throughout the world. The most well known of these assets is the country's unique music. In addition to its music – and often associated with it – are its fashions, rich visuals arts and literary traditions. Sadly, while these cultural assets are well known outside Jamaica, too much of the economic activity surrounding their exploitation takes place off shore and does not contribute to the national economy (7).

Jamaica has had sporadic international success throughout the history of our recorded music business but has never been able to sustain this on a continuous basis. However, other small markets, for example, Sweden, have done well in providing performers, songwriters and producers for the United States and British music industries.[2] The successes of artists such as Jimmy Cliff, Bob Marley and the Wailers, Peter Tosh, Black Uhuru, Damian 'Jr Gong' Marley, Shabba Ranks, Shaggy, and Sean Paul have not translated into the development of a strong domestic structure with the attendant pecuniary benefits.

It is my contention that while poor management structures and a lack of business acumen account for some of the failure to fully maximise the opportunities our international successes have afforded us, this, alone, cannot account for the obstacles which prevent us from translating our music product into the development of a viable domestic and international music industry. The Jamaican reality presents a very complex range of issues involving economics and history. The Jamaican music system has its roots in the legacies of our plantation heritage, colonial past and culture of resistance. Illustrating this reality was the role of race and class in determining the ownership structure of the business during its nascent years.

Also negatively impacting the business development of the domestic music industry was the fact that prior to 1993, Jamaica's copyright laws were essentially archaic and ineffectual, and far too many local entertainers were unaware of their basic rights in the intellectual property arena; a situation which still prevails. The stories of entertainers, songwriters and producers, who continue to sign away their intellectual property rights, in ignorance, are legendary. This failing is not entirely based on inadequate legislation. The mode of composition of text in the Jamaican experience has been influenced by many cultural and social dynamics which would render any analysis on the basis of intellectual property rights orthodoxy ineffective.

Up to the twenty-first century, collecting societies were noticeably absent from the local music industry with the British collecting agency, the Performing Rights Society (PRS), being the only representation on the island. Attempts to organise talent through agencies occurred at several junctures in the history of the music business. Among those who sought copyright protection were Tony Laing, The Conservative Connoisseur Limited (TCC) and Tommy Cowan's Talent Inc. These early attempts were never replicated nor entrenched in Jamaica's music business, primarily as a result of a lack of artist management expertise.

Weak Framework

Internationally, record companies, comprising the major and the independent labels, drove the music industry. Despite some attempts by the US-based Columbia Records in the 1970s (Power and Hallencreutz 2002, vol. 34), no record company was located in Kingston, the creative capital. The trend in Jamaica was the formation of production houses and recording studios. Some outfits had a complement of acts that recorded solely for them, while most operated an open-house policy and recorded any artist with whom they had a relationship. Some of these talents ended up being represented by the owners of the production companies, but the vast majority of musicians were 'freelancers' who recorded for anyone, sometimes even recording the same material for several producers. Understandably, while these production houses were creative juggernauts, they were not *au fait* with proper business models and were neither prepared nor equipped to take on the management of talent in a professional music context.

Perhaps the most fundamental, but often overlooked, factor impacting the growth of Jamaica's music industry from the 1950s to the present was the organisational structure within which it evolved. This is an area to which contemporary researchers have paid scant regard in their analyses of the sector's development. However, the influences of the management environment on the business culture that emerged during the embryonic stages of the music industry, and which persists to date, are unquestionable.

This study examines 50 years of Jamaica's musical development starting in 1956, the beginning of the making of popular music in Kingston, and ending in 2006. It focuses on music production in Kingston, long established as one of the music centres of the world.

In so doing, it traces the varied sociocultural, economic and political variables that have influenced the emergent management structures and business cultures characteristic of the industry and also probe the role of social status, wealth, educational and economic status on the types of management arrangements that existed in the early period. A comparison is made with the international contemporary realties and the extent to which the local arrangements differ from these.

The Issue of Copyright

Also of interest will be the effect of legislation relating to intellectual property, copyright and contract law on the development of the industry and more specifically, the attitudes of the major players in the industry towards the legal system. The Copyright Act of 1913, adopted from the UK Copyright Act of 1911, did not provide adequate protection for creators of intellectual property. This, in itself, created myriad problems for the business and promoted an environment of exploitation, ignorance and policy neglect. Dianne Daley (2001, 3) notes that copyright issues did not get any serious attention until 1978 when the country adopted the international framework for copyright protection provided by the World Intellectual Property Organization (WIPO). In 1977, with lobbying by the music fraternity, headed by the Jamaica Federation of Musicians (JFM), there were attempts to pass an updated Copyright Act. This draft was abandoned by the Manley administration after it was deemed 'silent on the rights of performers and the issue of moral right was never brought into force' (Daley 2001, 2).

The legal stalemate that persisted effectively crippled the proper functioning of the music business. I am also of the view, however, that the legal and business environment of the time, inadvertently, facilitated the development of artistic creativity and economic prosperity of some of the major players in the industry. It is my contention that the Jamaican artists developed as a counter hegemonic movement rejecting conventional norms of intellectual property rights and protection, freely borrowing from the vaults of Tin Pan Alley, Abbey Road, Motown, Stax and the juke joints of the southern United States and, in the process, developed an organic intellectual cadre of musicians and performers who became the driving force that developed the original works which have become a major economic asset.

This open environment, free of intellectual property protection and copyright legislative control, actually favoured the creative process as it facilitated innovation, creativity and ingenuity through countercultural resistance and cultural synthesis. Conversely, the areas of ownership of recorded masters, intellectual property rights ownership and artist management did not realise the phenomenal growth and development experienced by the creative side.

The Role of Technology

The role and the use of technology, for example, vinyl records, sound systems, jukebox, radio and the audio tape (recorded music) and dub methodology in popularising Jamaican music forms in the 1950s and '60s is another major aspect of the study. The rise of recorded music in the form of 78 rpm and 45 rpm vinyl records accounted for the development and spread of a music culture in the nascent years of Jamaican music. Jason Toynbee (2000, 74), in looking at the American experience with the popularity of recorded music and the distribution of records in the 1920s, cites Paul Oliver (1998, 9–10): 'The mass circulation of records led to a new kind of mediated orality, whereby young musicians learnt their craft listening to the phonograph as much as by reading music or watching performance.' Jamaican artists are familiar with this experience – a practice labelled by Toynbee (2000, 75) as 'dissemination of music through recordings' – where lyrics and styles are learnt by copying established talents, foreign and local. In fact, during the 1950s and '60s, many Jamaican artists had monikers such as the 'Jamaican Tom Jones' and the 'Jamaican Nat King Cole' acknowledging the respect they had for overseas acts, of all genres, whom they had encountered first through the radio and then on vinyl records.

My primary focus is on the microphone, the 45 rpm and 33 rpm vinyl records and the magnetic tape, technologies which were critical to the production system of Jamaican popular music. I also look, in great detail, at the role of the jukebox, which has largely been ignored in studies on Jamaican music development. In fact, to date, no serious interrogation of its important role has been attempted.

The literature available on the development of Jamaican music (Bradley 2000; Chang and Chen 1998) have all canonized the roles of the sound system, live performance, and talent extravaganzas such as the *Vere Johns Opportunity Hour*. However, very little documentation is to be found on the role of the jukebox in promoting Jamaican music and its significance as a site of resistance and identity affirmation. No serious scholastic effort has been attempted to interrogate the jukebox as a serious cultural phenomenon within the Jamaican pop cultural space. This book establishes iconic status for the jukebox in the development and sustainability of Jamaican popular music from mento to dancehall.

The sound system, on the other hand, has been studied from both the sociological and anthropological perspectives and, more recently, the economy of the sound system within the context of dancehall culture (Stolzoff 2000) was investigated. This study also takes a brief look at the sound system as an instrument of dissemination, as an agent of Black Electronic,[3] its role as facilitator of symbol production and, finally, its position within the political economy of popular music production globally.

Radio, also, plays an important role in the cultural industry as a promoter of popular music. The major conglomerates of the cultural industries all have major radio networks and are integrated within the marketing and promotion of music produced by their subsidiaries. The resistance to the music of the ghetto by the middle-class owners of radio is addressed demonstrating that ska, rocksteady and reggae were not given major airplay. In fact, Anglo-American music, reflecting the tastes of the middle and upper classes, dominated the airwaves. There was never a symbiotic relationship between radio and popular music and radio played a big role in ostracising the music by discriminating against it on the basis of class and race, even when it relented to give exposure to the indigenous music.

While the contribution of Jamaican music to world culture has been celebrated in academic circles for some time now, very little emphasis has been placed on its contribution to mainstream music production techniques. Only a handful of scholars (Toop 2001; Veal 2007; Alleyne 2002; Davis 1996)[4] have attempted to examine the influence of Jamaican production techniques on the global music industry. I contend that innovations within Jamaica's music space, born out of a combination of creativity and economic and technological expedience, have influenced global pop music production techniques significantly and I will explore the role of 'economic and technological expedience' in fostering the development of Jamaican innovations such as versions, the remix version, dub and dub-driven mixing techniques.

The recording studio experienced a metamorphosis and became an instrument of innovation in the hands of King Tubby, Errol Thompson and Lee 'Scratch' Perry. In what I call the ghetto laboratory, this group of engineers and producers created dub and in the process opened the world to an alternative soundscape that has influenced the music industry up to the present. Tubby appropriated the technology and did a masterful job of manipulating the equipment and sound to rewrite what constitutes composition. While dub has been recognised internationally for its influence, it is usually within the context of Third World expressionism, suggesting inferiority to innovations and inventions of the developed world. This is addressed with the aim of correcting the practice of appropriation with recognition. This study also aligns disparate views of the Jamaican music business by closely exploring issues of economics, the political economy of popular music and copyright which have been neglected or skimmed over by cultural studies and ethnomusicology scholars (Bilby 2006; Bradley 2000; Cooper 1993, 2004).

Central Questions

In exploring the development of the industry a number of issues were considered.

1. What was the recording technique employed in the earlier periods of production and how is it different today?
2. How were contractual agreements between producer and recording artists framed?

3. Why were the roles of the sound system and jukebox, as agents of commerce, so important?
4. Why was the studio system organised in the way it was?
5. In what way did the Copyright Act of 1913 influence the way business was done in the music industry?
6. How does the Copyright Act of 1993 represent the interest of creators and what factors accounted for the rapid developments in copyright legislation in the early 1990s, after decades of neglect?
7. What record companies, if any, existed during the 1960s and '70s and what kind of management culture existed in the Jamaican music business?
8. Were written/oral contracts in place between producers, distributors and recording artists?
9. What kind of recording technologies were available to Jamaica at the beginning of the business?

The fundamental goal of this work is to explain the relative underdevelopment of the Jamaican music industry despite its major contribution to global mass appeal. The book is timely and necessary in filling the gaps in data and analyses resulting from a general lack of attention paid by scholars to the business and legal aspects of the Jamaican music industry. Most major studies, to date, have focused on the creative development of the music with emphasis on the biography of some of its leading players. Other topical themes include issues of masculinity, sexuality, political and cultural identity and the economics of dancehall (Cooper 2004; Hope 2006; Stolzoff 2000). However, research initiatives have not adequately examined the economic, legal and management processes that paralleled the development of the creative milieu. Richard Peterson (1997) concurs:

> Recognizing that popular music remains plural, there is still a world of things we, as researchers, don't know about this plurality. There are, for example, enduring differences in the ways that music is made for the rap, rock, reggae, and country music markets, but we still know very little about the structure and sources of these differences…Thus, as I see it, the exciting research challenge now is to learn how this vast plurality of popular music is sorted and recombined by artistes, by the people in the

industry, and by diverse elements of the consuming public and to find what people popular music choice means to them (2).

Jamaica's music has helped to establish the island as a cultural superpower with an enviable reputation for its rich cultural production and has generated an astounding amount of revenue (Kozul-Wright and Stanbury 1998, 19). Bob Marley, in death, has achieved the coveted diamond status, signifying sales of ten million units for his *Legend* album.[5] Despite these statistics, an unsophisticated business culture and a weak legislative framework combined with the historical, political, social and cultural frameworks have diminished the sector's earning potential. In an era of rapid globalisation where microeconomies, such as Jamaica's, have little or no comparative advantage against major industrialised nations, it is imperative that we learn how to maximise the benefits of our creative industries.

As providers of content and primary material that benefits the North, too many members of the Jamaican music industry remain unaware of imbalances carried over from the old world order, imbalances that have existed in the areas of intellectual property rights, ownership and the way in which the ownership of these rights, mainly by major multinational entertainment firms, negatively impact developing countries. By examining the formations of institutions and systems within the music industry, this work establishes the causes of these imbalances, thus providing a context in which viable solutions to the current dilemma might be proposed. If Jamaica is to reap the full economic potential of the talents of her artists,, the music industry will have to operate in a more business-like manner with improved management practices and a full awareness of the laws governing the industry. The study, therefore, is targeted at music and copyright industry personnel, policymakers, academics, media managers, broadcasters, cultural activists, record executives and music enthusiasts with specialist interests in Jamaican popular music.

Cultural Production

In examining Jamaica's musical evolution, I identified several periods of cultural production – those periods which are marked by distinctive codes, practices, styles, sociopolitical and sociocultural developments that have impacted on the way cultural artefacts are produced. Jamaican music has evolved through a series of distinctive and complex periods of production including folk culture, appropriation, innovation, internationalisation, neo innovation, and global interaction. My divisions are as follows:

a. **Folk Culture:** Pre 1950s–1956. This period precedes the recording of mento songs by Stanley Motta, Ken Khuori and Ivan Chin for the overseas novelty market. The predominant popular sound of the common folk was mento. Also, during this period, the big band sound and Tin Pan Alley music were the dominant cultural forms of the elite.

b. **Appropriation:** 1957–60. This period is characterised by the inflow of American rhythm and blues, jazz and the beginning of the recording of non-mento popular music. The latter being Jamaican versions of American rhythm and blues which were made popular through the sound system, which was, at the time, the main vehicle of entertainment for the working class.

c. **Innovation:** 1961–69. Recordings became distinctively Jamaican, reflecting the influences of jazz, mento, rhythm and blues and nyabinghi. The creation of ska, rocksteady, reggae and dub took place during this period, considered one of the most creative periods in modern Jamaican popular culture. The music was exported to Britain to supply the immigrant markets in cities such as London and Birmingham.

d. **Internationalization:** 1970–80. During this period Jamaican music production began to make inroads, internationally. The music was exported to South America, Japan and Europe and increasingly made the popular charts in Britain and the United States. Jamaican production techniques were adopted by American and British pop music acts and indigenous reggae bands began to emerge, especially in Britain. Jamaican music became truly international. The recording facilities were now sufficiently advanced to attract British and American acts, including the Rolling Stones, Herbie Mann, Eric Gale, Johnny Nash and Roberta Flack, to record in Jamaica. Reggae performers, including Bob Marley and the Wailers, Jimmy Cliff, Burning Spear, Peter Tosh, The Gladiators, Culture and Dennis Brown, were touring globally.

e. **Neoinnovation:** 1981–2000. Dancehall emerged as the dominant art form in Jamaican music and the deejay replaced the singer as the dominant performer. However, reggae was still dominant on the international front. Inroads were made by King Yellowman, but this was not enough to make a major impact on tastemakers internationally. It was also the beginning of the digital era which heralded a new kind of artist – the programmers – who threatened to put musicians out of work. The music reached its highest level of commercialisation and began to attract corporate sponsorship and the attention of international record labels, resulting in a slew of record deals by some of the top artists. The most successful include Shabba Ranks, Patra, Cobra, Super Cat and Shaggy. The compact disc (CD) was introduced but vinyl was still king. The levels of management and marketing improved significantly and several production companies and individual artists realized a more organised business culture.

f. **Global interaction:** 2001–present. This is the post-modern era of music production where the Internet and digital technology have begun to change the music industry's business model. These technological advances have allowed for the democratisation of music distribution and promotion. Jamaican music is enjoying international exposure with the rise of Sean Paul, Beenie Man, Wayne Wonder and Elephant Man. Domestically, CD sales are nonexistent and a paradigm shift has been made towards airplay and live performances as indicators of success. The Internet has opened Jamaican culture to the world to unparalleled degrees.

Organisational Structure

The structure of the local music industry has been a significant factor in its inability, so far, to maximise its earning potential. A look at international norms will assist in clarifying the effectiveness or lack thereof of our domestic model.

Bill Ryan (qtd. in Hesmondhalgh 2007, 64) delineates the organisational structure of the cultural industries during the complex professional period, suggesting that the making of the creative product is not done by individual effort but by a group or 'project team'. He also outlines various roles of team members as follows:

a. ***Primary creative personnel*** include musicians, composers, lyricists, authors, video directors, screenwriters, engineers and record producers (remixes and the creation of dub) and programmers (gaming).
b. ***Technical craft workers*** perform technically-oriented functions such as sound engineering, videography, floor management, music mastering and copyediting. While there is some level of creativity, it does not reside in the original idea of the text.
c. ***Creative managers*** are the intermediaries between the owners and executives on one hand and the creative personnel on the other.
d. ***Owners and executives*** are motivated by profit. They set general policy direction, have the power to hire and fire and usually finance the creative process, but are divorced from the conception and development of texts.
e. 'A vast body of ***unskilled workers*** are also involved in the creation circulation and reproduction of products' (65).

This division of cultural production is used as a template to outline an organisational structure for the Jamaican industry, which highlights the significant differences reflected in the local system. It presents a compelling case for a counterhegemonic movement, rejecting the conventions and norms of the North Atlantic production of culture and reinforcing the production of culture perspective that culture is shaped by environmental factors. Additionally, issues of creolisation and hybridity also come into play.

Rather than attempting a strict chronological outline, the focus is more on the systems and methods which were employed in the making of Jamaican popular music and the variables which have contributed to the creation of the unique characteristics of the Jamaican music business during different periods. I have outlined seven stages of production of music, which will form the basis for the analysis of the production of music in the Jamaican context.

Additionally, while there is some discussion of distribution channels and how they fit into the economic structure of the Jamaican music industry, the work makes a priority of the production trajectory.

NOTES

1. According to Dizzy Moore, trumpeter for the Skatalites, the white British population did not warm to the sound quickly as they found it too fast. Personal conversation at the Don Drummond Symposium, UWI, 1999.
2. USA share of world market value 30–35 per cent, United Kingdom Share of world market value 6.4–9.1 per cent. IFPI, 2000.
3. See Erik Davis, *Roots and Wires: Polyrhythmic Cyberspace and the Black Electronic*. http:www.techgnosis.com/cyberconf.html 1996.
4. http://www.techgnosis.com/index_cyberconf.html 1996.
5. Shaggy also sold 6 x platinum (6 million copies) of his *Hotshot* album. He received a gold certification (500,000 copies sold) with the *Lucky Day* album in the United States.

Surveying the Soundscapes: Writing on the Jamaican Music Scene

The available literature on the structure of the Jamaican music industry does not adequately reflect the degree of its contribution to popular music-making globally. This work maps the development of income streams, music industry models, and music value chain dynamic on forms of cultural use of music in Jamaican cultural life.

The work on this area of research, from an international standpoint, is extensive. From a Jamaican perspective, the gap in research on the economic, legal and social perspectives of popular music production must be addressed in order to place it in its proper role as an important part of an overall framework that places the creative industries at the forefront of economic development of a lesser developed country (LDC) like Jamaica. UNESCO sees the cultural industries as critical to economic development, especially in LDCs:

> The cultural industries, which include publishing, music, cinema, crafts and design, continue to grow steadily apace and have a determinant role to play in the future of culture.
>
> Their international dimension gives them a determining role for the future in terms of freedom of expression, cultural diversity and economic development. Although the globalization of exchange and new technologies opens up exciting new prospects, it also creates new types of inequality. The world map of these industries reveals a yawning gap between North and South. This can only be counteracted by strengthening local capacities and facilitating access to global markets at national level by way of new partnerships, know-how, control of piracy and increased international solidarity of every kind.[1]

It is my intention to extend the theoretical body of work already positioned by the leading academics in the various disciplines examined in this study. Consequently, a review of the current body of work is critical as it provides a vehicle for honing the precision with which questions are formulated to address a particular area of empirical inquiry (Yin 2003). It also allows researchers 'to develop sharper and more insightful questions about a topic' (Yin 2003, 9). Patrik Wikström (2006) suggests a useful approach to reviewing research initiatives that focus on the popular music industry, stating:

> One way to structure a review is by level of aggregation, in other words whether the research initiative is focused on individuals in the music industry; on intra-organisational issues; or on inter-organisational issues (74).

Biographies

Biographies comprise the overwhelming content of the literature on Jamaican music and biographies on Bob Marley dominate. Numerous writers and scholars have chronicled his work and life. These include: *Catch a Fire*, Timothy White (1983); *Marley and Me*, Don Taylor (1994); *Bob Marley: Conquering Lion of Reggae*, Stephen Davis (2008); *Bob Marley: Lyrical Genius*, Kwame Dawes; *The Book Of Exodus: The Making and Meaning of Bob Marley and the Wailers Album Of the Century*, Vivien Goldman (2006); *Before the Legend: The Rise of Bob Marley*, Christopher John Farley (2007); *Bob Marley: King of Reggae*, Malika Lee Whitney and Dermot Hussey (1994); and *Bob Marley*, Jason Toynbee (2007). This should come as no surprise as Marley is still the only international Third World icon (Toynbee 2007, 2). However, there is reason for concern, considering the plethora of music greats that have come out of Jamaica.

The Bob Marley biographies are presented in a variety of styles with differing areas of focus. Of particular interest to this study are the works by Goldman, Toynbee, and Whitney and Hussey. Goldman's focus on the making of the album *Exodus*, which was designated the album of the century by *Time* magazine, provides a useful insight into Jamaican music that was produced in an international context and insightfully chronicles the merging of the two disparate cultures of the British rock industry and the Jamaican music production system from an aesthetic and commercial perspective. Goldman's semiotic device is powerful in explaining the story behind each song and is very convincing due to her insider perspective that allows readers a unique insight into the making and meanings of this landmark album.

Toynbee's work is a serious inquiry into the life of Marley and the Wailers which addresses the notion of social authorship which Toynbee believes was one of the mechanisms that was characteristic of the popular music production in Kingston of that era. Using *critical realism*, he (2007) explores the making of Bob Marley as a celebrity and suggests that the labelling of Marley as a Third World star served, 'to reduce Bob to the status of third world mystic', thus belittling him and missing 'his true significance' (2). The text is not merely a biographical look at Marley, as Toynbee extends his approaches to the political economy of music and social authorship which he had started in 2000.

Don Taylor's (1994) *Marley and Me* presents one of the only moments which examines Marley's interface with the rock industry from a contractual and creative perspective. Taylor's accounts are incisive, detailed and told from a perspective that fieldwork would not attain. The same assessment could be made about Malika Lee Whitney and Dermot Hussey's account of the life of Marley. Hussey, in particular, interviewed Marley as a journalist numerous times during his career and was a personal friend. This comes across in the book and is important not only for its critical analysis and its chronological accuracy but also for its attention to nuances and sensibilities that only a Jamaican could tap into.

Other biographies include David Katz's work on the legendary Lee 'Scratch' Perry – *Perry People Funny Boy* (2000); *Bob Marley and Peter Tosh Get up Stand Up Diary of Reggaeophile* (2003), by Fikisha Cumbo; *Reggae Rebel Life of Peter Tosh* (2003) by Chris Salewicz; and *Deep Down With Dennis Brown* (2002) by Penny Reel. There are few works on dancehall luminaries, but the only two of note are *King Jammy* (2002) by Beth Lesser and Steve Barrow and *Who Am I: The Untold Story of Beenie Man* (2008) by Milton Wray.

Intraorganisational Research

There are several texts that focus on the individual needs of artists, composers, managers and lawyers; two key texts are *This Business of Music* by Sidney Shemel, M. William Krasilovsky and John M. Gross and *All You Need to Know about the Music Business* by Donald Passman. These two books are essential to understanding the music industry from an international perspective. However, these texts would have been more instructive with some historical references and they do not provide any theoretical perspective on copyright, intellectual property rights management or management practices. Despite these limitations, the texts are essential to providing a framework and a reference point for key issues such as copyright and various recording industry contracts such as producers' agreements, label deals, management contracts, and distribution and merchandising deals. They also provide important models depicting the organisation of the international (Anglo American/Europe) music system.

Texts on the history and development of Jamaican music have not enjoyed a long history. This is, in part, due to the relative youth of the music as well as its social and political history. For a long time the music was not considered worthy of academic pursuit and the early academic inquiries were all foreign based. With the exception of Garth White, Sebastian Clarke and Carolyn Cooper, Jamaican and Caribbean analyses of Jamaican music have been very recent with most works looking at the historical, political and social development of Jamaican music. Important contributions to this trajectory of inquiry include Kevin O'Brien Chang and Wayne Chen, Lloyd Bradley, David Katz, Peter Manuel with Kenneth Bilby and Michael Largey, Sebastian Clarke and Steve Barrow, and Peter Dalton.

Chang and Chen (1998) provide a fair analysis of the development of music genres and the role of artists and innovations, like the sound system, in establishing Jamaican music; however, their study of the evolution of the music business may be deemed inadequate. They, too, skimmed over the pivotal role of the jukebox in exposing mento/ska/rocksteady/reggae performers and recording artists to the Jamaican audience. In reviewing the work of the early mento performers they state, 'most performers were previously known only to live local audiences but [that] radio had made them famous island wide' (15). Such an assertion is problematic on two fronts.

First, radio would not have done an effective job of exposing mento, given the biases against indigenous music forms, especially in the 1950s and through the 1960s. More fundamentally, though, as mentioned by Chang and Chen (1998), many of the better and more popular mento records were viewed as 'bawdy' and 'suggestive' and deemed 'not fit for airplay' (15). Hence, the role of radio in exposing early forms of Jamaican music is questionable.

Second, Chang and Chen failed to acknowledge the significance of the jukeboxes in popularising these 'bawdy' mento/calypso recordings among the masses of Jamaicans. Owing to its strong roots in rural Jamaican folk culture, mento records became an important part of the jukebox compilations played in the bars of western and eastern Kingston as well as in rural communities across the island.

Bilby, in *Caribbean Currents: Caribbean Music from Rhumba to Reggae*, lauds the role of the sound system in promoting the new music, '(t)hese early efforts at recording mento were soon overshadowed, in the late 1950s by a new phenomenon, the "sound system", which would play a crucial role in Jamaican popular music over the next few decades' (Manuel with Bilby and Largey 2006, 155). While acknowledging the central role of one technology, Bilby, like other scholars, remains mute on the equally crucial role of jukeboxes as disseminators of the music and as one of the focal points of the urban inner city culture. Given the aforementioned, it is easy to share Mike Alleyne's perspective in his critique of Manuel, Bilby and Largey's work (qtd. in Ho and Nurse 2005):

> The imperatives of cultural anthropology assume so much of the textual foreground that commercial realities, vital to the dissemination of the evolved folk forms, become an invisible undercurrent (289).

Bradley, similarly, overlooked the value of the jukebox as a major tool in the promotion, socialisation, camaraderie and cultural hybridity in the formative years of the Jamaican music industry. His omission is particularly surprising given that his book focuses on Prince Buster who was first a jukebox operator and whose popularity as a recording artist was boosted by this fact. Buster's jukeboxes were unique as only his own recordings and those of artists he produced, such as the Skatalites, Big Youth and the Maytals, were available on them. This gave Buster a distinct advantage. Manuel, Chang and Chen, and Bradley were all found wanting in their analyses of the production modalities, organisation, legal structures and customs of the Jamaican popular artist and music scene.

Value Chain Dynamics

Value chain analysis, pioneered by Michael Porter (1985), provides a useful tool for the investigation of the economic activities within the music industry. Porter suggests that organisations add value to the products and services they produce by engaging in certain activities that should be run at optimum levels if the organisation is to realize a competitive advantage. If efficiency is achieved, the value created should exceed the cost of running them. Porter suggests that there are five primary activities and four support activities that organisations engage in to optimize their profit potential. Primary activities include inbound logistics, operation, outboard logistics, service and marketing and sales. Support activities include firm's infrastructure, human resource management, technology development and procurement. We will look briefly at four models of value chain dynamics to establish the work done in this area. They will include work done by Paul Hirsch, Andrew Leyshon, Roger Wallis and Michael Witter.

The Popular Music Industry Model

Although Hirsch did not explicitly label the model a value chain, it has the prerequisite linear structure that demonstrates activities within the value-added process that is associated with value chain systems.

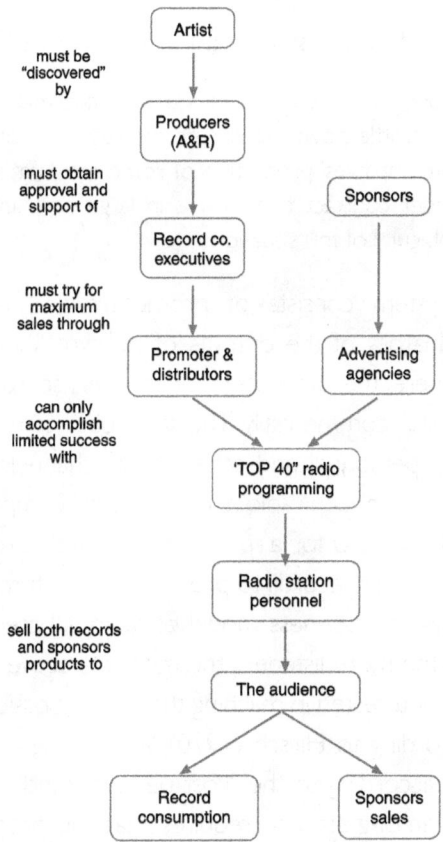

Fig. 2.1: Organisation of the Pop Music Industry (Hirsch 1970, 17A)

Hirsch identifies four subsystems within the recorded music industry through which an artiste has to negotiate in order to be successful. The creative sector is the first of the subsystems and includes the artiste, the producer and the artiste and repertoire (A&R) agent. The song is created at this point with the A&R agent acting as mediator between the artiste, the producers and the record label, performing the function of cultural intermediary. Ryan refers to this role as the creative manager (qtd. in Hesmondhalgh 2007, 64). The A&R is responsible for discovering the artistes and ensuring that their best work is presented (this usually means what is best commercially).

The record company is the second subsystem in Hirsch's model; it is the decision-making apparatus that determines which records are produced, marketed and released. Hirsch states (qtd. in Wikström 2006, 67):[2]

> While the decision to release a record is theirs, policymakers have little control over media, little power to ensure the exposure of a particular release. Record companies' promotion of some artists at the expense of others (all under contract to them) is in large part an attempt to structure the ambiguity of this situation.

The third subsystem consists of promoters and distributors who function as disseminators of the outputs of policymakers. There is also a filtering process where the promoter selects the records that are more likely to be successful commercially. The last subsystem is comprised of radio stations, radio personnel and other media channels; here there is a symbiotic relationship between radio and the record companies. The record companies depend on radio for airplay and, ultimately, promotion of their records while radio utilises records to provide content through radio shows with popular deejays. The business model of radio is based on delivering a sizable listenership, the more listeners the more attractive it is for potential advertisers who are interested in reaching the largest possible audience with their products. According to Hirsch (1970), 'advertising agencies place ads with radio stations according to the "cost per thousand" listeners' (6). The fierce competition among stations requires that the programme director selects a group of records that will appeal to the widest possible audience.

This model is one of the first of its kind and addresses what is known in the industry as the top 40 format and is centred on the artist and the song (Wikström 2006). It is also significant that there is no mention of a copyright and intellectual property regime in the Hirsch Model, which suggests that the main source of value is the actual record and the attendant value of playing it on radio. This results in music sales for the record companies and increased advertising value for the radio stations, based on the level of listenership.

Traditional Music Industry Value Chain

Wallis's (2004) traditional value chain model focuses on the composer and intellectual property rights and 'where various intermediaries (collection societies) are established to collect and distribute revenues arising from these rights' (104). A work is created by a composer who can register the work 100 per cent, known as manuscript registration; or can assign the work to a publisher. The publisher's role is to exploit the work and perform the administrative activities of registering it and issuing licences to collecting agencies. There are two types of collecting agencies. On the one hand, the public performance of copyright-protected work incurs a cost for its use on radio and television, for example. The payment is given to performing rights agencies such as Broadcast Music Incorporated (BMI) in the United States, the Copyright Office of Trinidad and Tobago, (COTT) or the Jamaica Association of Composers Authors and Publishers, (JACAP) in Jamaica. The publisher generally gets 50 per cent of the proceeds from the work as compensation for his input.[3] Publishers also work with record companies to record compositions under their portfolio; this is facilitated by the A&R Department of record companies.

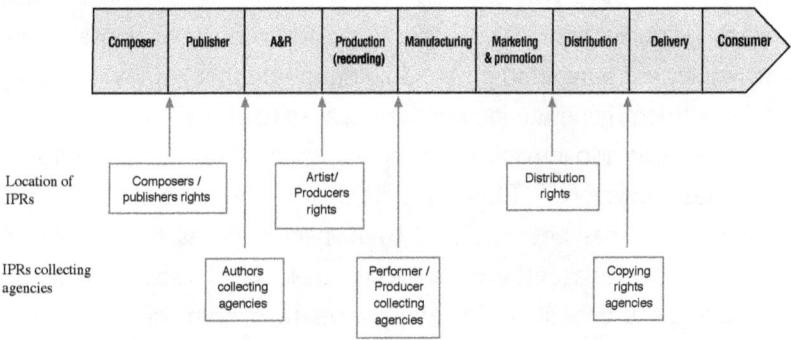

The traditional music industry value chain, linking composers, artists, producers and distributors, in parallel with a series of intermediaries (collecting agencies) which collect and distribute revenues based on intellectual property rights.

Fig. 2.2 The Traditional Music Value Chain (Wallis 2004, 104)

Once the recording process is in full swing, the record company is then responsible for the manufacture, marketing and distribution of the work. The promotion of the record in the media and at concerts generates the income discussed above. The record company is also liable to pay a royalty to the rights owner in the form of a mechanical fee, based on the use of the composer's work on any physical storage device, e.g., records, tapes and CDs. Mechanical rights societies, the other type of collection agency, enters the picture at this point. Examples of these are Harry Fox in the United States and MCPS in Britain.

The 1911 Copyright Act in the United Kingdom recognised the rights of music producers through the ownership of the sound recording. This new area of copyright legislation generated new ways to collect revenue for the exploitation of works, centred on the rights known as neighbouring rights (Laing 2004). Performance rights societies are responsible for the collection of these incomes, for example, ADAMI in France and JAMMS in Jamaica.

Wallis's model focuses on the composer and is the classic copyright industry orientation of the recording industry in North America and Europe. The artist is not the focus, as in the Hirsch model, but the song and the composer are the foundation of this value chain. It shows how value accrues along the chain with a number of intermediaries collecting and distributing revenues at various points. What this chain does not reveal is the fact that the composer receives the least of the revenue generated by his/her work. The big publishing companies are the ones who benefit from the exploitation of copyright-controlled works. Wallis (2004) notes, 'it is certainly arguable that the large publishers have become, in effect, investment houses: rights and catalogues are purchased on the assumption that they will, without any further investment, generate income for decades to come' (107).

The value chain also introduces the concepts known as disintermediation and re-intermediation (Tuomola 2004, 33–34; Frost 2007, 4). Disintermediation has been defined by Robert Frost as the 'process of removing superfluous agents in a transaction chain'. Frost also states that this process 'offers the benefits of lowering prices to consumers and a better feedback loop between producer and consumers'. The digital explosion in the music industry has facilitated the removal of unnecessary intermediaries in the recorded music value chain and it is suggested that this would make music cheaper and more accessible to the consumer who can deal directly with the creators of music, ridding the chain of bean counters and out-of-touch record executives. The process, however, is by no means unidirectional, as new or old intermediaries can be introduced into the process through reintermediation. Wallis (2004) notes, 'much rhetoric has emerged from the record industry regarding the difficulties they are suffering as a result of file sharing and other "misuse" of digital networks' (106–107). This process has introduced disintermediation but Wallis notes the strong position of the copyright industry and concludes that while the value chain has been disrupted, somewhat, by digital technologies, the impact at this point is negligible (109). While the status quo has not significantly shifted, the signs are clear that revenue generated from the publishing and copyright industry have been adversely affected by the mushrooming of digital file sharing. This has prompted the music industry to implement several measures such as lawsuits and encryption to resist the continued onslaught of file sharing and other piracy.

Musical Networks Value Chain

In their value chain of the recorded music industry, Andrew Leyshon and Brendan Scott identify four distinct systems that they label musical networks – creativity, reproduction, distribution and consumption. Leyshon (2001) states, 'One of the advantages of this approach is that it offers the possibility of analysing the various functions necessary for the reproduction of the musical economy' (60). It is also a tool to interrogate the complicated organisational structures that are evident in the recorded music industry and provides a theoretical framework for analysing the impact of issues such as software formats and for 'locating these functions within geographical space'.

Drawing on the work of Scott, Leyshon creates an organisational structure of the recorded music industry that is centred on the artist and the record company and places the production of recording in the realm of what Scott calls the *creative field* and the *musical scene*.

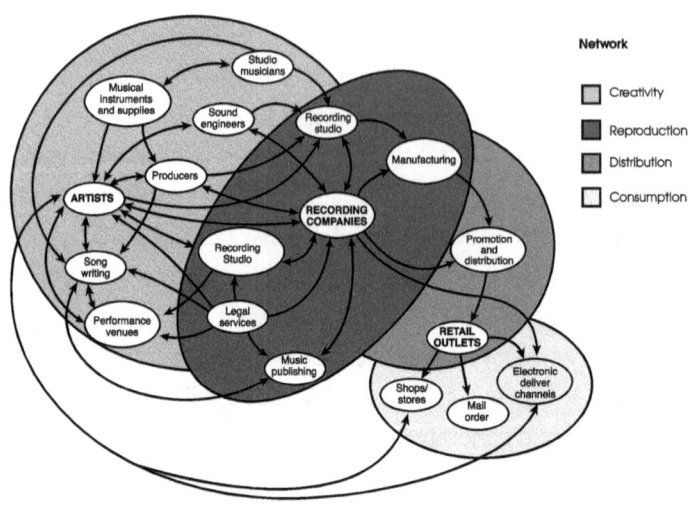

Fig. 2.3: Musical Networks (Leyshon 2001, 61)

These are all part of the network of creativity which, 'suggest that networks of creativity take the form of dense, spatially agglomerated interactions between relatively large numbers of actors, institutions and technologies' (Leyshon 2001, 61). It is within this network of creativity that all the players are working toward the recording of material that can be exploited by the record companies who have provided the personnel and technologies to produce music. 'They provide the initial contracts and money needed to hire the specialist workers such as record producers, sound engineers and studio musicians, and the dedicated institutions such as rehearsal and recording studios' (63). Networks of reproduction entail the mass production of recorded materials for mass distribution to consumers, 'where the emphasis is upon economies of scale' (64).

Record companies are all owners of major manufacturing plants that are usually located within 'global regions'. These plants offer the benefit of large-scale production, which are overhead savings, and management of 'volatile orders' which can fluctuate from week to week, based on the popularity of a recording. Networks of distribution, 'ensure that copyrighted products are delivered to final markets', allowing record companies to 'exploit the property rights they hold over sound recordings' (64).

'Networks of consumption incorporate those locations in which musical products created within other networks are purchased' (64). This network involves the retail outlets where recordings are available and includes the consumers who provide feedback loops to the other networks.

Michael Witter's Circular Income Flow

Michael Witter's circular income flow represents a nonlinear value chain and one of the first representations of a value chain for the Jamaican music industry. It was part of an effort by the Jamaican government and several international development agencies to focus on the economic dimensions of the recorded music industry after decades of neglect on the part of the traditional private sector and the government. He notes that the flow of income moves in the opposite direction to the flow of goods and services (Witter 2006, 47).

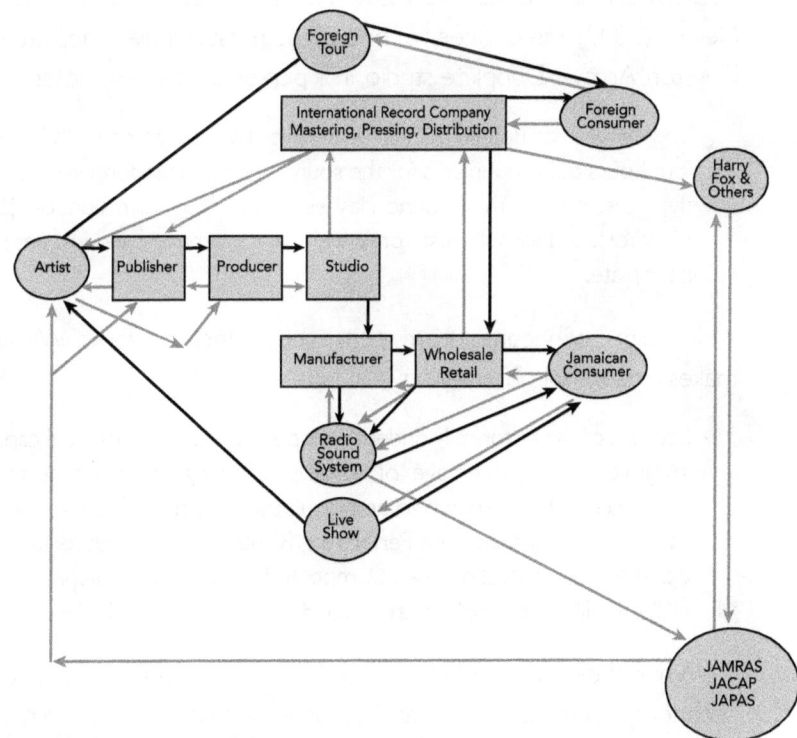

Fig. 2.4: Circular Flow of income in the Jamaican Music Industry
(Witter 2006, 62)

Witter's value chain is similar to Wallis's value chain in the sense that it is centred on copyright and the songwriter as the owner of the copyright in the work. It is also similar to Hirsch's value chain due to its reliance on the creation of musical works which are then moved up the value chain through the process of the manufacturing, packaging and marketing of finished products – CDs and vinyl. A critical income source in this value chain is the live performance both nationally and internationally. Secondary incomes are derived in the value chain through the exploitation of copyright-protected works and sound recordings. The inflows from finished products are usually questionable despite the success of artists such as Shabba Ranks, Patra, Shaggy, Sean Paul and Jr. Gong who, at various stages, have sold well. Shaggy has been the most successful, selling over 10 million copies of his *Hotshot* album worldwide.[4] These are the exceptions and not the rule in Jamaican music sale. There is no mention of the income flows from the dubplate studio which can be more lucrative than actual recordings. Donovan "Litter" Newby (2003), the engineer of one of the most popular dubplate studios in Kingston, Arrows Dupplate studio, in a personal interview notes:

> Bounty Killah or Beenie man can earn over two million dollar in less than four hours doing dubplates for the sound systems from foreign who want the latest hits for their sound clashes. Sound man from London, Japan, New York and Toronto just come with whack a money and just get plate after plate.

In terms of income from copyright-protected works, Witter (2006) makes a powerful observation:

> Because of the historically underdeveloped legal and institutional capacity in Jamaica, the percentage of royalties accruing to Jamaicans that is actually collected is known to be ridiculously low. In 1999, the last year of its existence in Jamaica, the Performing Rights Society, which for 64 years was the sole collecting society, reported collections of approximately US$2.5 million, most of which accrued to foreigners (48).

While the sound system is included in the flow, it is positioned as a secondary source of income and conflated with revenues from radio airplay, another sore point in the Jamaican reality as radio has been notorious for not paying royalties. This, again, does not reflect the reality of the Kingston value chain where the sound system and its activities are critical to the Kingston recorded music value chain through the existence of the dubplate culture. In this sector of the music industry, income is generated through the supply of dubplate specials to sound systems, worldwide, to feed selector activities such as juggling and the staging of sound clashes – where two or more sounds compete for supremacy by outplaying each other until a winner is crowned. Income is generated also through the auxiliary activities associated with the dance such as 'gate receipts, liquor sales, dance promotion and the sales of clothing for the dance attendees' (Stolzoff 2000, 117–21).

Interorganisational Research
Jamaican Music Industry

To fully appreciate how music is made in Jamaica, a serious examination of the social, economic and cultural conditions must be initiated. Research in this area is still developing and while some important work has been done, primarily in the form of position papers and studies commissioned by international development agencies such as United Nations Educational Scientific and Cultural Organization (UNESCO), United Nations Conference Trade and Development (UNCTAD) and World Intellectual Property Organization (WIPO), there is a wide gap that needs to be addressed. Zjelka Kozul-Wright and Lloyd Stanbury's paper, 'Becoming a globally Competitive Player: The Case of The Music Industry in Jamaica', (UNCTAD) Discussion paper No. 138, gives a detailed description of the music industry in Jamaica, with emphasis on the economic contribution to national gross domestic product (GDP). The paper also presents a case for the positioning of the industry in the global marketplace by identifying some of the obstacles it faces. There is a clear focus on the economic benefits of the music industry and the national system of innovation suggests that Jamaica's capacity is not yet sufficiently developed to ensure the viability of the music industry. While there is an in-depth interrogation of the structure of the industry by Wright and Stanbury, not enough attention was given to the social and cultural environment in which sound recordings are made. This leaves the researchers opting for several foreign models as examples of the possible solution to the identified weakness in the local recording industry.

The Structure of the Recording Industry

Geoffrey Hull's *The Recording Industry* provides a detailed outline of the structure of the recording industry and its role as the main catalyst of the music industry. Hull's contribution is focused on the economic spheres due to the notion that 'the most significant changes have been what would be generally described as economic' (Hull 2004, ix). Hull establishes the three income streams of the modern music industry which are the sale and use of sound recordings, the sale and use of songs (publishing) and live performances and touring.

The dominant themes of the book are consistent with the production of culture perspective, which is one of the underlying theoretical tools of the study. As mentioned before, the recording industry has become the focus of the music business. New technology has advanced the industry's ability to create better recordings more cheaply. This has facilitated the entry of an increasing number of players at this phase of production, thus democratising the creative process, by making 'those recordings and songs more accessible to more people' (Hull 2004, ix). These new entrants into the creative process are able to capitalise on new revenue streams. Hull suggests that despite the concentration of global music output in only four large multinational firms, the public enjoys diversity in genres and artists, i.e., more music and more variety. Finally, the book looks at the ever-changing structure of the industry and its global implications.

I disagree with Hull on two fundamental points. First, the notion of more diversity with the consolidation of the multinational conglomerate is myopic. With the mergers and the creation of these conglomerates that control all aspects of the industry, diversity has clearly been stymied with many independent labels finding it very difficult to get airplay and distribution. There are developing genres which are still trying to find a mainstream voice and although established genres, such as reggae and dancehall, have made significant strides, they are still on the periphery of the global music industry. Second, Hull, in defending the economic bias of his work at the expense of the cultural and social perspectives, notes that 'such a perspective is not particularly helpful in understanding how and why the industry functions the way it does' (ix). Again, this suggests a myopic viewpoint which privileges the economic over the cultural and social in understanding the working of the music industry. I contend that an economic analysis of the music industry cannot provide a complete picture of how the industry works. Cultural realties are critical. It is culture that provides the raw material for the recording industry and it is cultural and social trends that determine how and what kind of music is made. This happens, to some extent, independently of economic realities. To divorce the economic realm from the social and cultural is, indeed, a major flaw and this is the weakness of the work.

Technology and Popular Music

Equally absent in the research initiatives on Jamaican popular music is that which explores the impact of technology and the way in which it assisted or hindered the development of modern Jamaican music forms. However, a lot of the best music and technological innovations associated with Jamaican music are due to the limitations in the technology which drove creative and innovative musicians, engineers and producers to explore technological and production options that have become industry standards, internationally (Veal 2007; Alleyne 2001, 2002).

Dub is the technological wonder of Jamaican music. The creation of the dub soundscape through the manipulation of the recording studio and the production techniques have impacted on popular music and production and genre development internationally and have been the focus of intensive academic research and interrogation. Dub aesthetics and its assimilation in the Western pop mainstream global music trends have been a part of ongoing debate. Mike Alleyne (2001, 14–17) and Michael E. Veal (2007, 42–60) have investigated this phenomenon. David Toop's *Ocean of Sound* has explored the notion of the recording studio being a compositional tool through the work of Lee 'Scratch' Perry, Brian Wilson, Phil Spector and Joe Meek. Toop argues that all four studio innovators shared one thing in common and that was their state of mind at the peak of creativity, which conventional analysis described as madness.

Economic and Cultural Geography

Modern Jamaican music is the product of the inner cities of Kingston. It is within these ghettoes that our music was created, nurtured and developed for international consumption. Scholars such as Peter Hall, Charles Landry and John Macmillan have postulated the notions of a creative city or milieu.

Kingston, with its long history of cultural output, can be described as a creative city and is a cultural Mecca of the Western hemisphere. Charles Landry in *The Creative City: A Toolkit for Urban Innovations*, and Peter Hall in *Creative Cities and Economic Development*, examine the concept of the creative city and give insight into the development and importance of creativity to the economic importance of cities worldwide. John McMillan in *Trench Town Rock: The Creation of Jamaica's Music Industry* suggests that the creation of the music goes far beyond just music but involves issues such as the role of industrial clustering in fostering innovation in developing countries. This is one of only a few attempts to look at Jamaican music from an economic perspective.

Dominic Power and Daniel Hallencreutz in *Profiting from Creativity – The Music Industry in Stockholm, Sweden and Kingston, Jamaica* present a comparative analysis of the production of popular music in Kingston and Stockholm. While they found that both Kingston and Stockholm are at the forefront of creativity due to factors such as the clustered nature of the music centre in both cities, they discovered that Kingston, due to the fragmented nature of the small firms and the lack of a proper copyright framework, did not benefit economically in the same way as Stockholm did. The absence of organised record companies in Kingston was also identified as a major obstacle. While Power and Hallencreutz made some very salient observations about the music industry in some critical areas, they did not do justice to the dynamic and unconventional nature of the Jamaican reality. They note, quite erroneously, that the low level of technology serves as a deterrent to the development of the industry and cite the lack of high-tech recording studios, the lack of CD manufacturing facilities and the low level of computer saturation in the country as other areas of underdevelopment.

Yet, Power and Hallencreutz failed to recognise the phenomenal contribution of dub and its studio techniques that have revolutionised studio production techniques. These will be addressed later in this work. The Jamaican recording industry, while not comparable to Stockholm, has had its fair share of state-of-the-art recording facilities during all the periods of cultural production. State-of-the-art studios started with Federal Recording Studio and Dynamic Recording Studio in the late '60s. By the 1970s, there were Dynamics and Aquarius recording studios and in the '80s there were Tuff Gong, Mixing Lab and Music Mountain, Grove Music and, in the '90s,

Anchor recording studios. All these studio facilities were comparable to state-of-the-art facilities anywhere in the Anglo-American industry. Power and Hallencreutz (2002, 1,848) also note the absence of an efficient rights management structure as a primary reason for the disparity in earning. This observation presupposes that success in the music industry can only be measured by economic indices that are based on copyright philosophy.

Copyright: A Cultural Perspective

Copyright and copyright laws present an intriguing study of intellectual ownership. Several works will be cited in this research including *Copyrighting Culture: The Political Economy of Intellectual Property* by Roland Bettig. The author explores the power relationship between copyright ownership and the capitalist class establishing a clear link between the two and shows how they control the relationships which govern modern technologies such as film entertainment, cable television, the Internet, radio and book publishing through their ownership of copyright within the entertainment sector. Hence, they have significantly increased their own wealth at the expense of creators of original copyrightable content and the general public. Mark Rose's *Authors and Owners* traces the development of copyright and questions the concept of the author. Rose (1993) sees an author as a recent construct which 'is inseparable from the commodification of literature' (1). In *The Cultural Life of Intellectual Properties: Authorship, Appropriation, and the Law*, Rosemary J. Coombe takes an ethnographic approach to the analysis of intellectual property rights and the role of law in influencing culture from an economic perspective. Again, a perspective of the Jamaican and Caribbean reality, which is critical to the development of a theoretical body of work on copyright in the region, is lacking. Carter Van Pelt and Larissa Mann have done pioneering work on copyright in Jamaica. Mann's unpublished master's thesis, 'Intellectual Property and the Jamaican Music Industry', explores the development of Jamaican music without the implementation of a proper copyright regime. She posits that the music industry was based on notions such as a non-economic motivation for recording and a communal method of song composition, contradicting Western notions of copyright and its importance in the process of creativity as an incentive ensures that creativity is sustained. Mann focuses on the period before the Jamaican Copyright Act of 1993, although reference is made to the new act in the concluding chapters. Van Pelt's unpublished master's thesis 'Toward A Conventional Copyright system: The Jamaican Experience With Rights Management and A New Law', examines the post-1993 Copyright Act but looks at the development of practices of producers, songwriters and musicians before the new act in 1993. Van Pelt notes the changing attitude towards copyright but concludes that due to the uniqueness of the Jamaican environment, the effectiveness of a modern copyright regime and the benefits to creators will be tested on a regular basis.

Cultural Studies Perspective

A significant number of research initiatives have focused on the Jamaican musical scene from a cultural studies perspective and include some groundbreaking work. These focus primarily on sexuality, gender, cultural history and lyrical content analysis. Very little has been done on interrogating the business of the music, the management structures and the entertainment laws which governed and impacted on the development of the music business and the production of cultural artefacts.

Carolyn Cooper's pioneering work on the content analysis of both reggae and dancehall lyrics in *Noises in the Blood: Orality, Gender and The "Vulgar" Body of Jamaican Popular Culture* and *Sound Clash: Jamaican Dancehall Culture at Large* have provided important insights into the value of the Jamaican lyrical content and have proven that the lyrics of the top reggae stars, including Bob Marley and dancehall deejay stylists such as Ninja Man and Shabba Ranks, are powerful texts that are as potent and relevant to the cultural perspective as any other popular music. Cooper also makes the link between the lyrics of Marley and Shabba Ranks and the social and economic realities of the Jamaican space. The 'interpenetration of the oral and scribal forms' (117) are highlighted and Cooper also points to the significance of performance, songwriting and music within the Jamaican cultural space which, she posits, are 'organically integrated within an Afrocentric aesthetic' (117). Cooper also explores the notion of Jamaican popular music culture and the hegemonic struggles it faces. She points out that the music of the deejays, which she refers to as 'noise, can be simply dismissed as yet another example of the vulgarity of both rural and urban life in Jamaica, or, it can be recognized as a profoundly malicious cry to upset the existing social order' (5).

In *Noises in the Blood: Orality, Gender and The "Vulgar" Body of Jamaican Popular Culture*, Cooper outlines through the content analysis of over 50 song texts in five major thematic groupings: (i) 'songs that celebrate DJing itself'; (ii) 'dance songs that vigorously invite participants to 'shock out and party''; (iii) 'songs of social commentary on a variety of issues, for example, ghetto violence and hunger'; (iv) 'songs that focus on sexual/gender relations, – by far the largest number in the sample'; and (v) 'songs that explicitly speak to the slackness/culture opposition' (3). She concludes that dancehall is a discrete culture that is a space that is dedicated to the 'flamboyant performing of sexuality'. In both books, Cooper grapples quite controversially with the notion of the privileged position of Northern scholarship, Jamaican middle-class sensibilities versus southern/insider scholarship and working-class identity and expression. From the standpoint of the research initiative, the most important aspect of these works is the issue of consumption versus production. In the introduction of *Sound Clash*, Cooper painstakingly defends herself against the critique of three academics from the North – Norman Stolzoff, Henry and Ross – who question some of her readings and interpretation of various aspects of dancehall. Of the three, Stolzoff's critique is the most significant. Stolzoff (2000) states:

> What is wrong with many analyses of dancehall culture is the way that they either start at the level of the analysis of culture texts (song lyrics), or they go straight to an aesthetic or ethical critique of the work without examining the way the text is produced or consumed and what effects these processes have on the text (18).

While I agree that most of the work on dancehall is centred on historiographies and content analysis – hence the need for an initiative such as this – I don't agree with his assertion that there is something 'wrong with this approach'. This position assumes that such a cultural studies approach is invalid and not worthy of academic inquiry. This was pioneering work, which was necessary if one is to understand the nature of Jamaican society and the hegemonic struggles which have been the nature of popular music making in Jamaica. I, however, concur with the observation that 'the analytical pendulum has swung too far in prioritizing consumption in analyses of the cultural economy (Pratt 2002, 1).

This brings us to a point of deeper reflection on the work of Stolzoff. *Wake the Town and Tell the People: Dancehall Culture in Jamaica* is an ethnographic analysis of dancehall culture that asserts the primacy of the production process as 'A sphere of active cultural production that potentially may transform the prevailing hegemony' (15). Stolzoff suggests that the study of popular culture, and dancehall culture in particular, can benefit from the interrogation of 'everyday practice' and discounts the value of semiotic and content analysis interpretations which, he states, are inadequate. Stolzoff stretches the interpretation of the word dancehall to include all manifestation of cultural production within the last two centuries, yet, he never sufficiently addresses the issues of production, on which his thesis is centred, to other periods of Jamaican music output. He focuses on the narrow trajectory of sound system-centred production from the consumption in the dancehall space. Very little emphasis or interrogation is placed on the mainstream of production of dancehall music within the Kingston music scene geared toward radio play and international distribution and, ultimately, breaking into the British and US Billboard charts, leading to Grammy recognition. While Stolzoff claims to focus his ethnographic study on the production of dancehall, even outlining the political economic structure of dancehall in one chapter, and looking at dancehall artists 'from the beginning of their careers as 'no names' through the various potential stages that follow' in another chapter, the majority of the work takes the very same approaches that his work claims to find problematic.

The first three chapters are cultural histories of the dancehall phenomenon as defined by Stolzoff; chapter 4 presents the performance aspect of dancehall culture with particular focus on the 'relationship between growing social violence and the politicisation of the dancehall space'. In chapter 5, the focus shifts to the production trajectory of the work and highlights the production process of dancehall through the examination of a dubplate studio in Kingston. In addition, he attempts to establish the studio as a 'distinct social space' within the music scene of Kingston. The last three chapters cover issues such as the career path of the dancehall entertainer – from nobody to star – the sound system dance and its various performance modes and violence in the dancehall. Finally, the work looks at the relationship between dancehall and the social predicaments of Jamaica at the time of the study.

While Stolzoff has clearly identified the fact that many studies centred on dancehall are focused on the consumption trajectory at the expense of analysis of the production of cultural text in its social context, he fails to deal adequately with the very same thing he has identified as lacking. Certainly, a true understanding of the production process of dancehall and other genres of Jamaican music cannot be fully interrogated by a focus on the dubplate studio and the dancehall space. It presents a very narrow perspective, which does not do justice to the dynamic process involved in the production of popular music in the Kingston music scene. The dubplate studio, at best, represents a subgenre of dancehall in terms of music production and represents an economic device in the Kingston music value chain, but can never be elevated to the status of representing a major area of music production within the Kingston music space. What it represents is a repetition of the production process on a minor scale; the production process which is targeted at export and servicing the radio and lastly the sound system. While the economic value of the dubplate studio system can never be underestimated, it only represents a microcosm of the production ethos of the Kingston music scene, which is multilayered and multifaceted.

Dub Version

In this chapter, a survey of the literature in popular music study, popular music organisation, music production, Jamaican music history, intellectual property rights management, economic culture and economic geography was done. The glaring gaps in Jamaican popular music enquiry were established with a view to filling some of these gaps. The next chapter will establish distinctive periods of cultural production for Jamaican popular music output and will explore the hegemonic and counterhegemonic forces, which informed popular music production in Kingston.

NOTES

1. Http://portal.unesco.org/culture/en/ev.php-url_id=35024&url_do=do_topic&url_section=201.html.
2. More recent instances of media consolidation, for example, Time Warner and Viacom, challenge this model. Label acts were promoted through print publications and TV outlets owned by the conglomerates, demonstrating a significant degree of control over exposure. Viacom has reestablished the

record company, Columbia, which does not produce physical CDs of their signed acts but promotes them across multiple platforms – television (cable/network), newspapers, magazines and radio.
3. This depends on the constitution of the national collecting agencies as well as the deal which is negotiated between publisher and the songwriter; a more established songwriter has the power to negotiate a smaller percentage based on frequency of hit songs and his/her demand in the market.
4. http://bigyardmusic.com/index.php?option=com_bigyard&artist=1&Itemid=20.

Making Popular Music in the Creative Echo Chamber

Babylon system is a vampire sucking the blood of the sufferer.
                                                    Bob Marley

With 'Mother and Child Reunion' [on Paul Simon 1972], I went to Jamaica to record; I realized that if I want to write in that genre, for it to really work I had to go to the place and work with the musicians.
                                                    Paul Simon

Popular Jamaican music was essentially a response to rhythm and blues which was the music that the radio stations were playing.
                                                    Dermot Hussey

While not strictly chronological, this narrative describes the development of the Jamaican music industry by tracing the unfolding of the Kingston music scene through several periods of cultural development.

Periods of Cultural Production

Periods of cultural production are defined as those periods marked by distinctive codes, practices, styles, sociopolitical and sociocultural developments that have impacted the way cultural artefacts are produced.

Before examining the periods of cultural production in which the Kingston music scene might be divided, it is useful to look at the concept of cultural production in a broader sense. David Hesmondhalgh (2007), professor of media and cultural studies, adopting Raymond Williams's (1983) position provides a useful perspective on the development of cultural production in Europe. He recognises three distinct periods, 'each of them named after the main form of social relations between symbol creators and wider society prevailing at the time' (Williams 1983, 38–56).

The first period cited, *patronage and artisanal*, covers a series of systems that existed from the Middle Ages until the nineteenth century, during which musicians, painters and poets were retained and supported by the aristocracy and the church, thus releasing them from the humdrum activities of daily life that would distract them from their creative work. Artisans were skilled craft persons who exercised a significant degree of autonomy. The next period was known as *market professional*. Dating from the early nineteenth century, this was the period where symbolic work was offered for sale and the market became an important force in cultural production. The market professional period heralded the system in which 'more and more work was sold via intermediaries' (Hesmondhalgh 2007, 53).

Hesmondhalgh calls the next period *complex professional*. This refers to the early twentieth century, accelerating after the 1950s when creative personnel were organised under companies to which they were directly employed on retainer or contract. Along with the traditional creative activities such as authorship and music-making, new technology enabled the advent of radio, film and television. These various periods were not seamless transitions but, to this day, exist side by side with the first two periods and alongside the more dominant form of complex professional.

With regard to the development of Jamaican music, Michael Witter (2001) identifies three periods:

Period One: Pre 1950: before the recording of music
Period Two: 1950–70: production of recorded and live music for the Jamaican market
Period Three: Post 1970: supply of recorded and live music to the international market (4).

It is my contention however, that Jamaican music has evolved through a series of far more complex periods of production. As Pierre Bourdieu (1993) notes, 'cultural production distinguishes itself from the production of the most common objects in that it must produce not only the objects in its materiality, but also the value of this object, that is, the recognition of artistic legitimacy' (164). Before outlining the periods of cultural production that I have identified, some comments on Witter's timelines are necessary. There was some recording of Jamaican music pre-1950 by foreigners, although this was focused on folk recordings and was anthropological in orientation. Also, as will be discussed in detail in the ensuing narrative, songs were targeted at the British market during the late 1960s. Finally, to suggest, as Witter does, that the last period was dedicated to supplying international markets, without any mention of the domestic market, gives the erroneous impression that the domestic market was not important to the industry. It also blatantly disregards the role of the sound systems in the production process in the Jamaican recorded music industry. I propose a more detailed timeline:

a. *Folk Culture*: (Pre 1950s–56)

b. *Appropriation*: (1957–60)

c. *Innovation*: (1961–69)

d. *Internationalisation*: (1970–80)

e. *Neoinnovation*: (1981–2000)

f. *Global Interaction*: (2001–Present)

I thought it necessary to develop a periodisation for the evolution of music production that represents the dynamic nature of the creative process which emerged during the 1950s and continues into the present. The creation of so many styles and genres in such a very short period also 'provides a framework that will allow for the assessment of changes and continuities' (Hesmondhalgh 2007, 51) in the production of popular music on the Kingston music scene.

During each period of production, we can trace the development of popular music using technology, legislation and the organisational structures consistent with the production of culture perspective.

Folk Culture (Pre 1950s–56)

Prior to the recording of music in Kingston, Jamaican popular music consisted of mento bands that played in bars and street corners at community events. This was the predominant popular sound of the common folk which was influenced by African folk forms such as Junkanoo, Quadrille, Revival, Zion, Kumina and Pocomania (Chang and Chen 1998, 10–18; Barrow and Dalton 2004, 6–10; Bilby 2006, 185–87). Also, during this period the big band sound and Tin Pan Alley music were the dominant cultural forms of the élite and thus the predominant sound of radio. Mento music was the first music to be recorded when music pioneers such as Ivan Chin, Stanley Motta and Ken Khouri began recording the popular sound for the overseas market (Neely 2007, 5–7). The first of these, entitled 'Whai Ay', was recorded by Lord Fly in the early '50s for Stanley Motta. Another was the

1952 recording from the Ticklers (Chang and Chen 1998, 15; Barrow and Dalton 2004, 8). The recording of these songs was considered 'A landmark moment in the industry' (Neely 2007, 8). Ken Khouri, with backing from Alec Durie, proprietor of the famous Times Store on King Street, recorded and released his first mento record in 1951. It featured The Calypsonians with Lord Flea on lead vocals (Neely 2007, 8). This interest in recording mento was influenced by the calypso craze then occurring in the United States (Barrow and Dalton 2004, 9; Eldridge 2002, 621–22). Local mento producers took advantage of the opportunity to target the international market where there was a demand for calypso or mento music.

Most of the analyses on the mento period of recordings cite this period as the birth of the domestic record industry (Barrow and Dalton 2004, 7; Chang and Chen 1998, 15; Neely 2007, 2). This is being generous; as a real industry, one with the vertical integration and intermediaries that are required for proper recording industry, was not in place. No mastering facilities were available in Jamaica and Motta and the other producers had to send their acetates to Britain for mastering. This key ingredient in any recording industry structure was not a part of the Jamaican recording landscape at that time.

Market is also another important element of the recording industry; to be economically viable there must be a market in which consumers are available to purchase the recordings. By all accounts, the mento songs of this period were produced primarily for an external market. Daniel Neely (2007) states:

> Virtually everything Motta and Khouri manufactured in the early days of the industry evoked a sense of place linked to tourist entertainment… Of the 38 records Motta made between mid-1953 and 1955, 18 were made exclusively for hotels (these included Shaw Park, the Silver Seas [whose owner, Stuart Sharpe, was a close friend of Motta's] and the Montego Beach) Of the remaining twenty, only one was by performer (a Trinidadian, Cobra Man a.k.a. Joseph Clemendore) who had no traceable link to tourism (8).

While there was no doubt that mento music was a part of the fabric of the majority population handed down through folk songs and rural-urban migration, the music was not a part of the mass musical movement that had been ignited by the invention of the sound system dating back to the 1940s.

In addition, the masses did not participate in the consumption of the early 78 rpm records produced by Motta, Khouri and Chin. This was to come later with the introduction of the 45 rpm record, long after the mento tunes were current. The contractual arrangements, which were the hallmark of the complex professional period, were not yet developed and not much has been said about the early arrangements between the mento producers and the mento performers and musicians. Although Khouri had established the first pressing plant, label printing, recording facilities and limited distribution (Neely 2007, 9), all important components of any record industry, this was to service the limited mento recordings, with the first manufactured in November 1954. To label this early development as the start of the recorded industry is erroneous and creates confusion, so I prefer to call this period the birth of popular music recordings on the Kingston music scene.

The birth of the Kingston recording industry took place in the *appropriation* period of cultural production with the production of the early Jamaican R&B records. This period marked the origin of the relationship between the local music scene, through its independent producers, and the super structure of the Anglo-American music industry, with its hegemonic agenda of mainstreaming and homogenising the local music to fit North American taste as well as the capitalist aim of profit at the expense of cultural authenticity. This point is borne out by the fact that Jamaican mento was marketed in North America as calypso, although mento had its distinctive musical signature that clearly differentiated it from calypso and folk music.

Based on the early success of Trinidadian calypso in the 1930s, with top calypsonians such as Attila the Hun, Roaring Lion, Lord Executor and Harry Belafonte's 1956 album, *Calypso*, which was the first album by a solo artist to sell a million copies in American history, a calypso craze had begun in America (Alleyne 2009, 80, 81).[1] This led to the signing of Jamaican Lord Flea by Capitol Records and the release of the album *Swingin Calypso* in 1957. The album was clearly mento music and had no authentic calypso instrumentation but was labelled calypso to fit the exigencies of North American taste. John Connell and Chris Gibson (2003) make the following point about the Anglo-American music scene, 'every phase of the evolution of popular music displayed "alien" elements, though often substantially modified to suit Western tastes and prejudices' (145). Lord Flea himself was cognizant of this imposition of a cultural straightjacket for music of the other; in an article in the magazine *Calypso Star* he observes:

> In Jamaica, we call our music mento until recently. Today calypso is beginning to be used for all kinds of West Indian music. This is because it's become so commercialized there. Some people like to think of West Indians as carefree natives who work and sing and play and laugh their lives away. But this isn't so. Most of the people there are hardworking folks and many of them are smart businessmen. If the tourist wants 'calypso' that's what we sell them.[2]

Lord Flea appeared in two Hollywood movies in 1957, *Bop Girl Goes Calypso* and *Calypso Joe*. The Lord Flea contract with Capitol Records and the release of his albums and movie appearances marked another chapter in the ongoing discourse on the effects of the global music industry on the reformulation and distortion of Caribbean music to suit the international marketplace.[3] The mento recording had to fit into the exotic tropical illusions that were necessary to satisfy that market. Devoid of any masculine overtones and indigenous flavour or sensibilities 'the more successful introductions became occasional exotic additions to the lower levels of hit parades, culturally distinct, but ultimately little different from many other popular performances' (Connell and Gibson 2003, 145). Rebecca Leydon (2002) adds:

> [T]he elaborate fiction of the tropical paradise functioned as an exoticised complement to American suburbia: a colourful, dangerous, mysterious, heterogeneous Other which contrasted with the safe, predictable, homogeneous and sexually repressive environment at home (48).

Hence Adorno's culture industry analysis was critical to an understanding of these early interactions and negotiations between Jamaican popular music and the Anglo-American music industry. This use of Adorno's analyses is relevant in this instance as in many cases the industry had two general ways of commodifying and standardising music. First, they provided the context within which hit songs were produced by utilising a standard formula for songwriting, with critical elements of hook, melody and innocuous lyrics. Second, the corporations incorporated music of alien origins but subjected them to the industrial commercial logic of the modern culture industry (Negus 1996, 39).

Period of Appropriation (1957–60)

Connell and Gibson (2003) are correct in their observation that music has contributed to the increasing global nature of cultural and economic interconnection, 'mapping out new networks of commodity flow and entrepreneurial activity' (56). Within this nexus is the intermingling of different sounds, beats, harmonic, melodic and rhythmic resources on local national and transnational levels. On some levels it is true to say, as Simon Frith (1996) has, that:

> All countries' popular musics are shaped by international influences and institutions, by multinational capital and technology, by global pop norms and values...No country in the world is unaffected by the way in which the twentieth century mass media (the electronic means of musical production reproduction and transmission have...created a universal aesthetic (2).

The cultural production period, Appropriation, epitomised Frith's observations on the effects of transnational capital and technology on the South. The period was characterised by the inflow of American rhythm and blues, jazz and the beginning of the recording of non-mento popular music. These popular recordings were Jamaican versions of American rhythm and blues, which was made popular through the innovation of the sound system, the main vehicle of entertainment for the working class. Due to the reach of the amplitude modulation (AM) radio band, radio signals from as far as Florida could be picked up in Jamaica. Consequently, the stations that played this type of black music became popular among Jamaican listeners who could afford radio. The popularity of the music was cemented by the importation of the records by music buffs that had gone on farm work and other business on the American gulf coast. Included in this group were the pioneers of the sound system and popular music recording, Clement Dodd and Duke Reid. The American R&B songs became the popular sound at dances in the inner city areas of downtown Kingston and many of these were the exclusive prizes of the main sound systems that used them in sound clashes to defeat their opponents. It was common practice to disguise the real name of these exclusive numbers so as to prevent rivals from getting the songs in the United States.

> Sound clashes were the main motivation for these early importations of R&B recordings. Epic battles were contested between Sir Coxsone's Downbeat, Duke Reid's Trojan and Prince Buster's Voice of the People. The need for indigenous material arose when the main sound system Gladiators ran out of rhythm and blues material from New Orleans and Miami. This was primarily due to the emergence of rock 'n' roll in the

United States but dance patrons did not take to rock 'n' roll. So, the sound system operators were forced to do local recordings for use on their sound systems. These top sounds began to record songs and used them to win some of the most famous clashes in Kingston's popular dancehalls.[4]

One of the first non-mento songs, 'Lollipop Girl', which heralded the appropriation period, was recorded in 1956 by the Jiving Juniors – Derrick Harriott and Claudie Sang Jr. Harriott produced the 'single' on a dub plate (soft acetate)[5] at Stanley Motta's studio. This dub plate/acetate was given to a sound system from Maxfield Avenue in western St Andrew named Thunderbird, owned by Carlyle Hyoung. 'Lollipop Girl' created such a stir in the dancehall that producer Coxsone Dodd got the dub plate from Hyoung in exchange for some R&B records. Coxsone used the dub plate of 'Lollipop Girl' to conquer his rivals at the sound clashes which took place at popular dancehalls such as Forrester's Hall on North Street in Kingston (Katz 2003, 26).

Tired of being defeated by Dodd's sound system with 'Lollipop Girl', Duke Reid, reportedly, sent his cohorts to tell Harriott to send him a copy of the song. He played it at a dance and this resulted in some gun drawing between himself and Coxsone. Reid officially recorded the song for the Treasure Isle label after Coxsone had abandoned playing it on his sound system. Around the same time, a duo, Simms and Robinson, aka Bunny and Scully, made a track for producer, Dada Tewari entitled 'Till the End of Time'. This song and 'Lollipop Girl' are credited with starting the modern recording business (Bradley 2000, 40). 'Lollipop Girl' was a Jamaican interpretation of American rhythm and blues songs already popular in the Kingston dancehalls. Jamaicans had grown fond of the music of Fats Domino, Roscoe Gordon and Louis Jordan.

The popularity of 'Lollipop Girl', 'Till the End of Time' and other singles which shared the same timeline created a cottage industry of indigenous recording of rhythm and blues songs driven by the sound system culture. Many up-and-coming artists would record their original dub plates/acetates for sound system operators who were in search of good, indigenous hits for the dancehall. Lloyd Bradley (2000) explains the process:

Fig. 3.1 The famous Forrester's Hall, North Street, Kingston
© Dennis Howard 2009

> Any bartering would normally take place at a dance so the disc on offer could be road tested on the spot. If it moved the crowd, the artiste could expect five pounds or so for it; if it didn't, he'd be wise to go home and hide until the people in the area forget the shaming experience (25).

Thus, when songs like 'Lollipop Girl' and 'Till the End of Time' started the change in musical styling, the big three began to spend a lot of time at Federal to record some of the early indigenous recordings. This heralded the Kingston rhythm and blues/proto-ska period[6] of recordings. Notable hits include 'Mannie Oh' by Higgs and Wilson, 'Muriel' by Alton and Eddie and 'Oh Carolina' by the Folkes Brothers. Bradley notes, 'Although cut within the same few months, all three records displayed a noticeably different approach to contemporary cultural correctness, each one appearing to up the stakes as regards the definition of Jamaicanness' (51).

Around 1958 to 1959, led by Chris Blackwell and Edward Seaga, sound system producers began offering their records for sale to the public (Bradley 2000, 42–45) with the focus being on local consumption. Sales were made through the few record shops, barbershops, grocery shops and door to door (44). So began a thriving business in the production, manufacture and distribution of seven-inch records; a significant signpost in the evolution of the Jamaican music business and the development of a Jamaican sound.

The main producers/sound system operators were Clement 'Sir Coxsone' Dodd, owner of Sir Coxsone Down Beat; Arthur 'Duke' Reid owner of Duke Reid the Trojan; Lloyd Daley owner of The Matador; Vin Edwards owner of King Edwards sound system and Cecil 'Prince Buster' Campbell owner of the Voice of the People sound system. They occupied a unique position within the structure of the Kingston music scene.

Their sound systems performed the role of *feeder sound systems* which directly targeted the dancehalls, while they also made sound recordings exclusively for playing at dances in the Kingston metropolitan area and rural parishes. In addition, they were in a position to promote imported American R&B tunes on their sound systems then bootleg them for sale to other sound systems (Dodd 1995).

Fig. 3.2 Shang-Hi Solophonic Sound System at the Jazz Hut, West Kingston
© James Howard c. 1974

These owner/producers were distinct from other sound systems, like Tom the Great Sebastian, Thunder Bird, Sir Nick, Lord Koos, V Rocket and Thompson Hi Fi, which did not themselves produce sound recordings but played the regular R&B, mento records, custom acetates from local singers and copies of the sound recordings of the feeder sound systems to play at their engagements.

The latter sound systems I will designate *spreader sound systems*. They had the role of extending the popularity of many recordings that were done by the feeder sound systems. However, the effectiveness of the spreader sound systems was not uniform. A successful spreader system had to secure a good working relationship with the owners of the feeder sound systems, especially in the early days of the recording business, i.e., the R&B period. This was so because most feeder sound systems played their recordings almost exclusively on their own system for a considerable period of time before sharing them. It was only when they believed that they had optimised the benefits of a particular recording that they passed it on to the spreader systems (Howard 1990; Goodison 1990). However, during the later periods of production this feeder/spreader system became more sophisticated.

Non-sound system producers such as Leslie Kong, who operated the Beverley Record label, also played a significant role in the development of the music. Kong was responsible for many of the early hits by Derrick Morgan and Desmond Dekker and was the first to record Bob Marley. The appropriation of the R&B and boogie of southern United States of America was the critical starting point for the music production in Kingston and points to black diaspora movements across Paul Gilroy's Black Atlantic. Gilroy (2002) has also noted that along this Black Atlantic trajectory:

> Where African-American forms are borrowed and set to work in new locations they have often been deliberately reconstructed in novel patterns that do not respect their originators' proprietary claims or the boundaries of discrete nation states and the supposedly natural political communities they express or simply contain (98–99).

This points to the interconnection of cultures, through music, within the black diaspora, the hybrid nature of cultural reconstruction and a resistance to hegemonic forces which was a salient feature of the postcolonial Caribbean.

Innovation (1961–69)

Rex Nettleford's thesis on the creative imagination is an important tool of analysis in looking at this next period. Nettleford, in *Inward Reach Outward Stretch: A Voice from the Caribbean*, devised the term 'battle for space' (80) to highlight the conflicts faced by Caribbean people affected by North Atlantic marginalisation and oppression of the cultural, economic and political kind to make sense of their existence as human beings. He notes:

> The US penetration of the Caribbean Basin by way of political, military, intellectual, economic and telecommunications means in a latter-day version of the age-old attack on the space of the Caribbean people is likely to perpetuate the 'suffering' of dependency and powerlessness (82).

In his book *Identity Race and Protest*, Nettleford speaks of the rhythm of Africa and the melody of Europe in explaining the dialectical relationship between 'the largely brown biological and the black cultural hybrid' that placed European culture and traits in a superior position over the African in the Creole cultures of Jamaica. 'A Creole culture in which European and African elements persist and predominate in fairly standard combinations and relationships with things European gaining ascriptive status while things African were correspondingly devalued' (174). It is in this milieu that black, dispossessed youth 'survive as depressed people do anywhere through different forms of artistic expression, like music and dance' (97).

Armed with influences from jazz, mento, rhythm and blues, Jamaican rural folk culture and Rastafarian Nyabinghi, recordings from Kingston artists and musicians became distinctively Jamaican during this period, celebrated as the most creative and prolific period in modern Jamaican popular culture. It produced several new genres including ska, rocksteady, reggae and dub. In an effort to Jamaicanise popular music even more, the producers, players and performers of the day moved the Jamaican R&B sound to what is called ska. Important players in the creation of this genre include Coxsone Dodd, guitarist and arranger Ernest Ranglin, Prince Buster, bassist Cluett Johnson, drummer Arkland 'Drumbago' Parkes and pianist and vocalist Theophilus Beckford. This was the first distinctively Jamaican sound and it took over the dancehall and eventually radio from the American R&B and proto ska. Songwriters began to develop new styles of song construction (which will be discussed in chapter five); importantly, the indigenous studio production mode was fully developed during the ska period.

Fig. 3.3 Treasure Isle Studio, Bond Street, western Kingston
© Dennis Howard 2006

Local recordings were exported to Britain to supply the immigrant market of Caribbean residents and British-born youngsters settled in cities like London and Birmingham who were attracted to the sound and the beat. This initiative was led by Lee Gopthall and Chris Blackwell and implemented through distributors such as Trojan. Export to Britain became a primary economic outlet for the top producers and performers who exported records and performed at venues in London, Manchester and Birmingham.

This pointed to the fact that wherever music is played there are multiple networks at play (Connell and Gibson 2003). John Connell and Chris Gibson also note that, 'cities are nodes in international mediascapes – centres of production and retailing and hosts to multi-cultural communities and their diverse musical texts and spaces' (160). These cities, which hosted large Caribbean diaspora communities, became a major source of income for Jamaican producers of sound recordings. Paul Gilroy (2002) sees:

> England, or more accurately London, as an important junction point or crossroads on the webbed pathway of Black Atlantic political culture. It is

revealed to be a place where, by virtue of local factors like the informality of racial segregation, the global phenomenon such as anti-colonial and emancipationist political formations are still being sustained, reproduced, and amplified (95).

While the observation of an informal racial segregation in London is arguable, Gilroy's point is a potent one as London and other cities with migrant populations were important points of ethnic cultural expression, hybridity, appropriation and location. This cultural intermingling gave the descendants of the Caribbean a cultural centre they did not get from being British citizens, due to racism and police harassment. As William Henry (2006) noted, the British black used Caribbean culture, (reggae/dancehall in particular), combined with elements of African American culture of soul and hip hop 'as part of an outernational system of knowledge exchanges across the "Black Atlantic"' (26). 'The British born of Afrikan descent expressed a defiant attitude that questioned and challenged the seeming acceptance of their lot by the parental generation' (27). By adopting the cultural codes of Kingston, the young generation of British blacks were able to express a rejection of their own reality as the 'silent unwanted other'.

The first international breakthrough for ska came in 1964 with the Blackwell-produced 'My Boy Lollipop' sung by Millie Small, which reached number two on the British charts and sold six million copies worldwide (Bradley 2000, 151). 'My Boy Lollipop' was a critical signpost for Jamaican popular music in the modern era;[7] it was the first song to manifest the cultural dilution, which became the hallmark of the relationship between local industry and the Euro-American music industry and here the issues of authenticity, co-optation and appropriation became part of the discourse. The song was not even recorded primarily by Jamaican musicians. The only Jamaican musician included in the production process was Ernest Ranglin, brought in to produce and arrange the song. It was a watered down version of the authentic ska, which was being performed by groups such as The Skatalites, but this was an intentional ploy aimed at attracting the British pop market. Jimmy Cliff was signed by Island Records after his trip to the World's Fair in New York in 1964 and was marketed to the British pop market. He became the first Jamaican to be marketed that way and the first Jamaican artist to be signed to Island Records since the proto-ska period of Wilfred 'Jackie' Edward and Laurel Aitken. Cliff's first nominal success by way of airplay with Island Records came with the song 'Hard Road to Travel' in 1967 from the album of the same name.

The rocksteady genre transition was even more influential. The shift to drum and bass, the bass driven instrumental, the birth of the deejay/singer combination and the rise of the deejay as an individual talent all took place during this innovation period. With the rise of younger musicians, the ska beat began to slow down, and with the introduction of the electric bass; rocksteady was created in 1966. The rock steady period is significant for the development of major smooth vocal singers such as Alton Ellis, Ken Boothe, Desmond Dekker, John Holt, The Techniques, The Paragons, The Gaylads, The Uniques, and The Jiving Jrs, who made their most significant contribution during this very short transition period. Commenting on the influence of Rastafari on popular music development in the 1960s, Nettleford in *Mirror Mirror: Identity Race and Protest*, notes:

> The ska as a music and dance form emerging from the urban lower classes in 1965 has its initial responses of sneer and snobbery from the more privileged society, only to be thoroughly appropriated by the wider society and commercially promoted at home and abroad [and into oblivion]…(97).

The American influence was also significant during this period. Many of these groups were inspired by their American counterparts, for example, The Temptations, Tom Jones, James Brown, Jackie Wilson, The Beatles, Impressions, The Platters, The Drifters, The Supremes and The Four Tops. They borrowed the vocal styles, song composition and attitude from these American and British acts. Overseas success came again in 1967 and 1968 when Desmond Dekker's '007 Shanty Town' hit the British charts at number 12. In 1968, also, Dekker struck yet again with 'Poor Mi Israelite' (released internationally as 'Israelites'). The song, produced by Leslie Kong, reached number one in the UK, Sweden, West Germany, Holland and South Africa. By 1969, it went to number nine on the US Billboard Top 100 chart (Chang and Chen 1998, 44), entering the chart on June 7 and spending seven weeks on the charts (Whitburn 1996, 171).

The year 1968 proved to be another significant signpost in genre development on the Kingston music scene as this was the period when Jamaica's most enduring musical expression – reggae – was officially recognised. Influenced by the exigencies of the sound system culture, new production techniques were established through the creation of dub. These new production techniques revolutionised popular music production internationally and have endured to the present. The Beatles recorded a rocksteady/reggae song for the *White Album* called 'Ob La Di Ob La Da' in 1968. It was inspired by their visit to the Jamaican music scene and their exposure to the sound that had developed (Holness 2002). This, undoubtedly, is the most important creative period in the history of popular music production, influencing everything that followed in popular music production in Kingston and, by extension, London. The Beatles' transmigration to experience Jamaican music was not a one-way process and many Jamaicans moved about the Atlantic to the UK and the United States as part of transnational movements which manifested in various forms, one such is the island ceiling.

Internationalisation (1970–80)

Critics of cultural imperialism have argued that the effects of cultural imperialism on former colonies are exaggerated and that local cultures are not being decimated but are involved in a relationship with the American culture which is not homogenous but taken from various roots and different cultures including non-Western sources. They argue that cultural imperialism is no longer relevant because cultural flows cannot be identified with any single nation. Additionally, David Hesmondhalgh (2007) makes the point that:

> [M]uch of the popular music that traverse the globe is the result of creativity of the African Diaspora and very often African-American. Transnational corporations may control the circulation of this music, but it would be wrong to identify it culturally as simply the product of a dominant Western culture (235).

These perspectives do not take into consideration the effects of cultural imperialism/globalisation on non-Western others and how it affects every aspect of life in these societies. It was during the period of Internationalisation that Jamaica's music production began to make inroads, internationally, outside of the ethnic markets of immigrant Jamaicans. Reggae is the established music of Kingston and has a distinctive sound, beat and style. It has been exported to South America, Japan and Europe and, intermittently, made the popular charts in Britain and the United States. These forays into the mainstream are characterised by 'the Western control of the capital through which reggae artists must seek access to global discourse, and its creative consequences for the process of negotiation through the predatory environment of the record industry' (Alleyne 1998, 65–66).[8] In other words, the interaction between Jamaican popular music and the Anglo-American recorded music industry was mediated through the control of conglomerates which resulted in a lopsided relationship based on the crossover imperative. These negotiations led to 'recurrent instances of textual transformation as a primary characteristic of reggae's international outreach' (65).[9] Jamaican production techniques were adopted by American and British pop music and indigenous reggae bands began to emerge, especially in Britain. Jamaican music became truly transnational during Internationalisation, reaching countries such as Brazil, Panama, Columbia, Japan and Germany. The recording facilities were now sufficiently advanced to attract British and American acts to record on the island. The Rolling Stones, Herbie Mann, Eric Gale, Johnny Nash and Roberta Flack were some of the acts that took advantage of Jamaica's facilities. Reggae performers were touring globally and making significant inroads.

Jimmy Cliff had his first taste of international success with songs such as 'Wonderful World Beautiful People' from the album of the same name (1969) that includes tracks such as 'Vietnam', 'Many Rivers to Cross' and 'Better Days Are Coming'. Other albums on the Island Records label included *Goodbye Yesterday* (1970) with the song 'Trapped', produced by Cat Stevens and 'Bongo Man'. This was followed up with *Another Cycle* in 1971. Many of these early Cliff albums were compilations of earlier material he had done for Leslie Kong and which had been released by Trojan Records. The last of these tracks resurfaced on the album *Struggling Man* in 1973, his final Island Records release of the 1970s. Cliff is, arguably, the most cultural artist in Jamaican music history, for although he is identified as a Jamaican musician, his international work is a prime example of the crossover imperative gone bad. Despite his success, Cliff's music and sound cannot be viewed as entirely authentic Jamaican as those coming out of the Kingston music scene. In fact, in many cases it was a dilution of the reggae aesthetic for the much sought after crossover sound to fit the ideals and taste of the larger white markets of Britain and the United States. Mike Alleyne (1998) sums it up in the following way:

> The inconsistencies characterizing the career of Jimmy Cliff who has probably been signed to more labels than any other reggae artist (at least five) are indicative of this type of pressure. In his case, the big breakthrough seemed perpetually imminent but never arrived, largely due to the inappropriately commercial revamping which occurred at each major label transit point, especially during the early to mid 1980s phase with Columbia/CBS (69).

The release of the Perry Henzell movie *The Harder They Come* in 1972, starring Jimmy Cliff, was a significant milestone for Jamaican music. It portrayed the hard ghetto life of Kingston and also gave a peek into the difficulties associated with breaking into the Kingston music scene. The movie became a cult favourite and was responsible for the biggest international exposure for Jamaican music at that time. Cliff became an international figure and the soundtrack for *The Harder They Come*, which contained some real rocksteady and reggae gems, became the biggest selling reggae album at that time. It contained four tracks from Cliff, 'The Harder They Come', 'Many Rivers to Cross', 'You Can Get If You Really Want' and 'Sitting in Limbo'. Toots and the Maytals hit songs, 'Sweet and Dandy' and 'Pressure Drop', Scotty's 'Draw Your Brakes', the Slickers' 'Johnny Too Bad' and Desmond Dekker's '007 Shanty Town' were also on the album. Cliff parted company with Island Records after the eventual success of the film and moved on to EMI Records. Cliff released three albums on the EMI label, *Unlimited* (1973), *House of Exile* (1974) and *Brave Warrior* (1975) and on the Reprise label, (a subsidiary of Warner Brothers), *Music Maker* (1974), *In Concert: The Best of Jimmy Cliff*, *Follow My Mind* (1976). He left EMI for Warner Brothers and released *Give Thanx* in 1978 and *I Am the Living* in 1980 for yet another record label, MCA Records. This period was his most unproductive as he made no significant breakthrough, leading Chris Blackwell (1991) to note that Cliff had made a mistake in leaving Island.

In response to Cliff's pop-influenced 'Vietnam' and his stated intention to record a ska song,[10] Paul Simon made a reggae record in Kingston using Jamaican musicians; the resulting 'Mother and Child Reunion' was his first solo single from the album *Paul Simon* (1972). He recorded with the same Jamaican musicians that Cliff had used. They included Jackie Jackson (bass), Hux Brown (guitars), Neville Hinds (organ) Denzil Laing (percussions), Winston Grennan (drums) and their distinctive style can be heard in the heavy bass line of the song. The album entered the charts in the UK, Japan and the US and was the first encounter that many Americans had with reggae. Here, again, the trope of collaboration comes into play as Simon's interaction with Jamaican musicians can be viewed as a major Western star being fascinated by the music of 'A particular ethnicised, racialised Other and want to participate in making it' (Taylor 2007, 128). It can also be viewed from the standpoint of being 'A deliberate absorption of non-Western forms and traditions into Northern popular music' (Connell and Gibson 2003, 144–45) at the expense of makers of this 'new' form of musical expression. This type of collaboration involved some level of exploitation of the non-Western performers. Connell reminds us:

> Numerous western performers turned to other musician to play (usually) supporting roles, and imbue their own music with new sounds and some supposed elements of authenticity, in a growing complexity of music making and collaboration (150).

On the other side of the coin, these collaborations can be seen as an important juncture in the trajectory of non-Western popular music development as they opened the door for entry into the biggest markets for popular music – the United States and Europe. It also introduced into these markets, through an 'acceptable' medium, new soundscapes, cultural traditions and methods of music making that have been appropriated by the Western industrial machinery. One of the earliest adoptions of the Jamaican sound and aesthetics was done by Aretha Franklin who did the funk-driven, tribute to the Jamaican dance style rocksteady, titled 'Rock Steady,' in 1971.[11] The single went to number nine on the Billboard Top Single chart. Johnny Nash continued his chart success with the release of the album *I Can See Clearly Now* in 1972. Six of the cuts are backed by Fabulous Five including four Bob Marley compositions: 'Stir It Up', 'You Poured Your Sugar on Me', 'How Good It Is', 'Comma Comma', 'More Questions Than Answers' and 'Guava Jelly' (Campbell 2009). 'Stir It Up' went to number 13 on the UK chart and to number 12 on the US Billboard singles chart. 'More Questions Than Answers' also did well on the British charts, peaking at number nine. The album *I Can See Clearly Now* went to 39 on the British charts. In 1972, JAD Records released two Wailers records 'Reggae on Broadway' and 'Oh Lord I Got to Get There' on the Columbia Record label in the UK. 'Reggae on Broadway' was another single I discovered in the belly of the Jamaica Broadcasting Corporation (JBC) music library.[12] They were terrible flops in the UK (White 1984, 253). Nash's 1973 follow-up album *My Merry Go Round* featured a Wailers' composition, 'Nice Time' and the reggae track 'Ooh What a Feeling'. He continued his reggae explorations with the 1975 album *Tears on My Pillow* which featured three Marley compositions: 'Reggae on Broadway', 'Mellow Mood' and 'Baby We Got a Date'. Other reggae tracks include 'Cream Puff', 'Let's be Friends' and 'Tears on My Pillow', a cover of Ernie Smith's obscure debut recording. In 1975, the single reached number one on the British charts for one week.

The biggest event of 1972 was the release of *Catch a Fire* by Bob Marley and the Wailers on Island Records in Britain. Originally panned by some British rock critics, *Catch a Fire* was heralded as the *tour de force* of reggae productions, elevating the 'primitive milieu of reggae' to rock *auter* status (Toynbee 2006, 5).[13] That same year the Wailers followed up with *Burnin,* which featured the anthemic 'Get Up Stand Up'. This was virgin ground for reggae. Having two internationally released albums in one year was unheard of in the Kingston music scene and never done before in reggae or any other Jamaican genre. Mike Alleyne (1998)[14] sees this album and the circumstances surrounding its creation as 'indicative of the form of compromise necessary to negotiate major market access' (67). Alleyne documented the process through which the album was created, noting that after the album was recorded by the group in Kingston, the tapes were taken to London where the album was significantly altered by adding rock guitars and synthesiser phrases by American and British musicians. The album was also given a treble-oriented mix similar to rock, 'in effect, what was represented as reggae was western commodified reformation of the textual format' (67). Alleyne also points out that in subsequent albums there was 'the increased proportion of love songs on *Exodus, Kaya* and *Uprising* accompanied by much lighter melodies' (97). This amounted to cultural dilution, geared towards a white market in Britain and the United States. While there was some level of dilution in terms of the reggae aesthetic to meet the commercial imperative of the Anglo-American music industry, as Alleyne has noted, 'the anti-capitalist themes dominating the Wailers' lyrics remained both potent and intact on *Catch a Fire* – and on most subsequent albums.' This observation is critical to the overall picture of the negotiation between the Wailers and Island

Records. While the instrumental text was compromised, the lyrics had the desired effect on the British markets. Marley's militancy and anti-imperialist stance which was critical to its authenticity and value as a musical text was evident even in these aesthetically diluted tracks.

The issue of love songs on the album, while a deliberate ploy on the part of Island, is not cause for concern about commercial transformation as throughout their career the Wailers and Bob Marley did ballads and love songs. The haunting 'Hurts to be Alone', the suggestive 'Stir It Up', the sensuous 'Guava Jelly' and the playful 'Ketchy Shubby' are songs from their repertoire that are non-militant and point to the fact that as a group and as solo acts, the trio expressed their artistry with versatility and range. The influence of R&B and soul music of the United States was evident throughout their career;[15] hence, it was not far-fetched or compromising to do non-militant recordings. To suggest otherwise would border on straight jacketing the Wailers and Bob Marley to being unidimensional in their creative output. They were artists and artists first influenced by the creole society in which they grew up and while being anti-capitalist and anti-Babylon, the Wailers were participants in the 'blurred focus'[16] of the Caribbean cultural dynamic reflecting the ambiguity inherent in the Jamaican identity. An identity characterised by its mix of African and European retentions, with the European assuming a position which is desired and revered as superior by many in the postcolonial Caribbean society (Nettleford 1972, 173).[17] This is often overlooked in the discourse surrounding cultural identity and expression in favour of an essentialist position. I prefer to embrace a more post-modern approach, which allows for the expression of the Wailers and Marley to be viewed through multi-focus lens. Antonio Benítez-Rojo (1996) reminds us:

> That Caribbeaness is a system full of noise and opacity, a nonlinear system, an unpredictable system, in short a chaotic system beyond the total reach of any specific kind of knowledge or interpretation of the world (295).

A truly post-modern construct developed and sustained by various processes including creolisation, hybridity, exploitation, appropriation and identity construction.

Reggae's international status was given another boost in 1974 when Barbra Streisand released her album *Butterfly* with a reggae version of

Bob Marley's 'Guava Jelly'. Streisand's album, a selection of covers of great American hits from various periods of music, includes a brilliant version of the Jamaican favourite 'Let the Good Times Roll' by Shirley and Lee and 'Crying Time' by Ray Charles. To place Marley's composition (a US hit for Johnny Nash in 1972) in such a respected group of compositions was indeed a major achievement;[18] underscoring the often overlooked fact that Marley was recognised as a great songwriter long before he made it as an artist.

The release of the Rolling Stones' *Goat Head Soup* was another important event of 1973. The album was partially recorded at Dynamic Sounds, Jamaica in 1972 and eight tracks from the Dynamic Sounds session made it on to the album. The internationally renowned Rolling Stones[19] recording in Kingston validated the technical facilities and the creativity of the music scene. While the Rolling Stones did not record any reggae tracks for the album,[20] Kingston's music scene got the approval of one of the biggest rock bands in the world at that time. Ron Wood of the Rolling Stones also attempted, with very mediocre results, to record a reggae song on his solo album, *I've Got My Own Album to Do*. The 1974 album reggae track was titled 'I Can Feel the Fire', which featured co-lead vocals with Mick Jagger. Kingston's profile as a creative hub was squarely and solidly established. Jazz flautist Herbie Mann's 1974 *Reggae* was recorded and mixed at Dynamic Sounds with Jamaican and British musicians led by Tommy McCook and including the Rolling Stones, Mick Taylor (guitar), Winston Wright (organ), Michael Richards (drums), Bobby Ellis (trumpet), Gladstone Anderson (piano) and Jackie Jackson (bass). Mann's *Reggae* was a blend of jazz, pop and R&B and reggae tracks including 'Rivers of Babylon' (Melodians), 'My Girl' (Temptations) and 'Ob La Di Ob La Da' (Beatles).

In 1974, also, Eric Clapton released his album *461 Ocean Boulevard*. Clapton put the spotlight on Bob Marley by making a big hit of his song 'I Shot the Sheriff' from the 1973 album *Burnin*. Clapton's cover of the song reached number one on the Billboard Hot 100 and was his only chart topping song in the US. Marley was, again, recognised as a good songwriter and it gave the Wailers a boost in the UK and the US. Also in 1974, Stevie Wonder made his first reggae song with the hit song 'Boogie On Reggae Woman' with the line 'I like to reggae but you dance too fast for me', from the album *Fulfillingness First Finale*. In 1977, Roberta Flack displayed her continued attraction to the Kingston music scene with the production of her seductive reggae track, 'Fine, Fine Day', from the *Blue Lights in the Basement* album. The funk band Shot Gun also recognised the power of Marley's lyrics and did a reggae cover of 'Concrete Jungle' in 1977 on their album *Shot Gun 2*. Orleans, a folk rock group from Woodstock, New York, did a bass-driven reggae track called 'If' on their album *Let There be Music*. Soul pop duo, Daryl Hall and John Oates covered Stanley and the Starlights' mento-flavoured, reggae song 'Soldering' on their eponymously titled album; the track was the b-side for their hit single from the album *Sara Smile* which also used the Jamaican flavour that was influencing musicians all over the globe. Rod Stewart, not one to shy away from experimenting with different genres, made a reasonably executed reggae track entitled 'So Soon We Change' on his 1980 album *Foolish Behaviour*.

Serge Gainsbourg brought reggae to France with his first reggae album, *Aux Armes et Caeter* featuring Jamaican musicians Robbie Shakespeare (bass), Sly Dunbar (drums), Mikey Chung (guitar), Ansel Collins (organ), Radcliffe 'Dougie' Bryan (rhythm guitar), Robbie Lyn (piano), Uziah 'Sticky' Thompson, (percussion) and the I Threes (Judy Mowatt, Marcia Griffiths and Rita Marley). The album, recorded at Tuff Gong Studio in Kingston, caused some controversy in France as the *Legion d'Honeur* took offence to Gainsbourg's reworking of the national anthem.[21] He also, reportedly, angered Bob Marley who discovered that his wife, Rita, had sung some erotic lyrics on some of the backing tracks.[22]

Dutch flautist Chris Hinze hooked up with Mikey Chung in the late 1970s in Kingston when he was introduced to reggae legends Peter Tosh and Sly and Robbie. This led to his work in Aquarius studio in Half Way Tree with the Tamlins, Tosh, Sly and Robbie, Chung and many other musicians in 1980. Tosh provided lead vocals on two songs and background vocals on several other tracks.[23] The album, released on CBS Records in 1980 as *Word Sound and Power*, was a big seller in the European market. Hinze later re-released the project on his own Keytone label as *Kings of Reggae* and *Bamboo Reggae*.

The adaptation of reggae by, primarily, white Western artists can be heralded as validation and a potential windfall for Jamaican artists like Bob Marley and the Wailers and Jimmy Cliff who benefited from this process (Hebdige 2000, 95). However, there is a countervailing perspective which posits that the forays by Euro-American artists into the reggae aesthetics has resulted in its dilution and 'an ongoing disintegration of the reggae text' (Alleyne 2001, 15).[24] Yet another perspective sees these moments as 'deliberate absorption of non-Western forms and traditions into Northern popular music' where in this type of appropriation, very little is done to recognise the native performer and the origin of the appropriated text (Connell and Gibson 2003, 145).

While many North American and British acts were adapting to the reggae sound, Jamaicans were taking the music further than the US and the UK. The Germany-based pop group Boney M, who had two Jamaicans in their ranks, did a couple of reggae-influenced records and even did a cover of the Melodians big hit 'Rivers of Babylon'. Also in 1979, hotelier and arts promoter Keith Foote took a Jamaican ensemble to tour Germany, based on their album released in Germany titled *One Love Get Up and Reggae*. The Kingston music scene produced several singles that made an impression on the British and US charts. They include Bob Andy and Marcia Griffiths with 'Young Gifted and Black' in 1970 and Althea and Donna with 'Uptown Top Ranking' in 1971.[25] While it did not enter the British charts, 'Breakfast in Bed' by Lorna Bennett, a remake of the Dusty Springfield song, was very popular in Britain and was a favourite of sound systems and local radio in 1973.[26] Dennis Brown also broke into the British charts in 1977 with his biggest hit 'Money in My Pocket'. Ken Boothe's remake of Bread's 'Everything I Own' (1974) went to number one on the British Charts and his follow up 'Crying Over You' went to number ten. Peter Tosh and Bunny Wailer left the Wailers in 1974 to pursue solo careers and, practically using the Wailers band, Tosh released 'Legalize It' in 1976 on the Columbia Records label. In that same year, Bunny Wailer released the classic *Blackheart Man* on Island Records, again using the same musicians from the Wailers band. Island Records, encouraged by the success of *Catch A Fire* and *Burnin*, signed several Jamaican acts to the label including Burning Spear, Max Romeo and the Upsetters, Junior Marvin, Toots and the Maytals, Aswad, Steel Pulse, Linton Kwesi Johnson, I Jahman Levi and Third World. They all released albums during this period.

Richard Branson of Virgin Records also wanted to cash in on the reggae train. He created a new reggae label called Front Line and signed several reggae acts including U Roy, Johnny Clarke, Prince Far I, Big Youth, the Gladiators and the Mighty Diamonds. Virgin also licensed albums from Bunny

Lee, Prince Tony Robinson and Jo Jo Hookim (Barrow and Dalton 2004, 145; Chang and Chen 1998, 48–52).

The cultural dilution of Jamaican popular music was not only done by white, foreign musicians, but also by Jamaican musicians and producers in the hope of scoring a big hit in the UK or the US. The earliest attempts were seen with Chris Blackwell's Island Records and continued with Trojan Records where Lee Gopthall, along with Blackwell, made a serious attempt at crossing over by softening the roots sound of Kingston in favour of a pop-flavoured sound with string and lush horn arrangements.[27] This continued through all the periods of production and became one of the main motivational tools for the production of music on the Kingston music scene, a fact that has not been given enough attention and academic scrutiny.

The unwavering pursuit of the crossover market has also played a significant role in the blurring of genre distinctions. This has led, gradually, to the homogenisation of popular music soundscapes which, in turn, led to the use of genre classification as more a function of politics, corporate marketing and identity formation than true artistic differentiations.

Neoinnovation (1981–2000)

The 1980s saw the complete adaptation of the neoliberal agenda of the Reagan/Thatcher era by the Government of Jamaica. It was capitalism in its new manifestation, neoliberalism against socialism and communism; the political divide was never so wide. In 1980, Edward Seaga came to power after the bloodiest election in Jamaica's modern political history. His victory at the polls was secured, some say, by the intervention of the United States through state agencies such the Central Intelligence Agency (CIA) and the US State Department, as the US Government was becoming increasingly uncomfortable with the political leanings of the Michael Manley administration which had developed close ties with Cuba's Fidel Castro and the Soviet Union. Manley was also one of the main advocates of the non-aligned and the anti-apartheid movements (Manley 1982, 75–182). Speaking on the emergence of this economic agenda Hesmondhalgh (2007) states:

> Western economies, governments made permanent a set of anti-inflation strategies that had been tried in 1974–1975. Emergency cutbacks in public spending and the stripping away of regulation by democratically elected were promoted from emergency measures to permanent policy.

> The view that human needs are best served by an unregulated "free – market" – a view that had been popular with various nineteenth-century liberal economist, but had mostly been confined to cranks and nutcases for much of the twentieth century – made a comeback, hence the term *neo*-liberal economics and *neoliberalism* (86).

The Chicago School economic thought and the neoliberal policies of the International Monetary Fund (IMF) and the World Bank, which were imposed on Jamaica through loan agreements, had a debilitating effect on the economy and cultural life. It was under these conditions, of suffering and hardship under economic programmes such as structural adjustment and divestment, that a new music form emerged. It eventually became the dominant genre, with the deejay replacing the singer as the primary performer and star, prompting another occupational shift within *the creative echo chamber*. Dancehall emerged out of the inner cities of Kingston where new entrants in the music business developed, once again, around the sound systems. Reggae remained dominant on the international front and attracted mainstream attention with many established reggae acts touring globally. The new entrants were not connected to reggae and the move towards a new style and sound was influenced in significant ways by the sound system culture. Performers included singers and deejays who were regulars on many sound systems where they performed for dance attendees on a nightly basis. The phenomenon developed new cadres of performers expressing new styles and lyrical content including singjaying, popularized by performers such as Johnny Osbourne and Barrington Levy and the new wave lyrics of Sugar Minnott, General Echo, Michigan and Smiley, and King Yellowman.[28] The roots and Rastafarian themes of reggae; the love songs of Dennis Brown and Gregory Isaacs were replaced by lyrics about relationships, gang life, inner city experiences and the realities of the dancehall the space for entertainment for rural poor and inner city youth.

There was a neoinnovation revival of many rhythms of the '60s and '70s as young producers and artistes struggled to get their identity in the entertainment business. Sugar Minott and Henry 'Junjo' Lawes are considered the fathers of dancehall music and culture which began to shape itself in the late 1970s with releases from a young Barrington Levy. Early dancehall gems include 'Dances are Changing', '21 Girl Salute' and 'Mine You Mouth'. The last was produced by Lawes who worked out of The Channel One studio.

He began to develop the new style with artists such as Coco T, Michigan and Smiley, Eek-A-Mouse, Frankie Paul, Josie Wales and the first superstar of dancehall, King Yellowman. Lawes also operated one of the top sound systems of the period, Volcano Hi Power, that had a huge following and influence in the inner city. Sugar Minott is credited as the first artist to record a dancehall album, *Live Loving*, produced by legendary producer Clement 'Coxsone' Dodd in 1977. However, it was Minott's work as an independent producer and sound system owner that secured his place in history. Minott left Studio One after 'Live Loving' and two great singles 'Mr. DC' and 'Vanity' using some of the classic Studio One rhythms of the '60s. He began his sound system, Youthman Promotion, and produced several landmark singles on his own label; the most important are 'Dancehall We Deh' and 'Dancehall Stylee'.

Minott also began the first dancehall crew that included artists such as Yami Bolo, White Mice, Jr. Reid, and Michael Palmer. The first modern dancehall clash was won by Youthman Promotion going up against Black Scorpion and King Jammys. Youthman Promotion defeated the two giant sound systems by using the now classic 'Ring the Alarm' by Tenor Saw. Other early dancehall stars included Tristan Palmer, Little John, Robert Ffrench, Half Pint, Charlie Chaplin, Early B, Super Cat and Burro Banton. Like reggae and rocksteady before, early dancehall was first recorded at the Studio One recording facilities with the Sugar Minott release of 'Live Loving' which laid out the blueprint for early dancehall music. Coxsone Dodd also released two major dancehall classics, 'Rub-a-Dub Stylee and 'Nice up the Dance' by Michigan and Smiley. These two releases marked a major departure from the revolutionary and lover's rock lyrics of mainstream reggae and brought back a down to earth approach to writing lyrics backed by some of the old classic rhythms from the Studio One vault. Michigan and Smiley's lyrics spoke to the new reality of working class folk. 'Nice up the Dance' painted a picture of dancehall and described the entertainment and business transactions that were critical to a successful dance. It was King Yellowman who legitimised the genre when he broke big by 1982 with major hits including 'Over Me', 'Mr. Chin' and 'I'm Getting Married'. His break out to stardom was a major signpost for dancehall as within two years dancehall became the dominant force of youth culture in Jamaica and introduced a new form of cultural production in the recorded music business on the Kingston music scene.

Yellowman became the first dancehall star to sign an international record deal when he signed to Columbia Records in 1984.

King Yellowman made inroads into the US market in terms of touring, but it was not enough to make a major impact on tastemakers internationally and Columbia never figured out how to market and promote the new sound.[29] In addition, the album was not considered a very good representation of the new dancehall genre.

The year 1985 was another landmark one for dancehall as it was the year when digitisation of the studio production took hold. Prince Jammy established the digital sound with the release of the 'Sleng Teng' riddim. Keyboard player Noel Davey discovered the pre-set beat of Eddie Cochran song 'Somethin Else' in his MT 40 Casio keyboard Digitised production was more economical and did not necessitate a large group of musicians to play numerous instruments, as was the tradition in reggae. The number of musicians was reduced to a drum programmer and a keyboard player. The rhythm tracks were stripped down to drums, keyboard bass, piano ska and a keyboard phrase requiring a maximum of three musicians, in many cases only two musicians were required and sometimes, just one. The reduced costs facilitated the entry of more new producers into the business.

A new set of deejays, singjays and singers emerged and the output of traditional producers, such as King Jammy's, Jack Scorpio and King Tubby, provided the main catalogue for the early dancehall period. The list of new stars included deejays Lt Stitchie, Super Cat, Admiral Bailey, Shabba Ranks, Red Dragon, Tiger, Ninja Man, Papa San, Sister Nancy and Lady G. Singers included Admiral Tibet, Michael Prophet, Anthony Red Rose and Wayne Smith. John Holt saw resurgence during this period, so, too, did Dennis Brown, Leroy Smart, Beres Hammond and Johnny Osbourne. The music reached its highest level of commercialisation with new levels of fashion, lifestyle, dancing and community involvement never before seen on the Kingston music scene.

Henry 'Junjo' Lawes was at the forefront of this movement. While not the first to profile in expensive European sports cars, he did that and more, parading on high-end Japanese motor bikes and dressing in the latest fashion and outlandish jewellery from the US. This was at the height of the global neoliberal agenda which was being pushed by Reagan and Thatcher who found an ally in Edward Seaga. This neoliberal, globalised corporate capitalism fuelled the rabid individualism and materialism that characterised the dancehall music and lifestyle of the period.

Crossing over by Collaboration

While the 1980s was the period of growth for dancehall in terms of production modalities, the 1990s represented the golden era in the areas of marketing, distribution, product development and international outreach. The genre and its stars began to attract corporate sponsorship, for both talent and events, and international record label attention that resulted in a slew of major record label deals for some of the top artists. At one point, practically all the major dancehall stars were signed to deals with international record companies, both independent and major. This sparked another period of collaboration between American hip-hop groups and dancehall artists of Jamaica. The most successful of these artists included Shabba Ranks, Lady Patra, Cobra, Super Cat and Shaggy. In 1988, Lt Stitchie signed a record deal with Atlantic Records which resulted in the release of three albums over a five-year period. Shabba Ranks was signed to Epic Records and became the first dancehall star to sell gold and platinum and have several, massive crossover hits. He released five albums before his career was interrupted by the gay rights organisation GLADD.[30] Buju Banton was the top deejay among the new hotshots of the 1990s who included Cobra, Patra, Spragga Benz, Tanya Stephens, Bounty Killer, Beenie Man, Capleton, Mega Banton, Chaka Demus and Pliers, Professor Nuts and Cutty Ranks. After the raw slackness of the 1980s, gun lyrics, bad man tunes and materialism, the 1990s saw a revival of Rastafarian sentiments in the lyrics of some artists. Tony Rebel, Garnet Silk, Anthony B, Everton Blender, Sizzla and Capleton led the charge in this regard. By the mid-1990s, the compact disc (CD) had been introduced, but vinyl was still king due to the high cost of CD manufacturing on a commercial level.

The level of management and marketing were significantly improved and several production companies and individual artists began to cultivate a more organised business culture.[31] With the success of Shabba Ranks, led by his manager Clifton 'Specialist' Dillon and his Spec/Shang management outfit, several new entities were established to handle the numerous artists who were being signed by independent and major record companies in the UK and the US. Marketing and publicity strategies, which had not been fully developed during the other periods of production, were now being implemented, creating a major international buzz and interest in dancehall. Again, the period saw renewed interest in Jamaican music. Again, the interactions and negotiations were characterised by the textual reshaping of the dancehall aesthetics in the interest of crossover and mainstream appeal. During this process, the authenticity of dancehall was compromised in the interest of the global recording music industry. Most of the songs that made it big were reshaped versions of dancehall that attempted to infuse elements of R&B and hip hop so as to appeal to wider markets, again entrenching a separate production modality from the distinctive sound of Kingston dancehall, a phenomenon that will be examined in more detail in chapter five. Apart from the collaborations between American artists and dancehall artists, all of the instrumental rhythm tracks were non-dancehall R&B/hip hop reformulations, which bore no semblance to the authentic dancehall sound coming out of the Kingston music scene. The only component of some of these aural texts was the distinct Jamaicanness of the vocal stylings of Shabba and his hardcore semi-patois lyrics.

Concurrent with dancehall's rise was the ongoing production of reggae music primarily for the international market. Island Records continued to release albums from Black Uhuru, Burning Spear, Ijahman Levi, Toots and the Maytals, Grace Jones, Sly and Robbie and Pablo Moses. Reggae was the international sound and its main stars were touring the globe. Touring, as a major revenue earner, became a necessity for reggae acts which, due to poor marketing and lack of reach, had to go on the road to reach established fans and to gain new ones. The lack of consistent radio and television promotion in the US and Europe made it harder for reggae acts to sell in major numbers. Very few were signed to big labels and they missed results on the international front.

Global Interaction: 2001–Present

In his analysis of the phenomenon of the cultural dilution of the reggae/dancehall text, precipitated by the crossover imperative of the major record labels of the West to ensure its success in the wider market, Mike Alleyne (1998) notes in *Babylon Makes the Rules the Politics of Reggae Crossover*, that the 'conformity to mainstream trends' (74) was not limited to particular tracks but extended to 'the level of digital music technology application'.

Alleyne also suggests that digital technology has resulted in a 'pervasive textual homogeneity' (75), due to use of the drum machines, samples and the synthesiser. He argues that these instruments are made for and by Anglo-American aural sensibilities which implicitly stack the process in favour of 'the cultural perceptions of the place of origin'. This, according to Alleyne, has resulted in 'a common ground within which reasonably accurate rhythmic replication can more easily occur in the case of sampling, exact duplication becomes a reality.' While Alleyne's emphasis was on the 'susceptibility of Jamaican music to cultural pilferage' an equally important fact is that this mediation between dancehall and digital music technologies has resulted in a similar process where Anglo-American sound aesthetics (hip hop) are easily replicated and (re)presented in a Jamaican cultural context.

This is the dominant feature of this period of cultural production. It is also the post-modern era of music production where the Internet and digital technology have begun to change the music business model and 'core boundary models'[32] of genre classifications are being challenged. Digitisation and the emergence of Mp3 technology have allowed for the democratisation of music distribution and promotion. Jamaican music has enjoyed international exposure with the rise of Sean Paul, Beenie Man, Wayne Wonder and Elephant Man. Domestically, CD sales have been non-existent and a paradigm shift has been made which has placed airplay and concert performances as indicators of success. This period is marked by the development of what I call, the genre diffusion period of symbolic production where, through the processes of *genre blending* and *genre defiance*, it has become increasingly difficult to differentiate genres due to homogenisation of digital music technology and performative norms. Genre blending is the deliberate infusion of various elements of other genres to add to the foundation of one distinctive musical genre.

This process has been a feature of *the creative echo chamber* since the Appropriation period of cultural production but has escalated during the Global Interaction period due to digitisation and strides in telecommunication. Major proponents of this movement included Sly Dunbar and Robbie Shakespeare, Lloyd 'Gitzy' Willis, Steely and Cleavie, Danny Brownie, Robert Livingston and Sting International. Dunbar, along with Willis and Shakespeare, blended Indian bhangra, Latin salsa and Nigerian high life with the Jamaican genres of rocksteady, mento, ska, reggae, dub and dancehall to create new soundscapes which were successful both nationally and internationally. This was the period where reggaeton, influenced by the Kingston music scene, developed in Panama and Puerto Rico. These developments replicated in London, New York, Miami, Port of Spain, Bridgetown, Kingston, Panama City and San Juan exemplified the manifestation of a transnational musical process. From this 'explicitly transnational perspective', artists and musicians from various nationalist orientations through their 'mentalities and activities,' are 'articulating and being articulated from a single field of social relations'. The movement of artistic personnel across borders in the global music industry has become so natural, JocelyneGuilbault (1996) notes, 'that at times it becomes difficult to identify where they "belong"' (7). Linda Basch et al. (1994) also state, 'researchers begin to use the terms "transnationalism" and "transnational" social field to describe this interconnected social experience' (5). The authors define the process as follows:

> The process by which immigrants forge and sustain multi-stranded social relations that link together their societies of origin and settlement. We call these processes transnationalism to emphasize that many immigrants today build social fields that cross geographic cultural and political borders (7).

I am using the term transnationalism in a particular invocation, as Guilbault (1996) states, 'it is used here to highlight not the practices that are the same everywhere, but rather those which cross borders, be it nations, nation states, or other traditionally-defined closed spaces' (8).

The process through which artists blend/bond elements of other genre styles across national boundaries is another of these transnational processes where musical codes and practices are adapted to suit local, national and international sensibilities and imperatives. So, several dynamic processes, facilitated through transnationalism, marked the global interaction period which has resulted in the development of decentredness of practice. This has raised questions of genre authenticity and origins manifested through the process of genre defiance which can be defined as the making of popular music that, through its aesthetic codes, practices and signification, defy classification as any particular genre associated with any particular scene or music collective. Its hybrid nature and influences suggest a universal sound, a Utopian pop aesthetics which is fast becoming a reality of the post-modern condition. A direct response to the continued pursuit of the crossover market has led to some degree of homogeneity which has been praised by some critics and also rejected by 'cultural purists'. The Internet has opened Jamaican culture to the world, and music production has become more democratic as digital recording technology has opened up the occupational structure thus facilitating the entry of more players, such as producers, engineers and distributors, into the business. While Jamaican music is still making some kind of impact on global trends, it is becoming harder to locate the origins of the music, with serious implications for notions surrounding identity, ethnicity and location.

Concluding Thoughts

The production of popular music in Kingston's *creative cauldron* can be viewed through the prism of six periods of cultural production, Folk Culture, Appropriation, Innovation, Internationalisation, Neoinnovation and Global Interaction. During these distinctive periods, the Kingston music scene experienced many processes that have facilitated, encouraged, constrained and retarded the production of popular music. The Jamaican output has been a phenomenal success in some tangible ways but in others it has not maximised its potential. Some scholars have answered this last observation by asking, 'what potential?' as Jamaica has performed far beyond its potential. No other country of similar size has had such a powerful and lasting effect on the production of popular music worldwide. This was achieved through hegemonic and counterhegemonic forces, the adherence to non-Western philosophical stance of creating original work through communal authorship and a disregard for European notions of the genius author, the key factor in copyright legislation.

NOTES

1. See Alleyne. 'Globalisation and Commercialisation of Caribbean Music,' in *World Music Roots and Routes*, ed Tuulikki Pietila. Studies across Disciplines in the Humanities and Social Sciences 6. Helsinki: Helsinki Collegium for Advanced Studies, 2009: 76–101.
2. http://www.mentomusic.com/flea.htm.
3. Ibid.
4. These popular dancehalls include Forrester's Hall, Jubilee Tile Garden, Success Club and Cho Co Mo Lawn.

5. Dub plates are recordings done on soft acetate, which was primarily used in the recording industry to check the quality of the stamper which was used to manufacture vinyl records.
6. See Garth White, 'Ska and Rock Steady,' in *Reggae International*, ed. Stephen Davis and Peter Simon (New York: Rogner and Bernhard GMBH & Co., 1982)
7. Success did not start with the ska era, as outlined earlier. Lord Flea who was signed to Capitol Records enjoyed some international exposure and even appeared in two Hollywood movies.
8. 'Babylon Makes the Rules: The Politics of Reggae Crossover.' *Social & Economic Studies* 47.1 (1998): 65–77.
9. Ibid.
10. See Mike Alleyne, '*White Reggae: Cultural Dilution in the Record Industry*,' *Popular Music Society* 24.1:15–30.
11. The single was also on her album *Young Gifted and Black* in 1972.
12. They are re-released on CD (BMG Complete Bob Marley and the Wailers) and included in Steffens and Pierson's Bob Marley and the Wailers discography.
13. 'One Step Forward? Translating Jamaican Popular Music in the Core.' *The Society for Caribbean Studies Annual Conference Papers*. Ed. Sandra Courtman. Vol. 7 (2006).
14. '"Babylon Makes the Rules": The Politics of Reggae Crossover.' *Social & Economic Studies* 47.1 (1998): 65–77.
15. Bob Marley redid The Impressions' 'People Get Ready' on the *Exodus* album extending his song 'One Love' that took lyrics from the Impressions. Peter Tosh covered Chuck Berry's 'Johnny Be Good' on his *Mama Africa* album. The Wailers covered several love songs including Tom Jones's 'What's New Pussycat'. This influence was, of course, central to the development of Jamaican popular music in general.
16. See Rex Nettelford, *Mirror Mirror: Identity Race and Protest in Jamaica* (New York: William Marrow & Company, Inc, 1972).
17. Ibid.
18. It is not a stretch to believe that Streisand might have been influenced to record 'Guava Jelly' because of Johnny Nash's hit version, underscoring the point that collaborations had the effect of opening doors for non-Western artists and preparing Western ears for new soundscapes.
19. John Connell and Chris Gibson (2003, 56) note that when some artists were labelled international this was limited to a few regions and they did not really reach an international market 'the rest of the world consisted mainly of some European countries and scattered Anglophone outposts.'
20. That was to come in 1986 with the cover of Half Pint's 'Winsome' renamed 'Too Rude'.
21. Http://www.francevision.com/nsltr/vf14/gains.htm.

22. Chrisafis, 'Angelique,' *The Guardian*, April 14, 2006.
23. Rhythm and Blues singer Luther Vandross provided lead vocals on one track. The project was taken to New York Electric Lady Studio where Vandross, Gwen Guthrie and Tawatha Agee added background vocals.
24. 'White Reggae: Cultural Dilution in the Record Industry.' *Popular Music & Society* 24.1 (2001): 15–30.
25. Kevin O'Brien Chang and Wayne Chen, *Reggae Routes: The Story of Jamaican Music* (Kingston: Ian Randle Publishers, 1998).
26. In 2009, Lorna Bennett was honoured in London for her contribution to the development of lovers rock in Britain when New Name Music in association with Executive Decisions presented The Lovers Rock Gala Awards 2009 – Music: Reggae 25th July; 02 Academy; Brixton – London 2nd August: 02 Academy – Birmingham.
27. Arguably, 'roots' was one of a number of tendencies within the broad field of reggae. Clearly reggae was adapted and marketed for international consumption. But the hard question is to establish what form this took and whether it then fed back into Kingston or was resisted. I'd say both these things happened reflecting the 'contradictory' nature of a hugely creative music scene in a small country which was at one and the same time dominated by the capitalist world system.
28. Johnny Osbourne recorded the single 'Singjay Style' in 1979 which gave the performance style its name.
29. This became a recurring feature of dancehall interaction with the Euro American music industry, where marketing departments found it difficult to development appropriate image and find a fan base for the music outside of the migrant markets in keys cites such as New York, Los Angeles, Toronto and London.
30. GLAAD and other gay rights organisations in Britain had objected to his anti-gay utterances on British television in defence of Buju Banton who was being protested against due to his song 'Boom Bye Bye', a song that promoted violence against homosexuals.
31. Due to the involvement of American record companies and improvements with the Kingston scene, Jamaican entertainment lawyers, publicists, road managers, public relations and advertising personnel, the level of professionalism was gradually improving.
32. See Holt, *Genre in Popular Music* (Chicago: The University of Chicago Press, 2007).

Value Chain Dynamics in the Creative Echo Chamber

Orange Street is the music street; it's the street that sells the beat...
                                                             Prince Buster

Kingston: Beat City, the Creative Echo Chamber

In the beginning, Kingston was the nucleus of Jamaican music, with most of the business concentrated in the area of western Kingston spanning Bond Street to the west and Love Lane to the east. Orange Street, known as 'Beat Street', was the centre of this musical activity. Most of the business activities were situated on Orange and King Streets and North Parade. Pioneer producers such as Bunny Lee, Winston 'Niney' Holness, Sir Coxsone, Theophilus Beckford, Rupie Edwards, Lloyd Charmers, Clancy Eccles, JJ Johnson and Prince Buster were based on Orange Street. Clement Dodd's Studio One was located at number 136, JJ Johnson at number 113 and Prince Buster at number 127. Niney 'Observer' Holness, Clancy Eccles, Leslie Kong, Phil Pratt and Rupie Edwards all had record stores on 'Beat Street'. At the lower end of Orange Street was Tip Top records and retail store, operated by Sonia Pottinger, the only female producer and record retailer.

Fig. 4.1 'Beat Street' Orange Street, downtown Kingston
© Dennis Howard 2010

North Parade, a busy transportation and shopping hub, was home to Joe Gibbs and Randy's, the kings of the retail trade; Randy's recording studio, Studio 17 recording studio (operated by Pat and Vincent Chin) and the famous Idlers' Rest (located at the corner of Chancery Lane and North Parade) so named because musicians, entertainers, songwriters singers and deejays hung out there on a regular basis. Performers who had enough money to press their own records, and which were not accepted by the leading outlets such as Randy's and Prince Buster, hustled at Idlers' Rest to make enough money to go back to the pressing plant operated by Jo Jo and Ernest Hookim at the corner of Chancery Lane and Beeston Street. Idlers' Rest was the principal space where ideas and innovation flowed freely among the new creative class. At the other side of North Parade was Joe Gibbs' record store, another major distribution outlet for the now popular 45 rpm, 7-inch vinyl records and 33 1/3 rpm long playing records.

Derrick Harriott had his retail store on King Street. Next to him was Tony Laing who operated The Conservative Connoisseur Limited (TCC), the first attempt at a collective management and booking agency. Below TCC was the Bancroft Hylton music store that provided emerging and established musicians with the tools of trade.

Peter Hall (2000) and Charles Landry (2000) refer to the concept of the 'creative city' which aptly describes downtown Kingston of the 1960s and '70s. According to Hall, creativity occurs in 'a special kind of city, a city in economic and social flux, a city with large numbers of new and young arrivals mixing and merging into a new kind of society' (648). John McMillan (2005) supports this concept stating, 'Innovation rests on information transmission among likeminded innovators' (3), which requires 'a certain density of communication' (Hall 2000, 644). Like Bourbon Street in New Orleans, Beale Street in Memphis, 42nd Street in New York and Denmark Street in London, Orange Street was a catalyst for innovation and a burst of creativity, which was pivotal to the development of the Jamaican music forms – ska, rocksteady and reggae. Landry (2000) expounds on the concept of the creative city:

> A creative milieu is a place either a cluster of buildings, a part of a city, a city as a whole or a region – that contains the necessary preconditions in terms of 'hard' and 'soft' infrastructure to generate a flow of ideas

and invention. Such a milieu is a physical setting where a critical mass of entrepreneurs, intellectuals, social activists, artists, administrators, power brokers or students can operate in an open-minded, cosmopolitan context and where face to face interaction creates new ideas, artefacts, products, services and institutions and as a consequence contributes to economic success (133).

While Orange Street and the downtown Kingston area was the creative hub of popular music production from the 1950s to the 1970s, by the early 1980s the hub gradually shifted upwards and music centres developed in Kingston 13 at the Channel One studio on Maxfield Avenue and Joe Gibbs recording studio located at Retirement Crescent in Cross Roads. Two of the top dub plate studios frequented by sound system men were operated by King Tubby located in Tower Hill and King Jammy's located in Waterhouse. Sugar Minnott set up a small studio and base for his Youthman Promotion sound system at Robert Crescent and developed the first dancehall crew in the process (Howard 2007, 20). The Aquarius studio in Half Way Tree Square was another important creative point in the city.

The retail businesses also started to move uptown with Derrick Harriott relocating his record store to Twin Gates plaza and Herman Chinloy operating Aquarius record store in Half Way Tree. By the 1980s, retail stores were scattered all over the Half Way Tree area and recording studios and labels were being located in Kingston 11 and 13. Mixing Lab Recording Studio, owned by producer Roy Francis, was built in the late 1980s at Dumbarton Avenue in the Eastwood Park Gardens area, marking the beginning of a gradual movement of popular music production into this area. Presently, a high concentration of studios, production houses, labels, promoters, distributors, sound systems and dub plate studios are located in this area. The latter include King of King, Q45, Star Trails, 5th Element, Jr Studio, Harmony House and Big Yard. Sound systems include Rebel T, Stone Love and Copper Shot. Promoters include Supreme Promotion, Irish & Chin Production and Solid Agency. Production facilities include Grizzly's Productions, Starlight Productions and I Print. This area is now a creative hub.

Kingston is not only a creative milieu. The unique features that can be attributed exclusively to the Kingston model have made it more of a creative echo chamber in which the energies of our ancestors, violently suppressed during slavery, oppressed during colonialism and subjected to racism and imperialist hegemony in the postcolonial period, finally found a space where echoes of the past and present were being exorcised, repossessed and reincarnated through the creative intellect and imagination. In reference to the Orange Street experience, Kevin O'Brien Chang and Wayne Chen (1998) note:

> Beat Street's high concentration of talent made for many such happy, accidental encounters. In its musically saturated atmosphere artistes exchanged and fed off each other's ideas on a daily basis and this 'hot house' effect accelerated Jamaican music's astonishingly rapid development (45–46).

The phenomenon in Kingston represented a creative emancipation and resistance to colonial and European aesthetic hegemony. The music was the expression of an oppressed and marginalised class which found both creative expression and economic independence through the production and sale of phonographic records and by performing. Musicians found a new avenue for income earning; no longer restricted to playing in the 'big bands' and mento ensembles which were commonplace in the 1950s and early '60s. The creative autonomy they experienced by being symbol creators was a new liberating, experience as well as one of resistance in the face of white supremacist dogma and colonial oppression. This more than compensated for the low income earned. For the first time in history, the descendants of enslaved Africans could express themselves and, with the aid of technology, compose the soundtrack for resistance against the hegemonic control which they had endured for centuries.[2]

Clinton Hutton (2007) has argued that the working-class neighbourhoods of west and east Kingston represented a crossroad cultural ethos which was unrivalled anywhere else in Jamaica and the Caribbean. It was the place where many regional traditional music/dance cultures met with urban working-class culture as a result of massive rural-urban migration into Kingston.

Agreeing with Hutton's analysis, it is clear that *the creative echo chamber* became the space where Afro-Caribbean religious and secular retentions, Anglo-American cultural influences, Eastern influences, through India and China, all converged. Manifested though practices such as Zion, Pocomania, Revival, Jonkanoo, Burru, Kumina Rastafari, Nyabinghi, nine night traditions, Ettu, Convince, Anglo-American urban lifestyles and Christianity, mainly through the Baptist and Pentecostal faiths, all synthesised to form the foundation of the creative cultural ferment which took place in *the creative echo chamber*. There is also a regional twist to the equation as many of the seminal figures of Jamaican music were from other Caribbean islands who brought their flavour and style to the mix. Lord Creator, Lord Laro and Lyn Taitt were Trinidadians, Jackie Opel was Barbadian and they all played important roles in the development of popular music making in Kingston. The result was the creation of a sound track that was internationalised through technology and transnational movements, resulting in the adoption of music by diverse cultures worldwide and the creation of new text and meanings to a message born out of oppression and exploitation.

The Creative Echo Chamber[4] represented a model which operated on multiple levels. At one end, it privileged creative expression and not the exploitation of art for commerce. On the other, it was an incubator for a unique supply of talent for the international recorded music industry dominated by the world capitalist system. The emphasis on the creative aspects, of what Pierre Bourdieu calls the habitus, in Kingston is significant. It was primarily about art, not for art's sake, but art for identity construction, colonial deconstruction, economic independence, bricolage and appropriation. The system was regenerative in the sense that popular music production involved a lot of repetition in terms of devices such as of covering of both local and international tunes, the reuse of rhythms and the signification of styles. This allowed for continuity, appropriation, innovation and reinterpretation, processes that have made the Kingston music industry, a significant contributor to innovative trends and styles in international music circles. It has also kept the industry vibrant and on the cutting edge of global music trends, despite its reality of being on the periphery of music industry power relations. The communal echoes reverberated with the ancestral memories of Africa, the creolised society and the styles and influences, enabled by Anglo-American hegemony, created a unique space in Kingston that produced popular music through very complex, multifaceted, ambiguous and multilayered processes. Kingston, more than anywhere else in the Caribbean, became a creative city, an echo chamber of 'creativity reception and transformation' (Connell and Gibson 2003, 144).[5]

Value Chain Dynamics in the Recorded Music Industry

Utilising value chain analysis, pioneered by Michael Porter (1985), the music industry can be deconstructed and examined to understand its economic value and organisation. Porter suggests that organisations add value to the products and services they produce by engaging in certain activities that should be run at optimum levels to allow the organisation to realise a competitive advantage. If run efficiently, the value created should exceed the cost of running them. Porter highlights five primary activities and four support activities that organisations engage in to optimise profit potential.

Primary Activities

1. Inbound logistics – material handling, warehousing, inventory control transportation
2. Operation – machine operating, assembly, packaging testing and maintenance
3. Outbound logistics – order processing, warehousing, transportation and distribution
4. Marketing and sales – advertising, promotion, selling, pricing, channel management
5. Service – installation, servicing, spare parts management

Support Activities

1. Firm infrastructure – general management, planning finance, legal investor relations
2. Human resource management recruitment, education, promotion reward systems
3. Technology development – research and development, IT, product and process development
4. Procurement – purchase of raw materials, lease of properties, supplier contracts negotiations

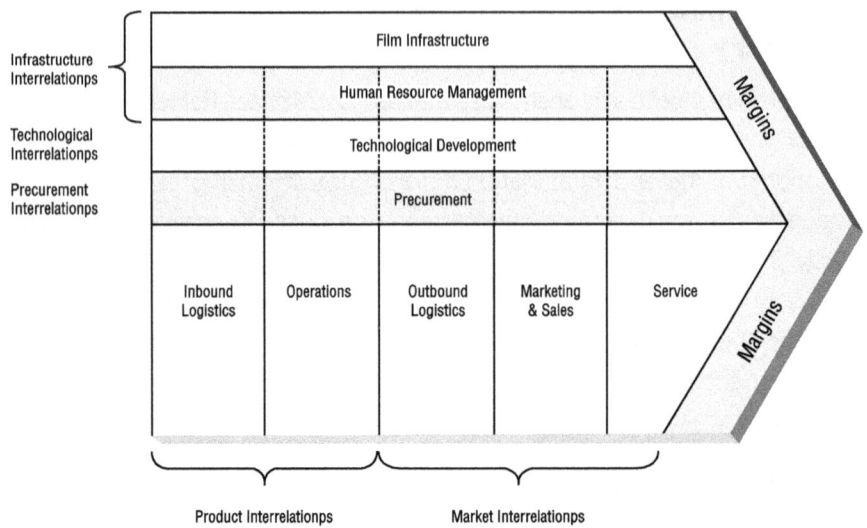

Fig. 4.2 Value Chain Analysis by Michael Porter

Various value chain models have been developed to analyse the Anglo-American and Jamaican music industries, each emphasising various key areas of the industry (Hirsch 1970, 126–35; Leyshon 2001; Wallis 2004, 49–77; Witter 2004, 47–56). Another useful tool for analysing the music industry is system theory which is employed by Geoffrey Hull (2004, 11). System theory outlines five facets that are essential to the proper functioning of any business system:

> (a) 'Inputs, (b) Some transformation process, (c) Outputs (the products which are the results of the transformation process), (d) a feedback process that will influence the selection of input into the next round of processing, (e) an external environment within which the organization carries out its processes.

Input includes songwriters, producers, studio engineers, performances and technology. Mastering, duplication and replication of CDs can be considered transformational processes, while outputs of the music industry include CDs, vinyl, DVDs, the profit and loss for the label owners and employees' satisfaction. Purchases by music consumers and attendance at live concerts with consumers making decisions, which are noted by record executives and artists, provide a feedback loop which is necessary for decision-making within the record company. The recording industry is motivated primarily by profits considering the fact that the global industry is controlled by four major conglomerates namely EMI, Sony/BMG, Warner Music Group and Universal/Vivendi which, through a process of vertical integration, has led to increased control over different stages in the production and distribution process (Wallis 2004, 6).

In outlining the three income streams of the recorded music industry Hull (2004) notes:

> At the heart of that economic model are three streams of income, generated through the utilization of a song, a particular recorded performance of that song, and live performances of that song. At the head of each income stream is a creative act: a song is written, a recording is produced, a live performance given. These creative acts give rise to legal rights associated with them. The songwriter's creative act results in copyright in a musical composition. The record label's, producers', and recording artist's creative acts result in copyrights in the sound recording. Performers have a right to keep others from recording or broadcasting a performance. Three distinct legal rights, three distinct creative acts, and three distinct treatment of a song produce three distinct income streams (21).

In the traditional music industry value chain based on a copyright philosophy, the composer is paramount (Wallis 2004, 104–109; Hull 2004, 22–23). The ownership and exploitation of the copyright in a musical work is one of the important income streams in the recorded music industry. The work is assigned to a publisher who then issues licences to end users who pay for the use of the copyright-protected material. The sale of recorded material as finished products in the form of vinyl records, tapes, CDs and Mp3/Mp4 is another source of income. This process involves a series of activities critical to the value chain. They include the recording of the song by the record company with the assistance of their artist & repertoire (A&R) representative and other intermediaries such as musicians, producers and engineers. The recording is then manufactured and packaged, a marketing and promotion campaign is developed and then the music is distributed through retailers who then sell to consumers. Roger Wallis (2001) commenting on the various ways income is generated by the copyright stream states:

Income is generated from physical and non-physical sources. Mechanical rights refer to moneys paid to composers and publishers when musical works are duplicated on physical carriers such as CD. Performance rights provide income to composers /publishers and in most territories to performers and producers, when recordings are performed in public (12).

This economic model approach of the value chain is useful in assessing the music industry. Allan Albarran (1996) states, 'the ability to attract revenue (and ultimately profits) enables different producers to continue to operate in media markets' (6). From a global standpoint, despite radical shifts in the way the recorded music industry operates, as Wallis (2004) notes, 'the value chain remains more or less intact' (106).

The structure and flow of the Jamaican music value chain is significantly different from that of the traditional Anglo-American value chain.

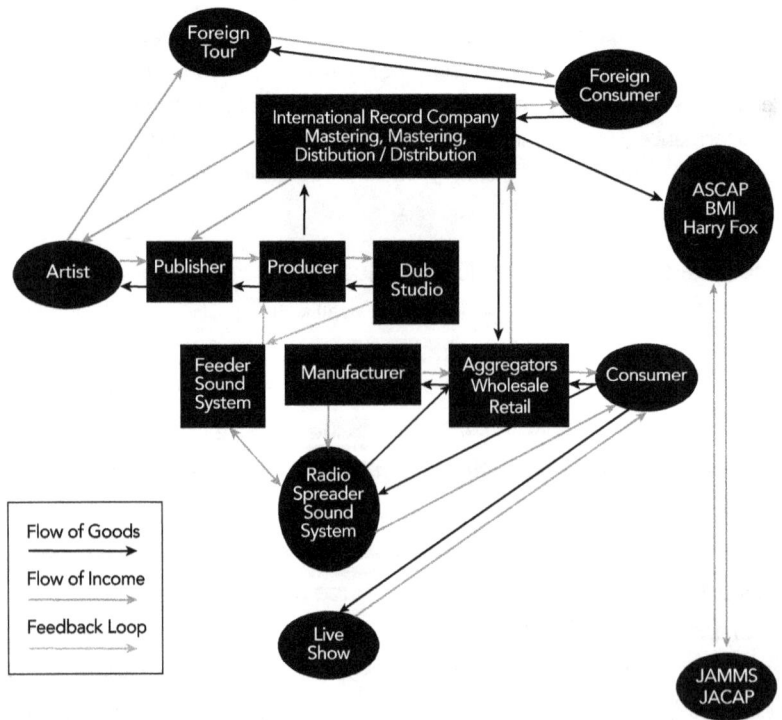

Fig. 4.3 Kingston Music Industry Value Chain

Kingston Value Chain

The Kingston music industry model has never adhered to the above mentioned value chain model and income streams in any of the various phases of cultural production. In fact, it has deviated in radical ways from the Anglo-American modality. While there are similarities in some streams of income in the Kingston model, the development of others are stymied by cultural and legal factors. Additionally, new income streams unique to the Kingston model provide an opportunity to interrogate these non-traditional income opportunities.

In the Kingston model, the copyright income stream is underdeveloped. In the instances where copyright protocol is observed, it is organised through a small minority. A brief overview of the development of the industry will explain the reasons for the non-adherence to the copyright modus operandi.

Voicing/Sound System Income Stream

The first income stream in the Kingston model was the process of voicing on rhythms at recording and dub plate studios and this has remained the basis of the model throughout all periods of cultural production. Artists earned income from voicing songs for producers on a song-to-song basis on rhythms that were owned by the producers. The system of advances was in play. Musicians received a flat fee for playing on the rhythm track while vocalists received an advance on payment, based on record sales and not on copyright of the song or the sound recording. In the dub plate studio, especially during the period of Internationalization, Neoinnovation and Globalization, artists earned money from recording 'specials' of their popular recordings. Specials were customised versions of popular recordings done for sound systems that played these specials in sound clashes and regular engagements. While this stream is somewhat similar to Hull's first income stream, (where artists get an advance from a record company for recording an album) there are several differences. Firstly, there is the absence of a recording contract between a record company and the artist. The contract, usually verbal, is for a single recording. Secondly, advances were not usually given to the artist as in Hull's income stream. The paying of advances was inconsistent and never guaranteed, as expressed by Winston 'Niney' Holness in a personal interview:

> I remember I do a song, I sing a song for Coxsone and Coxsone give me ten pounds and ten pounds was plenty money…no money don't run those days small money…you go to a producer him do audition. Don't care how you great, you could be a number one singer, when you do audition him have to hear the song you are singing. So you sing the song. Him like the song, him make arrangements to get musicians and him say 'yeah mi going to record this song.' In those days still is only verbal agreement, no one don't really take paper and sign paper. Is only man like Coxsone; Coxsone will have few papers on certain man, cause I remember when Coxsone give me the ten pound I did sign paper and them man don't throw away no paper. I did not sign in front no lawyer, but I know I sign whatever him give me to sign. I know I just sign and collect my money. So, therefore, is just so it run in them days. So you go the studio. Them record it. Them come and make label. Them start to sell the song. A man come an him want the song, him come and him license out the song to the company, or whatever.

Alton Ellis (2008), also, states:

> We knew very little about the business side, and those who didn't want to get wise, simple because it would taking bread out of his mouth if we get wise…I got fifteen pounds for 'Muriel' and the fifteen pounds shared for three of us. Alton and Eddie sing the song, as you know. And the guy who wrote the lyrics for us, a friend named Rookwood, I gave him five pounds too. And we buy some pretty shirts with frills on the front and of course we could get a change out of it.

Income was never guaranteed due to the informal nature of negotiations between artists and record producers. Additionally, the unlimited supply in the talent pool gave record producers the power to decide who got recorded, no matter the level of talent. This reinforced their gatekeeping function. Richard Caves (2000) states, 'the filtering of artists by gatekeepers and the promotion and distribution of their works goes on in all the creative sectors, leading to trouble-prone relationships between artists and the firms that link them with humdrum inputs' (52). This was particularly acute in the Kingston model, where artists were not motivated solely by pecuniary benefits. Factors such as artistic recognition, peer approval and community status played an important part in celebrity construction in *the creative echo chamber*. Aspiring artists were never in a position to negotiate with powerful producers who had an unlimited supply of talent; hence, income levels were low and irregular. Established stars were in a better position to earn a steady income from recordings; however, even in their case the income levels were uneven. Wallis (2004) explained the process which:

> Involves paying the artist/creator a lump sum covering both rights to the song as well as to the performance ('bundling of rights'). By signing such contracts, the composer has essentially allowed a process to start whereby his rights as an author can be transferred at will to other legal entities (13).

In later periods of production, the voicing of dub plates became an important source of income for both aspiring and established stars.

Recording /Distribution Income Stream

Once the consumers of the dancehall or radio have accepted a particular recording, the song is mastered and manufactured for distribution for national and/or international consumption. The main physical music format before the globalisation period of cultural production was the 45-rpm vinyl record. Popular recordings were exported to all the diasporic communities in Britain, Canada and the United States. Some recordings, specially produced for the overseas markets, were never released in Kingston. This was the primary opportunity for producers, who served as both creative and executive intermediaries, to make a return on investment. If the song was a big seller, the distributor first recovered all expenditure on distribution, packaging and promotion then paid the producer the remaining amount. The producer then recovered his expenses, e.g., advances to vocalist, studio time and musicians' fees, and the remainder split between the producer and the vocalist and according to Jason Lee of Sonic Sounds, the vocalist got five per cent of the unit price of each record sold. This process is called recoupment. Donald Passman (2008) notes:

> The process of keeping the money to recover an advance is called recoupment, and we say an advance is recoupable from royalties. The amount of unrecoupable monies is called your deficit or red position... since this is the amount that has to be recovered before you get paid (80).

It is at this point that some producers come into contact with the copyright industry due to distribution linkages with overseas distributors who are operating along the Anglo-American music industry value chain. Many local producers were introduced to the copyright/songwriting stream of income that was not represented in the Kingston model, when negotiating publishing deals with these overseas distributors.

Live Performance Income Stream

As soon as a recording artist had a popular song by way of airplay and sound system acceptance, the demand for live performances increased, establishing the next level of income stream in the Kingston model. Live performances were national and international, depending on whether the song was also a hit in the ethnic markets of Britain and the United States. In the early period of appropriation and internationalisation in the late 1970s, the main market for performances was Britain. In the period of Neoinnovation and Global Interaction, the United States became the major market for tours. Reggae, ska and rocksteady artists were popular on the west coast of the US, while predominantly white audiences preferred the reggae introduced by Marley and Burning Spear. Dancehall is popular on the east coast of the US due to the high concentration of Jamaicans in urban populations such as New York and Florida who reflect and follow the trends of their homeland. The immigrant population has invariably taken their cues from Kingston and most songs that are popular in Jamaica will be popular in these markets. Artists who do well in Jamaica are always in demand in the Afro-Caribbean diaspora and beyond.

In outlining the three income streams, it becomes evident that the Kingston system is based on a unique set of relationships which are influenced in significant ways by the historical organisational structure which is constantly evolving in the face of changing circumstances in *the creative echo chamber*. This heuristic political economy organisational structure that has developed, and which has been entrenched in Kingston's recording industry, has influenced the creativity/business binary in significant ways. We will now look in detail at how this system functions.

Organisational Structure

Bill Ryan's (1992) delineation of the organisational structure of the cultural industries during the complex professional period suggests that the making of creative products was not done by individuals but by a group or project team. Ryan outlines various roles played by the members of the team: primary creative personnel; technical craft workers; creative managers and owners and executives (124–34).

Primary creative personnel include musicians, composers, lyricists, authors, video directors, screenwriters. Also included in this category are engineers and record producers (remixes and the creation of dub) and programmers (gaming).

Technical craft workers perform technically oriented functions such as sound engineering, videography, floor management, music mastering and copyediting. While there is some level of creativity, this does not reside in the original idea of the text.

Creative managers are the intermediaries between the owners and executives on one hand and the creative personnel on the other.

Owners and executives are motivated by profit and usually finance the creative process. They set general policy direction and have the power to hire and fire but are divorced from the conception and development of texts (Hesmondhalgh 2007, 65). They are viewed as 'suits' by creative personnel. David Hesmondhalgh states that the project team exercises a great degree of autonomy at the conception and creation end and that this is critical to an understanding of the cultural industries. While there is some level of autonomy, Hesmondhalgh is quick to point out that this autonomy is by no means an absolute one and is carried out under the supervision of creative managers. He also points out that while there is some autonomy at the conception and creation stages, there is tighter control at the other stages of production, i.e., reproduction and circulation (56). The reproduction stage is heavily industrial, is often and increasingly reliant on technically complex electronic systems, and is strictly controlled, especially in terms of when master copies of films, books, records, etc., are scheduled to be copied and released, or when a programme is scheduled to be broadcast.

The analyses of Keith Negus (1996), A. Hennion (1983), J. Vignolle (1980) and J. Jenson (1984) are useful tools to be applied to Jamaica's music industry structure. By adopting a similar approach to the culture of production or the empathy and subjective feel approach of Hennion and Vignolle, a deeper understanding of the structure of this system becomes possible. This structure could be described as producing art in chaos, a fragmented, disorganised system influenced by racial and class biases. The division of labour in popular music production can be broadly divided into production and performance. The former involves the actual creation of the sound and the latter, the theatrical rendition of the sound. In the Jamaican industry, especially during the early periods of production, distinctions in roles were not as clearly defined and creators of popular music were and still are involved, to a lesser or greater extent, in the two forms. I will differentiate between five distinct groups among Kingston symbol creators in popular music. The first group can be designated the Primary creative/technical personnel, while the second, comprised of eight sub groups, can be designated creative managers/owners.

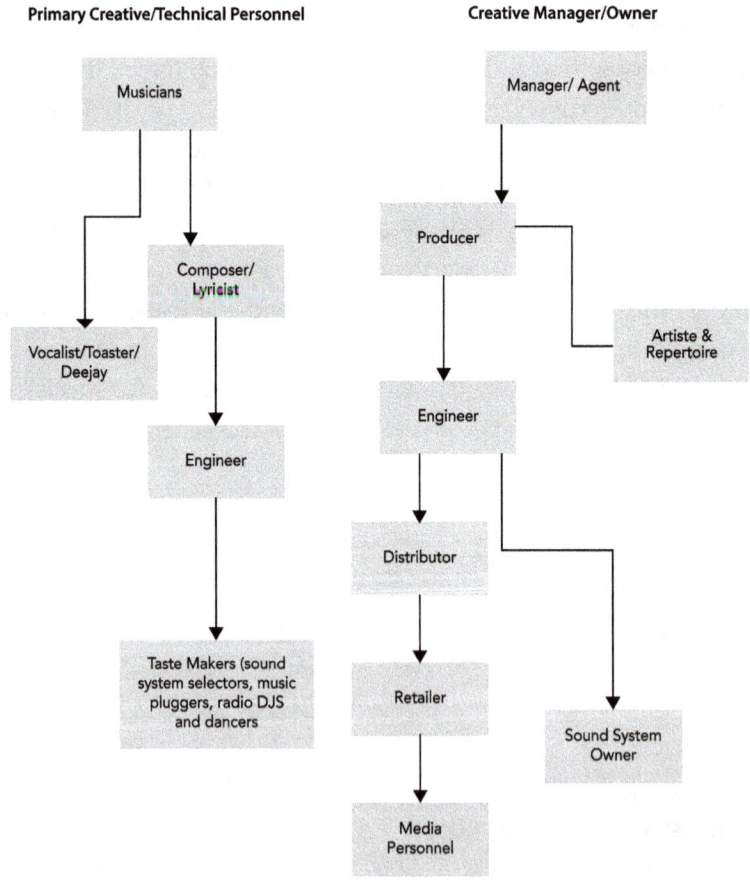

Kingston's Music Industry Organisational Structure

Fig. 4.4 Kingston's Music Industry Organisational Chart

Occupational categories in the Jamaican model were not clearly defined. The division of labour was, at best, blurred as many actors played multiple roles in a more radical way than in the Anglo-American popular music industry, which experienced similar shifts at particular junctures (Toynbee 2000). It was not unusual for some individuals in the industry to perform the roles of artist, producer, distributor, promoter, manufacturer and booking agent all at the same time. Several artists were singer producers, including Derrick Morgan, Derrick Harriott and Clancy Eccles (Barrow and Dalton 2004). Lee 'Scratch' Perry, Big Youth, Augustus Pablo, Prince Buster, The Wailers, Linval Thompson, Winston 'Niney' Holness, Kojak, Shaggy and Robert Ffrench are also among this category. Singers, like Errol Dunkley, supplemented their income by operating a jukebox businesses. Producers, such as Prince Buster, also had thriving jukebox business in addition to sound systems. While the Hookim brothers on Maxfield Avenue operated the Channel One studio and sound system, they also had jukebox and slot machine businesses to supplement their income and to finance their music production. In addition, one of the brothers, Ernest, was also the chief engineer for the studio. Byron Lee functioned as musician, bandleader, distributer, manufacturer, producer, artist-manager, concert promoter and music promoter.

Occupational roles evolved during the neoinnovation period with engineers becoming producers. Due to digitisation the number of musicians in a session decreased, requiring only a keyboard player who could programme sequencers. This fluidity of occupation significantly impacted the industry. The lack of specialisation, due to factors such as undercapitalisation and fragmentation, did not auger well for the organisation of the business, it was without structure and haphazard and was viewed by the Jamaican middle class as a hustle more than a business. Dominic Power and Daniel Hallencreutz (2002) note:

> [T]he production of music products involves a variety of inputs and agents all of which are intrinsic part of the 'creative' process which must be understood as essentially rooted in an industry based commercial logic that is highly spatialised (1,837).

Kingston's music industry was organised along spatial models with complex webs of occupational roles that were blurred and ambiguous. But, while in another context this could be viewed as a deterrent to creative productivity, it had the opposite effect in *the creative echo chamber*. Power and Hallencreutz notes:

> The complex and fragmented nature of the production system and the multiplicity of actors, most often working on an essentially freelance basis can be seen to have strengthened the role of interpersonal and informal contacts in the innovation process (1,846).

These observations are consistent with the culture of production analysis which addresses issues of race, aesthetic preference and division of labour, and explores how these issues affect development within the recording industry. While there is some level of control at the corporate level (national and international) of the Kingston music scene, the autonomy which many symbol creators exerted, in the face of opposition from the Jamaican power elite and international appropriation and dilution of Jamaican popular music, would suggest that there was more at play than organisational orthodoxy or corporate control.

Sound Systems in the Value Chain

The Kingston model developed around the nucleus of the sound system which was the main catalyst for its creativity and innovation. Songs were created specifically for play on the sound system and the response of the patrons determined whether it would go forward to actual production for sale. The song was created in either the recording studio or a dub plate studio for play on a sound system. Consumers' response in the dancehall provided an immediate feedback loop which determined whether or not it would go directly to market, adjusted in keeping with the comments and reactions of dance before release or simply discarded. This mechanism was critical to the production and creative process. It saved a lot of time and resources as producers had a direct link with the consumers through the sound system and dancehall mechanisms. Dick Hebdige (2000) observes:

> The sound system provides an opportunity for the grassroots people to talk back, to respond, to choose what they like and don't like. At the blues dances, the people can dictate the djs choice of sounds. And each sound system has its own toasting heroes who can express the feelings of the crowd (87).

The sound system provided a perfect feedback loop between production (artist/producer) and consumption (retail/distribution) within the Kingston value chain, a critical nexus, which determined how cultural artefacts are created and packaged for the recorded music industry in Kingston. As Hebdige (2000), again, notes:

> This process of feedback – of three-way flow between artists, record producers and the audience – is what helps to make reggae different from other types of pop music. The distance between the performer and the fans is never allowed to grow too great (88).

Thus, the Jamaican industry developed its own economic model, operating in a counter-hegemonic manner, disregarding North Atlantic canons of popular music production and distribution.

In Michael Witter's (2004, 62) circular flow of income of the Jamaican music industry, the artist is at the centre. Witter's value chain, although not linear like its Anglo-American counterparts, is based on the same principle of the copyright industry structure in which the song is the beginning and fundamental source of income from which everything else flows. Consequently, it fails to capture the real structure of the music industry and would present challenges in explaining the income flows if this value chain were to be used in any analysis of the business. In the value chain being presented, the nucleus of the flow is the sound system as that was what determined which songs were recorded, which artists become popular and what, ultimately, is the sound of Jamaican music. It was the driving force during all periods of cultural production, some more than others due to intermittent disintermediation of the value chain.[7] However, at all periods of cultural production, some level of reintermediation of the sound system in the value chain has occurred; hence, the centrality of the sound system to the recording industry of Kingston.

In a similar fashion the income streams of the Kingston model are different from the traditional value chain of the Anglo-America which is based on a contractual relationship between record companies and artists and on the control of copyright-protected creative work and the extent of the exploitation of such rights. In most instances, income streams in the Kingston model are inextricably linked with the sound system and its central position in the Kingston value chain.

The production/consumption trajectory of the sound system within the Kingston production model value chain presents the case for a very unique modality for music production. During the Appropriation, Innovation and Internationalisation periods, the relationship between the sound system and recordings played out in the following way.

The manner in which songs reached the public was as complex as it was fortuitous in the Jamaican business model. The process started with cultural intermediaries, called gatekeepers, who decided during the audition process whether a song was worthy of being recorded. Gatekeepers included the main producers or their assistants. The song then went to tastemakers who ran the sound systems and interfaced with the audience at dances and who determined if a song was hot or not. In many instances, the directions of sound selectors had a major influence over the audience. The song, based on the level of popularity, was then manufactured for distribution and sale. That process could take as long as a year and here, again, the influence of the retail agents was critical as they influenced the purchases of the public and jukebox owners.

Record touting was, indeed, a crucial occupation in the business. On any given day there would be touters in the major retail stores in Kingston encouraging buyers to get the 'next big hit'. Not only were they in the stores but some were positioned in front of all the stores. These touters usually worked for smaller producers who were trying to break into the business. Augustus Clarke (popularly known as Gussie), top publisher and owner of the Music Works recording studio, was among these upstarts. Gussie, in a personal interview, remembers leaving Kingston College in the days to go to Randy's storefront to sell his freshly produced song, as he was not able to get it into any of the leading stores. He had not yet gained the prerequisite respect and clout to get his song into any of the top stores. So, he, like many others, resorted to hustling, as a method of guerrilla marketing, to sell their records.

Radio was the ultimate channel of exposure for a new song. Songs played on radio were mainly the polished sound or gentrified *reggae* of uptown producers such as Byron Lee and Ken Khouri. This opportunity did not extend to the music of great roots symbol creators and, for the most part, the big hits of Treasure Isle, Prince Buster and Studio One did not enjoy any serious airplay. Radio was the preserve of 'good music' from America and Britain. Jamaican music was considered far too primitive and backward for valuable airtime. Hence, although Jamaican songs were regularly on the radio chart, a huge chunk of the catalogues of many top independent record companies did not receive any airplay.

In this context, the sound system represented an intriguing model for cultural studies scholars whose critique of the concept of creativity and cultural production has been the subject of an ongoing debate (Toynbee xvii).[8] The argument of the 'consumption orthodoxy' (Toynbee, xv)[9] articulates the position that culture is a significant facet of consumption. Supporters of this position conflate popular culture and consumption by arguing that culture can be defined by its ubiquitous commodification (Fiske 1989a, 1989b and Willis, 72).

Jason Toynbee (2000) argues counter to this position:

> ...The complexity and conflicted nature of cultural production is blithely ignored. Far from music just turning up in the market place it is the outcome of intense competition and struggle between, for example, record companies and musicians, radio stations and music publishers, disc jockeys and club owners. As well as affecting the economic wellbeing of the actors involved, these struggles have cultural outcomes. They have an impact on what kind of music gets made (xvi).[10]

Toynbee cites Willis's work on the Jamaican sound system, which contradicts his consumption orthodoxy proposition. Willis, along with Simon Jones, sees the sound system phenomenon as 'an institution where the activities of consumption merge into and become intertwined with more conventional forms of production' (qtd. in Toynbee 2000, 72). Toynbee concludes from this analysis of the sound system that:

> It is simply not clear whether reggae sound systems belong to the sphere of consumption or production...The consumption into production argument by Willis and Jones thus falls down because it does not engage with the professional, craft dimension of the sound system...There is a continuum of music-making activity in popular music as a whole, which stretches from the small scale and local to the global and fully industrial[11] (xvii).

The sound system seems to exist comfortably in both spheres of production and consumption, hence its critical role in the Kingston music model.

Musicians and their role in the Value Chain

Richard Caves outlines the process by which musicians enter commercial relationships. On leaving music school, musicians enter an apprenticeship period during which they hone their skills. Following this, they experience the dichotomy referred to as the A/B list of talent. The higher the level of musical talent and star persona, the better the chance of ending up on the A-list. Caves (2000) states:

> The A list/B list distinction begins in earnest as musicians listen to each other and interact in paid sessions and jamming on the side. The rankings that result depend mainly on playing skill, but also adaptability, versatility, and the interpersonal skills that are valuable for seizing the unpredictable and fluid opportunities open to these musicians (34).

The Jamaican recording industry, especially during the Appropriation and Innovation periods, operated within a similar studio system. Among the A-list musicians were the members of the Skatalites, including Cuban-born Tommy McCook, a trained musician who had the respect of all the other members for his ability as a saxophone player and a leader of men. Also represented on the A-list were saxophonist Roland Alphonso, Lester Sterling, Lloyd Knibb, Lloyd Brevett, Jackie Mittoo, Ernie Ranglin, Cluett Johnson, Rico Rodriguez, Gladstone Anderson, Boris Gardiner, Larry McDonald and Jackie Jackson. A-list vocalists included Alton Ellis, Derrick Morgan, Jimmy Cliff, Delroy Wilson, the Jiving Juniors, the Gaylads, the Paragons, the Techniques, the Uniques and the Wailers. Being an A-list musician or performer afforded certain privileges in the studio system of Sir Coxsone Dodd and Duke Reid who were the main players at the time. Smaller producers had smaller operations and were more flexible than Reid and Dodd but still applied the same studio code principle. A-list creators had ready access to the studio. They could record regularly and could even record songs that were not initially approved by Reid or Dodd. Talented A-list creators, who had proved themselves, became gatekeepers who conducted the auditions of new talent and decided who saw Reid or Dodd and who got the opportunity to record. Lee 'Scratch' Perry, B.B. Seaton, Leroy Sibbles and Jackie Mittoo became gatekeepers by the fact that they were arrangers and conducted auditions of new talent.

During all periods of cultural production, musicians were employed to perform on various rhythm tracks, the best of which provided the accompaniment for the performers. In some cases, however, as mentioned earlier, accompaniment was done to particular songs which were either original lyrics or a cover of R&B or pop songs from the United States and Britain. There was no guarantee that any song recorded was due for release within a specific timeframe; that decision rested solely with the producer. During later periods of production the number of musicians needed for a recording session was significantly reduced, due to aesthetic and genre shifts. With reggae and rocksteady, horns were not essential; with dub and dancehall, a minimalist approach to production took root reducing the number of musicians, a situation further exacerbated with the innovation of digitisation and drum sequencing.

Dub Plate Culture in the Value Chain

The dub plate studio is an essential part of the political economy of the Kingston recording industry. A critical part of the sound system aesthetics, the dub plate studio is the space where custom-made recordings of popular songs are made for the various sound systems nationally and internationally. It is a part of the recording income stream of the Kingston model and is dependent only on the demands of the sound system. Both new and old recordings are re-recorded to suit sound systems. These specials are of two types. There are specials that just 'big up' the sound system and its owner, selectors and crew. These are played by sound systems to establish the prestige of the system and its selectors. Then there is the clashing variety of dub plate special; recorded with the aim of defeating rival sound systems at sound clashes which are a feature of the dancehall and sound system culture. This becomes an important income stream for recording artists who earn significant income from doing specials. The level of earnings is directly proportional to the number of hit songs an artist has. The hits did not have to be current as many artists, who sometimes experience a hit drought which significantly reduces the demand for live shows, can always rely on the dub plate stream of income as they are always in high demand from the thousands of sound systems globally.

Manufacturing and Distribution in the Value Chain

Federal Records, operated by Ken Khouri, was integral to the development of the music industry in Kingston. Khouri provided all the technical services of recording, mixing and manufacturing, but did his mastering in Florida (Bradley 2000, 46–47). Apart from the small, low-tech studios operated by Stanley Motta and the first multitrack facility at the Jamaica Broadcasting Corporation, Khouri's Federal Records was the main facility for all the early producers. This changed when Reid and Coxsone set up studios for themselves and then, much later, Vincent Chin set up Studio 17 on North Parade. Reid, Dodd, the Pottingers and the Hookim brothers soon set up pressing plants. During most periods of production, Kingston was served by more than seven pressing plants, with Dynamic Sounds, Sonic Sounds, GG Pressing and Tuff Gong being the main producers. These manufacturers were also the main distributors for both local output and North American products which had a high demand in Jamaica and for many years, foreign music from the US outsold Jamaican music.[12] These top four distributors secured licensing agreements with most of the top labels in The United States including Sony, Atlantic, Warner Bros, A&M, Electra, Motown Stax, Def Jam and MCA. So, in Jamaica R&B, soul, rock, country and middle-of-the-road were outselling Jamaican popular music. Kingston, therefore, looked outside to sustain their business.

The Multiple-Simultaneity Modes of Production Model

Several popular music scholars (Roberts 2005, 24–46; Bynoe 2005, 200–213) have argued that popular music that is radical in essence, that speaks of the injustice, alienation and disenfranchisement, is usually made by independent record companies. These 'indies' are always finding, recording, marketing and selling new music. This has been the case with rock 'n' roll, rhythm and blues hip hop, reggae and ska, all new genres that have been developed by independent recording entities. Keith Negus (1996) argues that the rise of these genres posed a threat to the market dominance and recording control of large music corporations. This, he states, 'leads to tension that is resolved by the absorption of the independent, who are co-opted via processes of amalgamation, joint venture or complete buy out' (43).

The Kingston music industry was an independent one which comprised medium-, small- and micro-operations. At the medium level, there were Studio One, Dynamic Sounds, Federal Records and GG Records, all of which had manufacturing plants. Most owned recording studios, held auditions for talent and controlled major distribution in the island and the diaspora. The small- and microfirms were only able to finance recordings, do some promotion and relied on the bigger firms to carry out their distribution activities. However, it was these firms or individuals and producers who were the most innovative and creative. Not only were they influenced by the political and economic deprivation of the masses which was expressed in the music they made, but were also influenced by the profit motive in addition to issues of affirmation and identity. This led to the establishment of relationships between themselves and the bigger Jamaican firms as well as record companies in Britain and the United States to ensure economic viability.

Island Records, founded in Jamaica, was relocated to London in 1962 and became a part of the 'indie' scene in that city. Other independent labels with reggae ties included Virgin Records (1970s), Trojan Records (1960s), Creole (1970s) and Pama Records (renamed Jet Star) and Greensleeves Records (1970s). While Island and Virgin Records signed and recorded material along the lines of the Anglo-American rock tradition, they also engaged in the practice of licensing recordings that were the property of many of the top producers on the Kingston music scene (Power and Hallencreutz 2002, 1,843).

Negus (1996, 42–43) has noted that in many cases the distinction between majors and independent companies was blurred and their relationship should be viewed as symbiotic. This had implications for the relationship between the independent British companies like Island and Virgin Records, who were indirectly linked to the majors and Jamaican artists and producers.[13] While the majors did not have a direct presence in Kingston, their tentacles reached very far. This resulted in what Nelson George (2004) describes as the 'conglomerate control of black music' with 'overstuffed rosters of major labels' (167), which fostered the dreaded crossover mentality to reach a wider white audience (153). Surrender to this crossover mentality resulted in what Mike Alleyne (2001) calls the 'fragmented reproduction of reggae aesthetics' (16);[14] resulting in a 'cultural dilution' (16) that is at the heart of some of the stagnation and exploitation of many symbol creators noted by critics of the Jamaican music industry in the Kingston Creative Echo Chamber.

In the 1960s, international interest in ska came to a head with the release of 'My Boy Lollipop' by Chris Blackwell who had a licensing agreement with the Fontana Label, a subsidiary of Philips (Bradley 2000, 150–51). The song was recorded in England with British musicians led by Jamaican Ernest Ranglin. This record was produced in the Anglo-American pop tradition. Its subsequent promotion, distribution, with the pop/rock mainstream facilitated the record's ascendancy to international chart success, reaching number one on the British pop chart. Blackwell further developed the arrangement of Jamaican talent being co-opted into the British 'Indie' when he signed Wilfred 'Jackie' Edwards and Jimmy Cliff in the 1960s and the Wailers in the 1970s. This relationship reached its high point with the release of *Catch a Fire*. The production and marketing of this album changed the way in which rock music critics and radio deejays viewed reggae and eventually assisted in the band's international breakthrough (Toynbee 2006, 4–5).[15] This was the high point of the internationalisation period when reggae had ascended to international recognition and legitimacy.

This also marked the escalation of two distinct modes of music production in the Kingston Creative Echo Chamber (Power and Hallencreutz 2002, 1,843), which I have labelled the multiple simultaneity modes of production. Zjelka Kozul-Wright and Lloyd Stanbury (1998) commenting on the model note:

> The Jamaican music sector is characterized by a dual industrial structure, with a small minority of well known artists who have 'made it' in international markets, such as Jimmy Cliff, Shaggy, Inner Circle, Ini Kamoze, Patra, Third World, Diana King, and Buju Banton, who operate under modern competitive conditions analogous to those found in the rest of the developed world. However, the majority of local musicians, artists and producers function under far less organised and fortuitous circumstances. In addition to inadequate financial structures to support the industry, there is an absence of formal market institutional structures within the industry itself (16).

These modalities were present as far back as the 1950 with Lord Flea's Capitol release and later in 1964 with 'My Boy Lollipop'. However, the two distinctive modes of production experienced a marked development and consistency after the making of the *Catch a Fire* album.

On the one hand, there is the nonlinear mode of production based on economic and non-economic motivations, a totally indigenous mode of production based on the production of recordings to satisfy the sound system structure in a 'copyright law free' environment. In this case, the motivation for profits was not based on the capitalist/copyright model and the concept of identity and resistance of hegemonic forces was as critical as the ideals of success, fame and fortune. There was free borrowing of lyrics, (in what is called the *open domain*, explored in greater detail in chapter six), ideas and innovations which allowed for unparalleled creativity in the Kingston Creative Echo Chamber. This was 'a collaborative approach to innovation and a conception of music as continuous process rather than a set of discrete works' (Toynbee 2008, 3).[11] Within this mode, which I will call the *Beat Street* mode, there was a complex web of modalities in terms of production that will be elaborated on later in the chapter.

On the other hand, there was a hybridised system of engagement with the Anglo-American music industry mainly through independent record companies. The production of recordings were based on the pop/rock formula of the major record corporations. These relationships also involved the licensing of Jamaican recording through distribution deals with the major producers in the Kingston music scene, e.g., Lee 'Scratch' Perry, Bunny Lee, Jo Jo Hookim, Joe Gibbs and Clement Dodd. This relationship even spawned success on the British and American charts with Desmond Dekker's breakthrough with '007' in 1967 and 'Israelites' in 1969 (UK chart). These two recordings were produced by Leslie Kong in Kingston and were distributed in Britain by one of the 'indies' who handled Jamaican music. This modality I will call *Catch a Fire* as recognition for the groundbreaking album by the Wailers, co-produced by Island Records boss, Chris Blackwell.

We will now examine the two main modalities within the multiple simultaneity modes of production that were fully developed by the *appropriation* period of cultural production through the global int*eraction* period, to outline their fundamental divergence and similarities in terms of practices.

   1. In the Beat Street model the 'riddim' is paramount; the musical accompaniment is central in the recording process. Peter Manuel

and Wayne Marshall (2006), in describing what they call the riddim method, note:

> From the early 1970s reggae music – whose most popular form since around 1980 has been called 'dancehall' – has relied upon the phenomenon of the 'riddim', that is, an autonomous accompaniment track, typically based on an ostinato (which often includes melodic instrumentation as well as percussion). While dancehall song consists of a deejay singing (or voicing) over a riddim, the riddim which is not exclusive to that song, but is typically used in many other songs (447).

What Manuel and Marshall are describing is the unique model of music production that has been at the centre of song construction and the production process in the Kingston music model. However, they failed to point out that riddims were the starting point in the production process and riddims were not made for the sole purpose of what they call the riddim plus voicing system, where riddims are used over and over again. The critical distinction is that riddims are the starting point in the production and song construction process, which does not necessarily mean that a riddim will be used for multiple voicing.

Many riddims have been produced in all the periods of cultural production that were created under the riddim-plus voicing system but these riddims are exclusive to one song.

The role of the sound system in riddim's production is critical, the riddims' popularity and its autonomous nature rested squarely on the sound system culture. Riddims became popular due to the sound aesthetic in the dancehalls. For sound systems that competed on a regular basis, power in terms of wattage and fidelity was important. A sound system could destroy its rival on the basis of quality and loudness alone, so the availability of powerful riddims was essential. After versions were introduced in the '70s, sound systems began to use instrumental versions to showcase their audio quality and to drive fear into rivals who were not up to muster technically. In this area King Tubby's Hi Fi had no match and was famous for thunderous sound. Here, again, there is a deviation from the Anglo-American mode of production where lyrics, melody and rhythm are inextricably intertwined. In addition, during the ska period, instrumentals were very popular due to the studio session band the Skatalites. In the early period, many vocalists were not skilled enough to come up with good melodies nor could they voice properly if the musician played simultaneously. So, the musicians made the rhythm first and the voicing was done later. Stranger Cole (2008), ska pioneer, remembers his first set of recordings for Duke Reid and the difficulties he encountered:

> I did not know about studio and what you supposed to do so it was really hard to voice a song. I had the lyric but could not find the melody, so Lester Sterling tell me to just wait let him work it out and lay the track then I could sing when him find the melody for me. Lester help me a lot in those days is him help me on song like 'Bangarang'.

This highlighted the fact that many vocalists did not have sufficient music competence and relied on the musicians who were trained, entrenching the riddim as the first mode of production. Again, the copyright principle is diverted, suggesting a new modality for music-making, focused on the riddim and voicing on the riddim.

2. Artists were not restricted to any one label. There was free movement of artists from label to label regardless of any contractual obligations that were in place. Derrick Morgan notes that when he recorded the hit 'Fat Man' for pioneer producer Simeon Smith, after cutting tracks with Duke Reid and Coxsone, Duke Reid was upset with him, and related that:

> He sent some bad men to take me back to him, ask me why I do this, say I can't do that and so on. I said I didn't know it would be offending to him, I don't under no contract with nobody, but just stay back in his stable for a while (Katz 2003, 22).

In the *open domain*, the song was not protected as some singers recorded the same song for various producers. Between the years 1990 and 1991, the late deejay Baby Wayne recorded his hit song 'Mama' for over four producers including Pickout Records, but it was the Steely and Cleavie-produced recording which became the hit single. One of the determinants of this practice was the release date of singles. The timetable for release was very flexible so if a performer was frustrated by the lack of release time by a producer he would record the song for another producer in the hope that the release date would be more expeditious. It was also a deliberate ploy to ensure that the song was released, which was essential to the artist as release increased the possibility of sound system play or airplay. This would lead to greater popularity for the artist.

The major distribution networks were controlled by businessmen of the ethnic minority whose tastes mirrored their ethnicity or the Anglo-American culture. Many of them had no time for the roots music of reggae and the hard driving sounds of ska. Coxsone and Prince Buster did their own distribution and if the music was popular enough via sound system and radio, they had no problem making a profit from the music. Once artists were established they could get distribution deals, but even this was no guarantee of effective distribution and many artists suffered at the hands of these distributors who sometimes could not give good reasons for not distributing a particular record. Unknown producers and artists found it difficult to get distribution, on a regular basis, from the main distributors. Consequently, smaller, unorganised networks of distribution operated at various levels within the model. Many producers developed do-it-yourself systems. They pressed a number of records for sale then used the income raised to press additional records, and so on. This was a strain for many producers and accounted for the big turnover in personnel that was a feature of the industry. In fact, many great songs were never distributed properly and so did not make it on any credible chart.

However, over time, through sound system play, they have evolved into some of the best known songs in the Jamaican pop music repertoire.[17] During the cultural production periods of appropriation, innovation and internationalisation, the jukebox was a major avenue for promotion and did a more effective job than radio that was controlled by the power elite and discriminated against many indigenous recordings.

Table 4.1 Feeder Sound Systems

SOUND SYSTEM	PRODUCER	PRODUCTION PERIOD
Studio One	Clement Dodd	Appropriation Innovation Internationalisation Neo innovation
King Edwards	Vincent Edwards	Appropriation Innovation
Duke Reid	Arthur Reid	Appropriation Innovation
Matador	Lloyd Daley	Appropriation Innovation
Jack Ruby	Lawrence Lindo	Appropriation Innovation Internationalisation
Merritone	Winston Blake	Appropriation Innovation Internationalisation
Jahlove Musiz	Earl Belcher / Micky Mowatt	Innovation Internationalisation
Channel One	Jo Jo Hookim	Internationalization
King Tubby's Hi FI	Osbourne Ruddock	Innovation Internationalization Neo Innovation
Prince/King Jammy's	Lloyd James	Internationalization Neo Innovation
Volcano	Henry "Junjo Lawes	Internationalization Neo Innovation
Socialist Roots	Tony Welch	Internationalization Neo Innovation
Powerhouse	George Phang	Internationalization Neo Innovation
Gemini	Winston Dinall	Internationalization Neo Innovation
Black Scorpio	Jack Scorpio	Internationalization Neo Innovation
Heatwave	Bobby "Digital" Dixon	Neo Innovation
Silver Hawk	Wycliffe "Steely Johnson	Neo Innovation
Stur Marr	Kenneth "Skeng Don" Black	Neo Innovation
Renaissance	Delano Thomas	Global Interaction
Stone Love Movement	Winston "WePow" Powell	Neo Innovation Global Interaction
Shang-hi Solophonic	James Howard Dennis Howard	Neo Innovation Global Interaction

3. The sound system was critical to the recording, production, testing, promotion and success of sound recordings. The *feeder sound systems* owned by producers during all periods of cultural production were critical to the production process. They recorded material and got direct feedback from patrons at dancehalls, which determined what singles were released, based on the responses. Feeder sound systems set the trends and were in the front seat to see emerging trends and respond to them with amazing speed. In the periods of internationalisation and neoinnovations, producer-driven sounds included Channel One, Black Scorpio, Prince Jammy (later known as King Jammy), Gemini, Socialist Roots, Volcano, Red Man, Heatwave, Silver Hawk and Stur Mars. I observed this process both as a dance attendee and as a selector for the sound system Shang-hi Solophonic, a joint venture between myself and my father, James Howard.

Spreader sound systems were critical to the feedback loop and provided solid data on crowd response and aesthetic direction for both sound system producers and regular producers who did not own sound systems. This firmly situates the sound system as the primary focus of the Beat Street mode, moving away from the Anglo-American rock mode of production based on the 'writing-recording-performing unit' (singer-songwriter or band) focused on producing albums with the rise of the popularity of the long-playing record (Toynbee 2008, 4).[18]

4. The Kingston Creative Echo Chamber was, and still is, a singles-driven market; the recording of the album was never at the forefront of the production process with most albums being compilations of recorded material and not deliberate productions oriented around a concept, which was the standard industry mode in the Anglo-American system.

5. Within the *Beat Street* modality of production in Kingston, there was also a production mode that attempted to imitate the production aesthetic of the Anglo-American rock/pop mode. With the development of the business from a cottage industry to a more organised system with all the five facets necessary for a business

system (Hull 2004, 11), the ethnic business class, who were more educated, cosmopolitan and informed, attempted to make music that sounded like the music of North America and Britain. The main features of such productions were full orchestration with strings and wind instruments, three part harmonies with arrangements that emphasised melodic chord changes instead of the rhythmic fixity of regular roots reggae, ska and rocksteady. The mix was radio friendly with the vocal soaring over the 'riddim' while the bass and guitars were more subdued than was normal in the Beat Street modality. These were ready-for-radio tunes that did not have to be tested on the sound system. These recordings were consistent with the dominant sound on Jamaican radio, which were mainly American and British pop and rhythm and blues. Radio and popular music has had a very tumultuous relationship, which, incidentally, is not unique to the Jamaican experience. The cultural elite who controlled the media resisted all countercultural movements. Hence, popular music from the Kingston music scene was not given major airplay. Anglo-American music dominated the airwaves reflecting the tastes of the middle and upper classes which, as Stuart Hall (1996) notes of his own Jamaican roots, 'in a lower-middle-class family that was trying to be a middle-class Jamaican family trying to be an upper-class family trying to be an English Victorian family' (116).

There was never a symbiotic relationship between radio and popular music; in fact, radio played a big role in ostracising the music and discriminating on the basis of class and race, even when they relented and gave exposure to the indigenous music. The mimicking of the Anglo-American aesthetic in music production also had the ulterior motive of breaking into the British and North American markets and also to create a sound that was consistent with the Anglo-American production aesthetic which was considered by the power elite to be superior to what was going on in downtown Kingston. The prevailing philosophy in media in Britain and the United States was that the music out of Kingston barely made it as music (Bradley 2000, 256). They thought it was crudely mixed and the emphasis on heavy bass lines did not sit well with the British and American mainstream consumers who had a difficult time dancing to reggae with its emphasis on the offbeat (Chang and Chen 1998, 43). A case in point was the hit song 'Israelites' by Desmond Dekker. Even after the success of '007' (Shanty Town) in 1967, the BBC rejected the follow-up single, 'Israelites', because they felt the production was poor, which deemed it unfit for airplay. Graeme Goodall remixed the song for airplay, but even this did not result in any success and BBC only picked up the song, belatedly, after it became a big hit in the clubs (Bradley 2000, 241).

This new sound was adopted by the middle class, uptown Kingstonians who had only accepted ska when Byron Lee began playing a watered-down version at venues uptown. Instead of the pioneers of the music, the legendary Skatalites, Lee was asked by Edward Seaga to be the backing band for a group of ska artists, including Jimmy Cliff and Prince Buster, at the New York World's Fair in 1964. It is said that this was a clear case of class bias, as the Skatalites were ganja smoking, Rastamen and officials were nervous about such a band of revolutionaries representing the country. On the other hand, it was also felt that Byron Lee and his band were not good enough to represent ska at its best (Chang and Chen 1998, 36).

At the forefront of this music were Ken Khouri and Byron Lee, who produced a number of singles and albums which have been described by Chang and Chen as 'pop reggae'. At Dynamic Sounds, Lee released singles and albums for Boris Gardiner, Vic Taylor, the Blues Busters, Keith Lyn and Janet Silvera which were very radio friendly, with lush arrangements, backing vocals and lyrics which spoke more to love than the revolutionary and ghetto-oriented lyrics which had become the norm during the innovation and internationalisation periods. Gardiner's songs included the ballads, 'So Nice To Be With You', 'Love's Been Good To Me' and 'Don't Take Away', the mento-influenced 'Commanding Wife' and a string of cover tunes including, 'Groovy Kind of Love', 'Jean' and 'Strangers in the Night'.

At Federal Records, Ernie Smith was releasing songs such as 'I Can't Take It', 'One Dream', 'Pitta Patta', 'Duppy Gunman', 'Bend Down' and 'Ride on Sammy'. Pluto Shervington had a series of hit songs including 'Ram Goat Liver', 'Dat', and 'Your Honour'. Ken Lazarus also had a few hit songs with 'Hail the Man' and 'Cecelia'. Federal also had a band, Tomorrow's Children, which was marketed and packaged like a North American pop band that could appeal both to the international market and the middle-class and uptown Kingstonians who were slowly getting in this type of reggae. Groups like Fabulous Five and Third World continued this tradition producing what I labelled, *gentrified reggae,* in later years. Many of these songs, released mainly by Trojan Beat and Commercial Records, did well on the British charts. And, it was not only the uptown producers who had success with this type of production. Several *Beat Street* producers scored big with this type of production aesthetic including Harry J with 'Young Gifted and Black' and 'Pied Piper' by Bob and Marcia and Winston 'Niney' Holness; 'Everything I Own' by Ken Boothe; 'Love of the Common People' by Nicky Thomas; 'You Can Get it if You Really Want', and 'Wild World' by Jimmy Cliff and 'Liquidator' by Harry J All Stars. This was a distinctive sound that was cultivated alongside the *Beat Street* sound and the Anglo-American rock production style, practised by record companies such as Island Records, (Jimmy Cliff, Wailers, Third World, Aswad Burning Spear, Black Uhuru); Virgin Records, (the Mighty Diamonds, Hugh Roy); Arista, (Native); EMI, (Inner Circle, Matumbi); Columbia Records, (the Congos, Aswad).

These ethnic minorities had one thing in common – access to money and education. This they used to their advantage in terms of organising the business. While the 'uptowners' had an advantage in terms of business management, they could not compete with the downtown crew in terms of street smart and the ability to read the pulse of the people. Creative innovation rested more in the hands of the downtown artists and producers. Studio One and Treasure Isles were the leading outfits in terms of innovation during the early periods of cultural production hits and big star artists; however, the work of Prince Buster, King Edwards, Lloyd Matador, Simeon Smith, Derrick Harriott, Bunny Lee, Winston 'Niney' Holness, Joe Gibbs and later Sly and Robbie, Henry Junjo Lawes, King Jammy's, Steely and Cleavie, Mikey Bennett and Gussie Clarke cannot be ignored.

6. Within the Beat Street modality, several distinctive styles developed. A thorough interrogation is needed to show the dynamic nature of popular music production within such a small market and the amazing diversity it engendered. These styles are a testament to the creativity and inventiveness of the musicians, producers, engineers and songwriters who operated in the Kingston Creative Echo Chamber. It also signifies the versatility of Jamaican genres, especially rocksteady and reggae, which could be fused easily with diverse genres from North America, Latin America, Africa and the Caribbean. The styles include but are not limited to: country reggae, novelty tunes, gospel/revival, roots Rasta and slackness.

Conclusion

The value chain model for the Jamaican music industry is significantly different from the linear models proposed by music industry scholars such as Wallis (2004, 104–109); Hirsh (1970, 126–35); and Leyshon (2001, 49–77). It is also different from the circular flows of income set out by Witter (2004, 62) which focuses on the artist as songwriter going through the directional channels of publisher, producer and studio. The model I have proposed centres on the sound system which is the nucleus of the recording music business in Jamaica. The sound system is intricately intertwined with the recording process and directly influences the production of popular music during all periods of cultural production in *the creative echo chamber*. Sound system culture is directly responsible for the development of a sustainable recording industry based on commercial and popular sounds and vernacular, unlike the mento/calypso period, which was based on a product that was geared towards tourism, tropical exotica, Western flirtation with alien sounds and national identity formation (Neely 2008, 6). The sound system also facilitated the critical feedback loop to the recording industry, which was unique due to its position in the value chain. Feeder sound systems from direct feedback of the dance attendees who, through their rejection or acceptance, decided which song made it to manufacture and islandwide distribution.

The income streams which were also established, while similar to the Anglo-American model, as outlined by Hull (2004), were different due to the importance of the sound system and the additional income which came from the dub plate studio. The absence of regular contracts and the freelance nature of the recording artists were also significant departures from the Anglo-American model. The organisational structure of the Jamaican music industry was outlined as being divided into two main categories namely primary creative/technical personnel and creative manager/owner. Subcategories for the creative/technical personnel include musician, vocalist, toasters/deejay, composer/lyricist, engineer, taste makers (sound system selectors, music pluggers, radio djs and dancers).

The creative manager/owner taxonomy includes producer, manager/agent, A&R, engineer, distributor, retailer, sound system owner and media personnel. The fluidity of occupational roles due to the informal, fragmented nature of the business and issues of undercapitalisation were also noted.

Value chain analysis was used to interrogate the sound system musicians manufacturing distribution management and the dub plate studio system within the Jamaican structure.

The multiple simultaneity mode of production model was established as the distinctive feature of the Jamaican music industry and *the creative echo chamber* was the milieu within which the production models operated. There were fragmented webs of learning and creativity that was the source of innovation, creative synthesis and expression within the city of Kingston. Orange Street, the first creative hub, was the foundation of the rich legacy of Jamaican music that has endured to place Jamaica as one of the major contributors to world culture. This has been the big dilemma of the Jamaican music business – Bob Marley's catalogue is foreign owned; some of the greatest music produced in Jamaica is licensed to various overseas distributors who have shamefully exploited these treasures to their benefit, leaving the original creators to die as paupers. The next chapter will examine copyright culture in the Kingston Creative Echo Chamber to assess the influence of regulation within the circuit of culture trajectory of the study.

NOTES

1. Orange Street was also the location for one of the first record stores in Kingston, which was owned by businessman Jack Taylor. The store specialised in imported records from the United States.
2. Just how did agglomeration and clustering foster the type of creativity that is the essence of the Kingston creative echo chamber? As mentioned earlier, many young musicians gathered around the many music and knowledge

centres, which were scattered around Kingston. These *webs of learning and creativity* provided an alternative space for dispossessed young men and a few women, to get the kind of knowledge and education that was missing from the colonial education. Vocal duo, Alton Ellis and Eddie, had established themselves as the first set of Jamaican stars with their hit 'Muriel', produced by Clement 'Coxsone' Dodd circa 1956. Ellis's house soon became one of the spots where all artists and up-and-comers gathered; it soon developed the name *Room One*.

3. Many of the top Jamaican artists, past and present, and including Bob Marley, Peter Tosh, Jimmy Cliff, Toots Hibbert, Beres Hammond, Lady Saw and Luciano, have rural roots.

4. The *creative echo chamber* was not only about location but presents a theory for analysing the practice of music-making within the Jamaican sociocultural space, signifying a significant praxis/theory continuum.

5. In addition to Room One, there were many other locales (Fifth St, Trench Town) where the teachings of Rastafarians and the UNIA were enunciated by elders and brethrens such as Mortimer Planno and Alvin 'Seco' Patterson engaged young musicians in philosophical reasoning about colonial oppression and African redemption. Among Planno's students were The Wailers, Allan 'Skill' Cole, Ras Michael and Alton Ellis. In the east of Kingston in Wareka Hill/Adrasta Rd, Rasta Brethren would gather in a similar fashion under the leadership of Count Ossie and the Mystic Revelation of Rastafari. Members of the Skatalites, Roland Alphonso, Johnny Moore, Lloyd Knibb and Mystic Revelation members, Nambo Robinson, Cedric 'Im' Brooks and Joe Ruglas were among the regulars.

6. Sonic Sound was one of the top distribution outfits in Kingston, responsible for distributing labels such Taxi Records, Solomonic Records, Volcano and Powerhouse.

7. Disintermediation occurred at different periods due to the production of producers like Byron Lee and Ken Khouri, Chris Blackwell, Clifton Dillon and Harry Johnson whose main market was the United States and the United Kingdom. This happened during all periods of cultural production and reinforced the multilevel nature of popular music production. Reintermediation occurred when these same productions were reimported back into the Jamaican market after exposure in the international market, at this reentry point the sound system regained its important role of providing feedback and being a contributor to the popularity and success, the rejection and failure of these recording.

8. Jason Toynbee, *Making Popular Music: Musicians, Creativity and Institutions* (London: Arnold, 2000).

9. Ibid.

10. Ibid.
11. Ibid.
12. According to the IFPI report, *The Recording Industry in Numbers 2000*, of the top ten selling albums only four were Jamaican and only four songs were reggae or dancehall among the top ten selling singles.
13. At the high point of the involvement of Island and Virgin Records in reggae in the 1970s and '80s, both labels depended on the majors in Britain and the US for the distribution and promotion of their recordings. So, from a very early stage, the international conglomerates that controlled the industry since the 1960s influenced the Kingston music scene through various webs of connection.
14. Mike Alleyne, 'White Reggae: Cultural Dilution in the Record Industry,' *Popular Music & Society* 24, no. 1 (2001): 15–30.
15. 'One Step Forward? Translating Jamaican Popular Music in the Core.' The Society for Caribbean Studies Annual Conference Papers, ed. Sandra Courtman. Vol. 7 (2006).
16. 'Copyright and the Conditions of Creativity: Social Authorship in Reggae Music and Open Source Software.' CRESC Working Paper Series. Working Paper No. 60. CREWC, Open University, November 2008. www.cresc.ac.uk.
17. Included in this category are 'Here I Come' by Dennis Brown, 'Fade Away' by Junior Byles, 'Far East' Barry Brown.
18. 'Copyright and the Conditions of Creativity: Social Authorship in Reggae Music and Open Source Software.' CRESC Working Paper Series. Working Paper No. 60. CREWC, Open University, November 2008. www.cresc.ac.uk.

Too Much Mix Up Mix Up: Copyrighting Culture

Babylon system is a vampire sucking the blood of the sufferer.
                                                    Bob Marley

What is Copyright?

Copyright is defined as the bundle of rights, under law, that are guaranteed to owners of copyrightable works. These include the right to reproduce, distribute, perform the work publicly, make an adaptation or derivative work for broadcast or transmission on cable and the Internet. Copyright can be considered a limited duration legislative monopoly, which lasts the lifetime of the owner of the work and in the case of Jamaica, 95 years after death. Copyright in a work becomes effective if that work satisfies certain criteria including that the work be manifested in a tangible form and is 'sufficiently original'. An idea is not protected under copyright law; it is the expression of ideas to which copyright applies. In legal circles, this is known as the idea/expression dichotomy. A work is protected under copyright law and the author of the work is given exclusive rights by virtue of being the copyright owner and not the author.

Rights owners who are interested in exploiting their works will normally assign or license their right to a third party interest to perform these restricted rights. Rights owners assign their rights to a publisher who is responsible for the administration of these rights. This includes promotion of the work, issuing licences to other organisations such as collecting agencies. Performance and broadcasting rights are usually assigned to *performance rights agencies* and the right to record the work, known as mechanical rights, are assigned to *mechanical rights agencies*. The technology of recording necessitates the existence of a set of rights which are known as related or neighbouring rights, which are owned, not by the composer, but the entity that organises and publishes the recording, i.e., the producer. The owner of this right has the exclusive right to broadcast the recording, to be heard publicly and to make other recordings embodying the recording or any part of it. Another area of neighbouring rights involves the musicians and their right in the performance of a particular work and is known as the performer's rights. Simon Frith and Lee Marshall (2004) make the point that, 'the distinction between copyright and neighbouring rights is an important one, not least because they are intended to benefit different parties (though in practice this may not be the case)' (8).

Copyright within Kingston's Creative Echo Chamber

The story of copyright protection within the Jamaican music industry does not start with the enactment of the new Copyright Act in 1993. Contrary to the observations of many commentators (Bradley 2000, 41–42; Hebdige 2000, 86; McMillan 2005, 7) who have lamented the lack of proper copyright protection in Jamaica and have seen it as a major deterrent to the economic wellbeing of the music business due to the absence of any proper rights management mechanism. The fact is that Jamaica has had a copyright law since 1913. This first law was an adaptation of the 1911 Copyright Act of Britain. However, in colonial Jamaica, copyright protection was intended for the colonial masters whose composers and musicians needed protection for such works that were exploited in the colonies. In 1914, the Performing Rights Society (PRS) was formed in Britain to collect money for the public use of copyrighted works in an effort to curtail the unauthorised use of these works. A branch of the PRS was set up in Jamaica, again to secure the rights of English creators as part of the imperial copyright system created by the Copyright Act of 1911. The Jamaican branch, like all other British outposts, reported to the London office (Ehrylich 1989, 125).

Who Owns the Music?

The main business model for copyright in the Jamaican recorded music industry was based on a principle known in American copyright legislation as the *Work for Hire* principle which recognises two categories under Section 101 of the Copyright Act:

1. A work prepared by an employee within 'the scope of his or her employment', for example, work created by a conventional salaried employee.

2. A work specially ordered or commissioned for use as a contribution to a collective work, as a part of a motion picture or other audiovisual work, as a translation, as a supplementary work, as a compilation, as an instruction text, as a test, as answer material for a test, or as an atlas, provided that the parties expressly agree in writing that the work shall be considered a work for hire. Notice that nine types of work are specified in the second category. An independent contractor who has agreed, in writing, to such treatment generally creates a work of one of those types. Subsequent cases have determined that the written agreement must be completed before the work is created (US Copyright Act 1976).

Though the concept of work for hire was never specifically stated in the Jamaican Copyright Act of 1913, certain clauses within that Act operated under the same principle.

Ownership of Copyright

5. – (1) Subject to the provisions of this Act, the author of a work shall be the first owner of the copyright therein:

Provided that –

(a) Where, in the case of an engraving, photograph, or portrait, the plate or other original was ordered by some other person and was made for valuable consideration in pursuance of that order, then, in the absence of any agreement to the contrary, the person by whom such plate or original was ordered shall be the first owner of the copyright, and

(b) Where the author was in the employment of some other person under a contract of service or apprenticeship and the work was made in the course of his employment by that person, the person by whom the author was employed shall, in the absence of any agreement to the contrary, be the first owner of the copyright, but where the work is an article or other contribution to a newspaper, magazine, or similar periodical, there shall, in the absence of any agreement to the contrary, be deemed to be reserved to the author the right to restrain the publication of the work, otherwise than as part of a newspaper, magazine, or similar periodical.

19. – (1) Copyright shall subsist in records, perforated rolls, and other contrivances by means of which sound may be mechanically reproduced,

in like manner as if such contrivances were musical works, but the term of copyright shall be fifty years from the making of the original plate from which the contrivance was directly or indirectly derived, and the person who was the owner of such original plate at the time when such plate was made shall be deemed to be the author of the work, and where such owner is a body corporate, the body corporate shall be deemed for the purposes of this Act to reside within the parts of His Majesty's dominions to which this Act extends if it has established a place of business within such parts (Jamaican Copyright Act 1913).

Creative manager/owners used this 'loophole' in the act to claim the copyright in the sound recording and the musical works of R&B, ska and rocksteady. Consequently, leading producers such as Clement Dodd, Leslie Kong, Duke Reid, Byron Lee and Ken Khouri are presently owners of copyright for a number of works they did not compose. However unfair it may seem, they are the legitimate owners as this was done under the work for hire principle. There are songs, which were done under arrangements, which were neither clear nor specific enough and, as a result, have been the subject of many lawsuits. On a daily basis, creative workers would report to studio and work on songs and record rhythm tracks. The singers who were 'assigned' to the two companies would then utilise these rhythms and songs.

Musicians were paid per track, while vocal performers were lucky to get any money at all. They only received compensation in the form of an advance to be recouped from sales of the recording. This firmly established the first contractual arrangements between talent and producers. *Work for Hire* was the contractual arrangement between singers, deejays and musicians and producers in the Jamaican music business model and was the preferred choice for those producers who knew the law. Despite the picture painted by many scholars of a weak copyright framework, adequate copyright legislation was in place at the beginning of creative Jamaican music. However, writer's rights were subordinated to producer's rights which fell under related/neighbouring rights. In the Jamaican music industry, the first phase in copyright development, which was the protection of the interest of composers, songwriters, literary and dramatic writers (Laing 2004, 71) had been superseded by the rights of producers and broadcasters, which was the second phase in copyright development. Again, some clarification is necessary. Under related rights, singers, musicians and actors also had secure rights, derived from the role they played in any particular work. However, in the Jamaican experience only the producers and broadcasters rights had gained any traction. This had serious class implications and reflected the prevailing hegemonic structure of the colonial and postcolonial realities of Jamaica.

Again, the circumstances which created this business were unique and did not develop along a Western business paradigm that seamlessly fused art with commerce. The factors which created this music were based not on monetary gains but on localised entertainment for the marginalised lower other in a colonial oppressive environment. In an interview with Clement Dodd and Bunny Goodison (2000, 2005) it was revealed that some creative manager/owners did contribute to the original works in their catalogue.

The Performing Rights Society

With the creation of Jamaican original works it became apparent that there was need for intellectual property rights management. Producers, through their interaction with the British copyright system, realised that there was money to be had from performing and mechanical rights in original compositions. This led to the Performing Right Society (PRS) in Jamaica courting many of the composers to become members so as to ensure they collected on their works. Sonny Bradshaw recounts that the PRS was in Jamaica from as far back as the 1920s but had no link with Jamaican music as it had been established to protect the interest of English composers whose work was being played on radio and bandstands in Kingston and the north coast. Bradshaw remembers that he and other composers had been invited to join the PRS just after Jamaican composers began establishing themselves during the '50s. He became a member then.

The role of the PRS was to collect money from users of the copyrighted compositions of their members. This was another major institution in the development of the Jamaican music business culture and continuation of the synergetic dual nature of the Jamaican music industry.

Copyright Dynamics in The Creative Echo Chamber

Many of the early creators in the 1950s were not sufficiently knowledgeable about the protection of copyright and the potential pecuniary benefits.

Carter Van Pelt (2006) observes, 'the law was relatively modern in most senses, and many record producers abided by it to the letter. However Jamaicans in general, and musicians in particular, were not broadly aware of the meaning, much less the legal intricacies, of copyright' (7).

In addition, the music business in Jamaica did not start with an abundance of original works. During the 1960s, when the music really took off commercially, a significant number of the songs recorded were covers of American rhythm and blues, blues and British pop. This practice had started with the pioneer producers, who, as sound system operators, imported American and British records for consumption at dances. Many singers of this period were not proficient songwriters. Consequently, producers handpicked records from North America, and later Britain, for them to cover. This practice was largely enabled by the lack of enforcement of copyright legislation which protected owners of copyright from the infringement of their works. Additionally, infringement went relatively unnoticed as the American and British publishers and administrators of these rights generally did not know of the existence of these covers and even when they did know, the market was viewed as being so insignificant that the returns were not worth the effort of pursuing litigation.

Table 5.1 lists a number of songs which fell into this category.

Table 5.1 Jamaican R&B/Pop Cover Classics

SONG	JAMAICAN SINGER	ORIGINAL SINGER
1. Rain from the Sky	Delroy Wilson	Adam Wade
2. A Love I Can Feel	John Holt	The Temptations
3. (No, No, No) You Don't Love Me	Dawn Penn	Willie Cobbs
4. You Don't Care	The Techniques	The Impressions
5. No Man Is An Island	Dennis Brown	The Van Dykes
6. My Boy Lollipop	Millie Small	Barbie Gaye
7. Black Bird	The Paragons	The Beatles
8. Left With A Broken Heart	The Paragons	Four Tops
9. You Make Me So Happy	Alton Ellis	Blood, Sweat and Tears
10. Feel Good All Over	Delroy Wilson	The Drifters
11. Someone Loves You, Honey	J.C. Lodge	Charley Pride

Not only did the early producers cover the songs of African American jazz, blues and R&B and British pop through what Toynbee calls *phonographic dissemination*, but many musicians and singers developed their craft by learning the styles which they heard on the records (2000, 74). The importation of 12-inch 78 rpm, 12-inch 33 rpm and 7-inch 45 rpm records by the sound system boss/producer facilitated this new form of 'mediated orality' and 'enormously extended the possibility of participation in music-making'.[1] Toynbee cites the work of several writers (Small 401, Chanan 56–57) who noted the importance of African American 'race records' in the spread of idioms and styles in the United States in the early period of the recorded music industry. There is more than just the transfer of idiom and repertoire at stake here, the imitation of these foreign records by Jamaican artists actually created new styles of music in the *creative echo chamber*. Vocal devices such as falsetto stylings, two-, three- and four-part harmonies became very popular among many local vocal groups who imitated the R&B groups such as the Temptations and the Impressions. These styles became the standard modes for recording by many vocal groups which emerged, especially during the *Appropriation, Innovation and Internationalisation* periods of production. Anglo-American popular song structures were cemented due to the size of the 45 rpm which could not facilitate songs longer than four minutes. Toynbee calls this process phonographic crystallisation and traces its origin to the blues singers in the United States, citing the works of LeRoi Jones (1970, 95–121) and Michael Chanan (1995, 56–57).

Most Anglo-American popular recordings relied on the verse-chorus song structure in which the chorus is repeated several times with the same words and tune; while the verse is repeated with the same tune but different lyrics (Spitzer and Walters 2003, 4–5). Another style adopted by Jamaican performers was the use of a hook, a 'memorable verbal phrase set with a melodic fragment that seems to fit the words like a glove'.[2] The hook is repeated several times during the song, becoming the most significant part of the song. Through *crystallisation* vocal styles of American and British artists such as the Impressions, the Drifters, Al Green, Tom Jones and the Temptations were imitated and subsequently developed by Jamaican artists into a distinctive indigenous vocal aesthetic. The three and four-part harmony structure of groups such as the Impressions and the Temptations were widely copied by Jamaican groups such as the Paragons, the Wailers, the Uniques, the Gaylads and the Techniques. The Motown sound, with its commercial pop writing style, was a favourite source for many of the top producers and vocalists of that period. David Morse (1971) explains the structure of the Motown song:

> It is also characteristic of Motown music that it gives the chorus or refrain a more important position in the structure of a song. Rather than following a 32-bar pattern, repeated over and over with different words, the song is cleanly divided into separate section of verse and chorus, each verse serving as a bridge between repetitions of the chorus. Such songs appear not to move in a straight line but in a circle. Usually they do not come to a definite conclusion but fade out over a chorus which is freer and more improvised than anything which has preceded it (40).

The Temptations, Four Tops, Marvin Gaye, Diana Ross and the Supremes were all studied and covered by the top groups, both male and female, so when songwriters began to emerge in the industry, they adopted the writing styles of Motown and black-owned companies such as Spectre and Stax. The Motown sound was about great hooks and not about a narrative. They are, as Jim Curtis (1987) puts it, about 'lyrics, which state a principle'. Curtis also underscores the power of the Motown writing style by highlighting songs that 'employ a verbal twist which takes a public situation and transforms it into private situation.' 'Shop Around' and 'Second that Emotion' by the Miracles and 'Stop in the Name of Love' by the Supremes are good examples (99).

Creative Commune

The dynamic nature of the Jamaican content could not be explained exclusively by the above mentioned processes. While *phonographic dissemination* and *crystallisation* might have jump-started the creative process of popular music production, artists in Kingston eventually drew on the rich tradition of the oral expressions – the foundation of Jamaican cultural heritage. Mento (the popular music form before the emergence of ska) and other folk and religious music expressions, such as, Revivalism, Pocomania, Kumina and Nyabinghi, could be identified in ska, rocksteady and reggae. European styles were simultaneously being incorporated, with even the Rastafarians adopting the European hymns to create their own grounation music (Hebdige 2000, 55–56). This altered the composition structure, resulting in a deviation from the standard song structure of verse-chorus in favour of Afro-European retentions which also incorporated a *through-composed* structure – where neither words nor music are repeated, and a *strophic* structure, where the tune repeats several times with new words (Spitzer and Walters 2003, 5). Early songs composed by groups such as Toots and the Maytals, Burning Spear and later, Culture, fall into this category. These acts created new forms of composition styles by fusing the various styles of Anglo-American, African and creolised Caribbean methods of song construction, engaging in a process which I have termed *phonographic synthesis*. The lyrics of Toots and the Maytals' 'Sweet and Dandy' illustrates the shift which took place in the song construction:

> Etty in the room a cry
> Mama say she must wipe her eye
> Papa say she must be foolish like she never been to school at all
> It is no wonder, it's a perfect pander
> While they were dancing in that bar ballroom last night.
>
> Johnson in the room a fret
> Uncle say he must hold up him head
> Aunty say he must be foolish, like it's not time for his wedding day
> It is no wonder, it's a perfect pander
> While they were dancing in that ballroom last night.
> One pound ten for the wedding cake, plenty bottle of cola wine
> All the people them dress up in a white
> They go eat out Johnson wedding cake
> It is no wonder, it's a perfect pander
> While they were dancing in that bar ball room last night
>
> Etty in the room a cry
> Mama say she must wipe her eye
> Papa say she must be foolish like she never been to school at all
> It is no wonder, it's a perfect pander
> While they were dancing in that ballroom last night
> Johnson in the room a fret
> Uncle say he must hold up him head

Aunty say he must be foolish, like it's not time for his wedding day
It is no wonder, it's a perfect pander
While they were dancing in that ballroom last night
One pound ten for the wedding cake, plenty bottle of cola wine
All the people them dress up in a white
They go eat out Johnson wedding cake
It is no wonder, it's a perfect pander
While they were dancing in that bar room last night

Sweet and dandy, Sweet and dandy, Sweet and dandy, Sweet and dandy
Sweet and dandy, Sweet and dandy, Sweet and dandy, Sweet and dandy
Sweet and dandy, Sweet and dandy, Sweet and dandy, Sweet and dandy
Sweet and dandy, Sweet and dandy, Sweet and dandy, Sweet and dandy
Sweet and dandy, Sweet and dandy, Sweet and dandy, Sweet and dandy

The standard verse-chorus-verse structure is abandoned by the singer-songwriter for the unstructured format where he has three short verses. The verses are repeated once. Then the song ends on the hook 'sweet and dandy'. Toots Hibbert's structure is reminiscent of African field songs with emphasis on the hook and not the verse and vocal. Toots's high-pitched lead vocals with accompanying higher-pitched unison coupled with harmonies from the Maytals presents a complex interweaving of voices which are reminiscent of the vocal styling associated with dead yard singing at nine nights in rural Jamaica and certain areas in working-class Kingston. The mento riff is strong throughout the song, firmly establishing Toots and the Maytals country roots. The vocal performance on the hook exhibits a vocal dexterity in the phrasing and delivery, which employs the same virtuoso style of the jazz and blues musician, but maintains its revivalist roots.

Burning Spear's song, 'Foggy Road' is another example:

> My way is long but the road is foggy, foggy
> My way is so long so long
> but the road is foggy, foggy
> My head never swell,
> My heart never leap,
> I never have no fear from within
> My head never swell,

My heart never leap,
I never have no fear from within
so foggy, foggy
can hardly see
Jah Jah is my eye sight
Be with I, be with I, be with I
Jah Jah, Jah Jah be with I
I and I and I and a I
They and them that hate I
They and them that fight against I
Some of them judge I wrongfully
But never mind my brother I will go on
The road is foggy, foggy
road is foggy foggy
Guidance be with I and I
Going out and coming in
From all evil thing and evil doers
Let me tell you accidental clue
The road is foggy foggy, The road is foggy Foggy
So Foggy Foggy

Bridge
No more stumbling block
No more stumbling block
Forward my brother
Forward my brother come forward
Even thought the road is so foggy foggy
I and I will never turn back
no turning back in a I
the road is foggy foggy
the road is so foggy foggy
the road is foggy foggy
the road is so foggy foggy
the road is foggy foggy

Spear's use of a semistrophic structure is evident in this song with almost no repetition of the lyrics, apart from the hook 'so foggy' and the first two lines. Here, again, the fusion of African and European styles is employed to create a new method of songwriting. Even the hook is open to various presentations and is never really repeated in the same way throughout the song. Spear utilises the African call and response method in a unique way by responding to his own call, as evident in the first two lines of the song:

> My way is long but the road is foggy, foggy
> My way is so long so long
> but the road is foggy, foggy

His tonal projection gives the distinct impression that Spear is representing the finest tradition of the African call and response technique, but presenting it in the loner mode which has been the hallmark of his mystique. The altered call and response continues throughout the song, as in the following stanza:

> My head never swell,
> My heart never leap,
> I never have no fear from within
> My head never swell,
> My heart never leap,

Spear uses timbre to effectively create a solo call and response sensibility in the styling of the song. A critical part of this style of composition is not found in the lyrics but in the vocal performance itself. Both Toots and the Maytals and Burning Spear achieved a new form of compositional style through performance. Toots's improvisation on the 'Sweet and Dandy' refrain and Spear's solo call and response and melismatic techniques are as intrinsic to the composition as are the lyrics. In these compositional devices, the lyrics and vocals are intricately intertwined. Carolyn Cooper (1995) is accurate in her observation that:

> The reggae songwriter's art is a dynamic process in which words, music and dance are organically integrated within an Afrocentric aesthetic. The composition and performance of lyrics as transcript is monologic and thus somewhat counterproductive (117).

To extend Cooper's powerful observations, I explore another vital aspect of the compositional practice within *the creative echo chamber* – the construction of the instrument text known as versions or riddims. The instrumental backing track was much more than musical accompaniment with melodic chord progressions governed by Western notions of tonality. It was the sonic foundation in the construction of the song and, simultaneously, an independent aural text with its own identity and status as a work of art. It was a way for musicians in *the creative echo chamber* to insert their creative genius inside the technical system of the available recording technology to assert their counter-cultural desires of reordering the sonic architecture of the hegemonic pop styles of the Western cultural industries.

This suggests a rejection of the Anglo-American style of pop song composition, (chorus-verse-chorus) Motown sound, and Abbey Road, which was the standard format for the main producers such as Coxsone Dodd, Duke Reid, Bunny Lee and Prince Buster. Toots recalled being rejected by Duke Reid who felt his lyrics and vocals were too parochial and told him to come back in a year's time (Hibbert, 2005). Similarly, Duke Reid told Lee 'Scratch' Perry (2007) that his style was too 'country' and not ready for the business. However, once these artists got their break they went about reshaping the Anglo-American pop song prototype, through language and harmonic structure, resisting the North Atlantic norms for an Afro-Caribbean aesthetic which represented their identity. Bill Ashcroft et al. (1989) place this phenomenon in the postcolonial discourse of domination-subordination and note:

> The abrogation or denial of the privilege of 'English' involves a rejection of the metropolitan power over the means of communication. The appropriation and reconstruction of the language to new usage marks a separation from the site of colonial privilege…Appropriation is the process by which the language is taken and made to 'bear the burden of one's own cultural experience (38–39).

Another practice which had serious implications for copyright was the collaborative nature of the song writing process in *the creative echo chamber* which was not consistent with the individual genius notions posited by 'secular European enlightenment philosophy' (Van Pelt 2006, 51; Mann 2000, 26). Many songs were composed jointly by the performers, engineers, songwriters, producers and musicians, making it very difficult to decide on the authorship splits.

The Open Domain

These new forms of popular song composition and production were done in what I have termed an *open domain* environment, an integral component of the *multiple simultaneity production model*. This was an environment devoid of copyright enforcement and at that time Jamaica was not a signatory to any of the major conventions, which governed the copyright industry internationally. The *open domain* was characterised by the exploitation of creators who were neither aware of copyright protection nor concerned with its economic benefits. This created a situation in which some producers were able to exploit a creator's ignorance by cajoling or coercing him into signing away his rights without adequate compensation (Van Pelt 2006, 7). Nevertheless, as far as the domestic market was concerned, copyright protection was not paramount among the creative class, i.e., singers, producers and musicians who practised their craft in a communal environment, with more value being placed on the sound recordings and the vinyl records which were manufactured for consumption. The emphasis by lyricists and composers was not on ownership of lyrics and music. Indeed, this was one of the African retentions of the working-class, black majority who made up the creative class. Another critical issue was the fact that unlike its British counterpart, which was updated in 1956, the Jamaican Copyright Act was never updated to accommodate new developments in technology and industry practices.

For the present argument, what matters is that this traditional practice ran counter to the Anglo-European notion of property rights, the very basis of copyright legislation. It would also seem to suggest that there were also 'non-economic motivations' to the creation of musical works, and 'non-individualistic methods of authoring, based in a non-commodity understanding of music and performance' in the *open domain* (Mann 2000, 1). In the colonial context, in which the new music was evolving, emerging black entertainers from the slums of Kingston placed a higher premium on the notion of being a star, what Rex Nettleford calls the 'smaditization' of working-class Jamaicans, rather than a songwriter with copyright protected material. The 'promise' of delayed remunerations in the form of royalties, no matter how significant the amounts, was unimportant.[3]

Infringement of copyrighted works and piracy had always been integral elements of the indigenous recording industry structure. Producers and performers received no permission to cover the songs they freely used and, furthermore, they did not credit the author of the copyright-protected material. However, no serious attention or consequence resulted from these infringements due to several factors including the small size of the market, communal song construction and the practice of phonographic dissemination. The issue of coming to the market in a competitive environment was also crucial. Getting product to the market in a timely fashion was critical to success in a highly competitive space (McMillan 2005, 15; Toynbee 5). Also of particular significance was the notion of versioning/copying which created non-rival good benefits where rhythms were used and reused by all producers, which expanded the market for everyone and reduced the task of creating more original works. Versioning and the communal use of rhythms were critical to the dub plate/special culture which freely used musical works for the creation of dub plate specials to feed the dynamic and lucrative sound system industry.

Local producers and songwriters were not spared these acts of infringement. There were several cases of producers covering rhythm tracks of fellow producers. In fact, almost every major producer from the '60s up to the present copied the Studio One catalogue of rhythms. Coxsone allowed this to happen despite the fact that he knew he could stop this infringement. A plausible reason for allowing this infringement was that he was also aware of the disquiet among musicians and vocalists who accused him of not advancing them or paying regular royalties from record sales. Once a producer made a hit rhythm, other producers would do a similar version of the rhythm without fear of prosecution.

Some riddims such as 'Heavenless', 'Rockfort Rock', 'Throw Me Corn', 'Hot Milk' and 'Full Up' have been re-recorded more than 1,000 times by numerous producers over the decades. Like some 300 years before, Jamaica was a pirate's paradise! In the open domain system, this practice was never seen as piracy or infringement of material controlled by copyright.

Table 5.2 Jamaican Originals and Their Local Covers

ORIGINAL	COVER
How Could I Live – The Sharks	How Could I Live – Dennis Brown
Tribal War – Little Roy	Tribal War – George Nooks, John Holt
Every Nigger is a Star – Boris Gardiner	Every Nigger is a Star – Big Youth
Prophesy – Little Roy	Prophesy – Freddy McGregor
Movie Star – Delroy Wilson	Movie Star – Errol Dunkley, Wayne Wonder
Picture on the Wall – Freddy McKay	Picture on the Wall – Carl Dawkins and the Wailers
To be Poor is a Crime – Still Cool	To be Poor is a Crime – Freddy McGregor

In fact, many of these rhythms were never registered and, hence, were not protected.[4] Symbol creators viewed the unauthorised copying of rhythms as a means of paying homage to a great piece of work.

Producers who owned hit 'riddims' saw the 'licking over' (covering) of his/her riddim as a sign of respect for the quality of the work which afforded bragging rights among his/her peers. Some producers even added new instruments to the original and renamed the original riddim, in a sense claiming the work as his/her own property – a concept that is known in copyright philosophy as derivative works.

Some originals scored big for both the original performer and the cover performer. In many cases, the cover became the signature song of the composition while the original is little known.

Many scholars have noted the exploitation of the Jamaican symbol creators who were cheated out of their intellectual property by unscrupulous producers. However, this was not unique to Jamaica as a similar tradition was perpetrated by the big capitalist record companies in the US on a similar unsuspecting group of rhythm and blues and rock and roll African American writers. Many songwriters were robbed of their creation due to circumstances similar to those outlined in the earlier Jamaican experience. As Norman Kelly (2005, 8) shows, the big record giants in the US exploited scores of African American singer/songwriters, many of whom died penniless.

Simon Frith (1996) makes an important point here about the way in which composition by African American performers was simply not recognised historically by the US music industry:

> The pop industry is organized around music as composition – American copyright law protects composers rather than performers. It is songwriters who get royalties when records are sold or broadcast, not their performers, and black singers who were popular in the 1920s and 1930s were systematically cheated out of their due returns. Their music, however distinct, was in a legal sense 'composerless', and it was white publishers who rushed to copyright the resulting 'spontaneous' compositions. Such exploitation of black musicians by publishers and record companies continued into the 1960s, and in fighting for their economic rights, these musicians learned that if they couldn't necessarily make money out of the recordings of specific performances, they could make money out of their general performances, they could become part of the star system (17).

It is clear that this tradition of stealing[5] was an entrenched practice within the culture and Industry, and Jamaican producers were adopting an 'acceptable' metropole practice in the traditional hegemonic control practices of the colonial realities. Coxsone Dodd registered his publishing company, Jamaica Recording and Publishing Company (Jamrec) by the early 1960s to administer the copyright on his sound recordings, literary and musical work, though he was not, in most instances, the creator of the literary and musical works in his recordings. Other top producers such as Byron Lee, Bunny Lee and Winston Riley quickly learnt the benefits of copyright ownership and secured the rights to their sound recordings and also the literary and musical works in the recordings they produced, despite the fact that they did not create most of these works. While these producers did not earn any money, domestically, from copyright they certainly benefited in significant measure from copyright royalties in Great Britain, Europe and, to a lesser degree, the United States.

The question of ownership and authorship needs deeper investigation at this point as it is common practice, in hindsight, to demonise the producers for robbing artists and musicians of their works. On the one hand, the UK Act established the author as the first owner of copyright in his/her work; Van Pelt (2006) notes, 'this provision applied to musical works, i.e., musical compositions as distinct from sound recordings are the sonic representation of the written language of a composition' (21). On the other hand, the provisions for the protection for mechanical sound recordings were, at best, blurred and confusing. As noted earlier, the owner of the master recording was deemed the author of that specific recording, regardless of his or her participation in the creative process. Peter Jaszi (1991, 487) calls this the 'reverse-twist on individualistic authorship', where the necessities of commerce created the work for hire doctrine, where the employer is classified as the author and is seen as 'the visionary' while the artist or music arranger is reduced to 'a mere mechanic following orders' (489). This Anglo-American legal philosophy, derived from English common law and described by Porter (1985, 3) as the 'public interest approach', favours the interest of the owner class within the cultural industries. Dave Laing (2004) states:

> While this definition recognises that the Anglo-American notion of copyright gives greater weight to the interest of users of copyright works, it underplays the extent to which United States and the United Kingdom copyright law was framed to accommodate the interests of the corporate owners and distributors of cultural products, through the granting of primary copyright status to 'producers' of film, television and music products (75).

So the picture becomes clearer that while exploitation was indeed a feature of the *open domain*, the 1913 Copyright Act had obviously stayed too long on the books without being updated and certainly affected the efficient development of a copyrighting culture. The extent to which this exploitation was a major feature of the industry seems to have been exaggerated and in some cases has not been sufficiently addressed by the academy. There was clear confusion between the different rights, i.e., author's rights and the rights of the producers and this led to exploitation by some producers. Certain practices within the *open domain* also complicated matters. Practices such as the trading of backing tracks between producers, versioning, communal authorship and the production techniques of dub all created a phenomenon which was counter hegemonic to North Atlantic notions of copyright which had as its foundation the right of an individual to exploit his or her original creations.

Multiple Simultaneity Production Model (Copyrighting Culture)

The *open domain* environment persisted until the 1990s. Paralleling this counter hegemonic model were a growing number of Jamaican rights owners including Derrick Harriott, Jimmy Cliff, Bob Marley, Third World and Bob Andy, who sought the protection of the copyright system for their original works. Some later secured protection through signing with overseas record labels which allowed them access to reputable lawyers and managers who guided them. Operating within the Anglo-American mode of production model, these artists were obliged to adopt the copyright industry's insistence of control and protection for sound recordings. Marley's first publishing contract was with JAD Records who recognised his prowess as a songwriter. This resulted in Johnny Nash (a principal of JAD Records) recording a number of Marley's compositions including 'Stir It Up' and 'Guava Jelly'. Marley, according to his former accountant Colin Leslie, felt the deal was bad and when he signed with Island Records he found a way to circumvent that contract. It was mentioned earlier that Clement Dodd and other creative manager/owners operated within the copyright industry when interfacing with the international market. These creative manager/owners, through omission, exploited many artists who did not understand or care about the benefits of participating in the copyright industry. The PRS made it possible for its membership to receive some performance royalties, mainly from British airplay. Royalty payments from the PRS were, however, a sore point for many writers who felt that the collecting agency did not have their best interest at heart.

Jimmy Cliff, one of the first Jamaican acts to sign to a foreign-based record company, was able to secure ownership of the rights to his works. The bands Third World and Inner Circle were also signed to publishing companies overseas and secured this same privilege. Unfortunately, there were numerous examples of other writers who faced significant challenges in securing the rights to their works. A well-known example is that of Musical Youth's international hit, 'Pass the Dutchie', which was written by Lloyd 'Judge' Ferguson of the Mighty Diamonds. Several parties claimed rights to the musical works in the recording which had been done on a Studio One riddim called 'Full Up'. The reggae trio subsequently found themselves in a legal battle for ownership which is still not entirely settled (Howard 2007, 25).

It is clear that there was a duality of hegemonic and counterhegemonic practices within the creative process of the Jamaican music industry. This feature has not been given enough attention from scholars in ethnomusicology, cultural studies and anthropology. On one level, the hegemonic pop style of the culture industry targeted at a white mainstream audience fully entrenched in a capitalistic power structure was desired and attempted among some in the Kingston music industry. Simultaneously, the creative process was constructed on a more democratic framework where the creative worker practised music-making through alternative economic and non-economic modalities and whose agenda was influenced by the creation of the super ordinate personality. The 'star-bwoy' identity and resistance to colonial and postcolonial hegemony trumped what Jacques Attali (1985) calls 'the logic of the creation of value' (41).

A Call to Action on the 1993 Copyright Act

Between the late 1960s and the 1990s, many composers, musicians and producers, led by the Jamaica Federation of Musicians (JFM) and Affiliated Artists Union, began lobbying for a proper copyright law to ensure protection for the creators of original works. Desmond Young, president of JFM recalls, 'The JFM was the lone voice in the call for a new copyright law; when we invited other groups to support the cause, we got none. I must commend Sonny Bradshaw, who started the lobby which was continued by Headley Jones and me.' Sonny Bradshaw (2006), in an interview, recounted that his first battle was to get producers to start putting the credits on the records they manufactured. In the 1960s, many producers manufactured 7-inch 45 rpm vinyl records without including proper labelling. Bradshaw, therefore, felt labelling was the first step towards recognising the Jamaican author. 'The producers were up in arms when I started this campaign,' Bradshaw recalled. Clancy Eccles told Barbara Gloudon, then editor of the *Star*, 'Mi nah stop do blanks'. Bradshaw stated that after a sustained campaign in his 'Music Man' column in the daily tabloid The *Star* and meetings with the producers, he was able to secure an agreement with the main producers to credit the performers and writers of the songs they produced on the labels of the records they manufactured.

In 1977, the lobbyists achieved some success when a new Copyright Bill was tabled in Parliament. Attorney-at-law Earl Witter stated that the new law was not adequate and had taken too long to be tabled in Parliament (2006). Dianne Daley (2001) noted, 'This act was silent on the rights of performers and the issue of moral rights'. Bradshaw also noted that by the time it was ready to be tabled in Parliament, the law needed upgrading and suggested that the government should not to attempt to pass an outdated act. However, an important step was taken towards copyright development when the island became a member of the World Intellectual Property Organization (WIPO) in 1978.

Based on continued lobbying by the JFM, the Affiliated Artistes Union and the intervention of international agencies, the Copyright Unit was established in 1990. It was responsible for bringing together all the stakeholders – media, producers, authors and composers – to submit recommendations and to put the issue of copyright in the public sphere. This eventually led to the passing of the Copyright Law of 1993. Jamaica became a member of the Berne Convention for the Protection of Literary and Artistic Works (1886, revised in 1971), the Convention for the Protection of Producers of Phonograms Against Unauthorized Duplication of their Phonograms (the Geneva or Phonograms Convention) and the International Convention on the Protection of Producers, Performers and Broadcasting Organization (The Rome Convention) (Daley 2001, 3–4).

This was followed by agreements between the US and Jamaica on the production and enforcement of intellectual property rights in 1994. Through this agreement, Jamaica embarked on a total update of its intellectual property regime. In 1995, Jamaica became a signatory to the agreement on Trade Related Aspects of Intellectual Property Rights (TRIPS) through the World Trade Organization (WTO). These developments, as Daley puts it, 'cemented its commitment to an international and modern standard of copyright protection' (4).

Home-grown Societies

Having enacted the Copyright Law of 1993, Jamaica now had to move to the next stage. There was need to establish the necessary administration mechanisms and 'systems critical to successful implementation of its law, increasing public awareness on copyright, combating piracy and ensuring that the legislation keeps pace with the new technological digital revolutions' (Daley 2001, 4).

Hence, in a relatively short period, through the establishment of a National Task Force on Collective Administration of Copyright, four collecting societies were established between 1995 and 2000. These indigenous societies include the Jamaica Association of Composers, Authors and Publishers (JACAP), the Jamaican Musical Rights Administration (JMRAS), the Jamaican Copyright Licensing Agency (JAMCOPY) and the Jamaica Performers Administration Society (JPAS).

More compliance with the US came in 1999 with the amendment of the 1993 Copyright Act. The process was the final stroke towards reintermediation in the Jamaican music industry value chain, consistent with a capitalist-driven best practices agenda and the realignment of the counterhegemonic movement, which the open domain environment fostered for so long in the music industry.

In 2000, a report done by the International Intellectual Property Institute (IIPI) under a grant from the World Intellectual Property Organization, led by American Bruce Lehman, an intellectual property expert, made extensive recommendations for the modernisation and centralisation of the administrative functions of intellectual property rights within the government.

Table 5.3 National Collecting Agencies

SOCIETY	RIGHTS
1. JACAP	Performing rights composers, authors and publishers in their musical work.
2. JAMRAS[5]	Rights of producers and national record companies.
3. JAMCOPY	Reprographic rights of authors and publishers of work in print media.
4. JAPAS[6]	Administering rights of performers in their live and fixed performance

These led to the formation of the Jamaica Intellectual Property Office (JIPO), in 2001, to administer intellectual property rights in the island. With the establishment of JIPO, Jamaica was well on the way to a modern copyright protection regime in compliance with the WTO, the GATT and TRIPS agreements and the Jamaican lobby.

National Consolidation or International Coercion?

Champions of copyright saw these developments as a positive move towards the protection of rights for owners. However, one wonders if the passage of the copyright laws of 1993 had more to do with overseas interests, that is the US and the European Union wanting to protect the intellectual property of the major entertainment conglomerates, which had developed in the 1990s in the Jamaican and other important foreign markets, rather than putting an end to the upfront piracy of Jamaican, American and British works by Jamaicans for several decades. Indeed, the 1990s experienced a serious outcry from major record companies, film studios and cable content providers over the piracy and infringement of copyrighted materials which had been taking place in the developing nations, including China and the Caribbean.[8] This might have been the impetus for the Jamaican government to move with such speed, after years of apathy, to enact this new law and to comply with rules of the agreements and conventions to which they were signatories.

In light of the increasing importance of the core copyright industry's export earnings, which stood at US$626.6 billion in 2004 (IIPA, 1), countries which had trade barriers on the export of US copyrighted works in the form of records, CDs, film and television programmes were subject to greater scrutiny. The International Intellectual Property Alliance (IIPA), the membership of which included the Recording Industry Association of America, (RIAA), National Music Publishers Association (NMPA), and the Motion Picture Association of America (MPAA), was formed to lobby Congress. This resulted in the passing of the Omnibus Trade and Competitiveness Act in 1988. This Act also had a provision known as the 'Special 301' which permitted the United States Trade Representative (USTR) to label countries whose intellectual property rights regime was weak and did not offer sufficient protection for the United States copyright industry 'Priority Foreign Countries'. Any country so designated was subjected to trade sanctions if they did not upgrade their intellectual property rights regime and also improve their commercial and trading practices (Bettig 1996, 198–200; Laing 2004, 80–84). Brendan Scott's (2001) analysis actually supports this argument:

> The rules of the Berne Convention were quite simple – each country was accorded one vote without taking account of the relative economic power of that country or of the works produced by that country; whether the country was a net consumer or net producer of works. As a result, over time, as more developing nations became members to the Berne convention they formed voting blocs which were able to outvote the developed countries on resolutions. 'By targeting the individual countries beforehand, the U.S. was able to remove developing country resistance to the TRIPS initiative in the 1994 Uruguay Round of GATT (9).

This clearly shows that the intention of the United States to secure and enforce the protection of the intellectual property of the major entertainment conglomerates which control massive catalogues of music, books, movies, television programming and magazines that have been the victims of infringement globally. The attack was made at both governmental and individual levels. In the '70s, there were a few lawsuits against Jamaican producers by major publishers in the United States. The most famous was against record producer Joe Gibbs who had covered the Charley Pride song 'Someone Loves You Honey' performed by J.C. Lodge. The song went on the national chart in Britain, at which point it also entered the culture industry and the capitalist structure of the international music industry. Hence, the Gibbs-produced sound recording was now subject to the hegemonic ramifications of copyright philosophy. The owners of the copyright declared this an infringement of their work. This lawsuit literally put Gibbs (2006) out of the music business.

In the Interest of 'Babylon System'

It is, however, unclear whether or not the regulations and laws are to the benefit of the Jamaican composers and authors. In fact, many authors are still ignorant of their rights and the public education programme, which has been ongoing, has not been effective in reaching its target. Daley (2001) sums it up in the following way: 'a fundamental challenge for Jamaica in the decades to come is ensuring that a comprehensive copyright and related regime translates into national economic development' (5).

The verdict is still out on the economic windfall to be derived from copyright protection from overseas use of Jamaican works. In fact, during the 1990s, JPAS, the related right agency at the time, was involved in legal wrangling with French related right societies, *Spedidam* and *Adami,* which are reputed to have collected approximately four billion French francs in performances rights royalties on behalf of Jamaican musicians. The societies paid a portion of this royalty but did not hand over most of the royalties using a number of excuses, such as having no address for these musicians (Laing 2003). Since then some progress has been made and several performers have had some royalty payments.

There is no doubt that copyright protection can be of economic value. However, more foreign music is played on Jamaican radio than Jamaican music. Foreign music is played in public spaces including hotels, supermarkets, concert halls and in offices as elevator and telephone background music. Thus, users of these copyright protected materials have to pay these foreign owners and funds are repatriated to foreign countries. JACAP has estimated that the payment of royalties to overseas collecting societies constitutes 70% of its total earnings. The remaining 30% is paid to their members. Conversely, in the United States, Jamaican rights owners are not afforded the same respect by Broadcast Music Inc. (BMI), the American Society of Composers Authors and Publishers (ASCAP) and Society of European Stage Authors and Composers (SESAC). Invariably, these collecting agencies do not sample the outlets that play the most Jamaican music, namely broker stations, college radio, and block parties. ASCAP and BMI are notorious for their very low levels of royalties paid to Jamaican music. Overall, approximately '…10 percent and 6 percent, respectively, of ASCAP and BMI's distributions are to non-members.'[9]

Despite this entrenched inequity, Jamaican music released by major labels by internationally renowned artists such as Sean Paul, Shaggy, Gyptian, Beenie Man and Omi, are played on mainstream radio stations such as HOT 97 in New York and cable outlets such as Music Television (MTV) and Black Entertainment Television (BET). These works, when written by the artists themselves, have been reported by US collecting agencies. This is due to the heavy spin rotation on radio, and television outlets. These opportunities are very sporadic and many songwriters have enjoyed some additional income from related rights royalties from entities such as SoundExchange, which is a society that collects and distributes for digital performance for artists and copyright owners. Royalties from SoundExchange are now rivalling ASCAP and BMI with a reported pay out of $773 million in royalties in 2014 in comparison to BMI which paid $840 million in royalties. Jamaican right owners royalties from SoundExchange do not always translate into massive income. Table 5.4 outlines the income received by a popular Jamaican artist who scored a major hit in 2012. The period in question is between 2012 and 2015 and the income includes several other songs from his catalogue. In comparison, American artists would invariably earn more due to the spins received on more radio and Internet outlets. With such an imbalance, the economic benefits will always be skewed in favour of the North. To exacerbate the issue, Jamaica has not legislated any quota content rule which could go a far way in levelling the playfield to the benefit of Jamaican rights owners.[10]

Table 5.4 Featured Artist – Digital Performance Royalties, 2012–15[11]

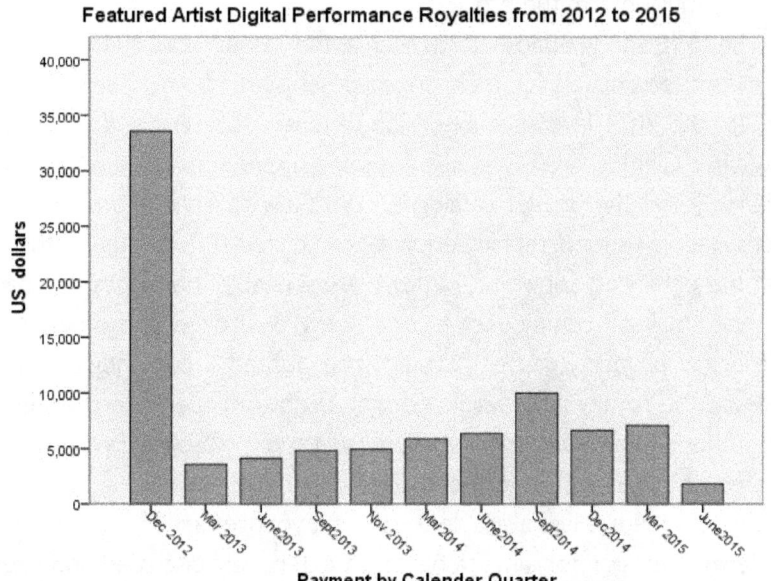

Copyright Extension 2015 - Legislative Overreach

The Jamaican creative imagination has never stalled. However, despite traditions and practice within the *creative crucible* of Kingston and the *open domain* framework, international and national pressure has steadfastly been exerted to extend the life of copyright from life of the author plus 50 years. In the United States this was achieved with the passing of the Sonny Bono Copyright Term Extension Act 1998 and in 1993, the European Union extended the term of protection for authors in 1993 and in 2011 for performers and sound recordings. Canadian legislation was amended in 2015 to extend the term of protection for performers and the owners of sound recording from 50 years to 70 years but no change was made to the period of protection for authors, which is life plus 50 years. This led to strong opposition by rights collection agencies such as the International Confederation of Societies and Authors and Composers (CISAC). The fact that Canada has not acceded to changing its protection of copyright term for authors' rights suggests that term extension is not a fait accompli for nations that have a vibrant music industry. The interests of the particular country must inform the process.

The 1998 Sonny Bono Act was seen as the Disney Corporation's attempt to extend protection for their prized possession, Mickey Mouse, while in the UK, the 2011 legislative extension of term protection – dubbed 'Cliff's Law' after Cliff Richard – was seen as safeguarding the sound recordings of Britain's jewel, the Beatles catalogue. Fran Nevrkla, chairman of the music licensing body Phonographic Performance Limited (PPL), noted at the time that the 'enhanced copyright framework will enable the record companies, big and small, to continue investing in new recordings and new talent'.[12] Intellectual property lawyer Daniel Byrne posited a contending view. He believed the royalty pool would not get any bigger due to term extension, but rather, 'the available money will be split more ways (and now to more estates of deceased performers). This rewards unproductive performers and means there is less available to support younger acts.'[13]

Term extension for Jamaica has been extensively discussed and interest groups such as the Jamaica Music Society (JAMMS), JACAP, JAMCOPY, and the Jamaica Intellectual Property Office (JIPO) have lobbied for its enactment for many years. This legislative change was achieved with the passing of an amendment of the Copyright Act in June 2015, extending the protection of copyright to life of the author plus 95 years (moving it from 50 years) with retroactive provisions to provide continued protection for works that would have fallen into the public domain from 2012. With this amendment Jamaica now has the third longest copyright term only behind Mexico and Côte d'Ivoire with 100 and 99 years respectively, from the death of the author. According to the Jamaican Ministry of Industry, Investment and Commerce, the amended legislation has 'created the framework for rights holders to realize the value in maintaining their intellectual property rights over their content'.[14]

This statement however, wrongfully conflates rights holders and original creators of works, and ignores the interests of the public good. Thirdly, there is an incorrect presumption that original creators possess the bargaining power to negotiate with major entertainment conglomerates who control the entertainment industry, thereby putting them in a greater position to benefit substantially from their creation. Jason Toynbee reminds us 'it is the power of capital that counts when it comes to copyright and the rights of the creator serves as a pretext for corporate control of music' (2004, 125). However, as record companies continue to struggle in their attempts to develop viable business models, creators of original work, battle to negotiate better deals that will see them getting a larger percentage of royalties. What this statement suggests, is not a plausible proposition in the foreseeable future.

Many observers – scholars, journalists, politicians and industry personnel – have questioned the validity of extending the Jamaican term of protection much farther than what exists in the United States and the United Kingdom in light of the symbiotic relationship that exists between the three major music producers. Jamaica is a net importer of American, Canadian and British musical works. Term extension of copyright protection therefore, does not translate to increased royalty collection but instead has the effect of stifling creativity and innovation by restricting available raw material which can be exploited for the good of the general public. Australia has a similar predicament. According to Philippa Dee:

> The net effect is that Australia could eventually pay 25 per cent more per year in net royalty payments, not just to US copyright holders, but

to all copyright holders, since this provision is not preferential. This could amount to up to $88 million per year, or up to $700 million in net present value terms. And this is a pure transfer overseas, and hence pure cost to Australia.[15]

The fact is Jamaican copyright owners are still not collecting substantial revenues in comparison with their British and American counterparts and only a few select major stars collect anything worthwhile in terms of copyright royalty revenues. In addition, many of the superstar artists, composers, lyricists and producers are not affiliated with national collective management organizations (CMOs) but are linked to CMOs in Britain and the United States and Canada, so that income generated by these rights owners are not directly linked to local music ecosystems and economic framework and so cannot be measured by national economic indices. In addition, British and American literary, musical works and sound recordings will enjoy 25 additional years (over Jamaica) for works that have entered the public domain in their territories. This status will continue the outflow of revenues to the detriment of the Jamaican music industry. Ultimately, copyright is and will continue to be of no major significance to the average music maker in Kingston's *creative crucible*.

Another dimension that has been ignored is the fact that many of the sound recordings that were to enter the public domain would have given the artists who made these recordings, the first real opportunity to earn from these recordings unencumbered by restrictive copyright laws. Many of these artists do not own the rights for many of these recordings and were never compensated for the work or the sound recordings although they are the original authors of the works. The extension of term on sound recordings benefits the owners of these recordings, which invariably are the record companies and the music conglomerates who licensed these sound recordings for international distribution. The potential therefore exists, of robbing the original creator of the first real opportunity to earn from their creation. When these sound recordings go into the public domain original creators would be able to sell these recording on multiple formats to earn some well-deserved income.

The expiration of monopolistic copyright ownership would also effect the resurrection of lost recordings, so called 'orphan works', for the benefit of the artistic community, the creative industries and the public interest.

Record companies have held back recordings with the ploy of building interests and waiting for revivals so that they can cash in. The catalogues of existing superstars are shelved to cash in at a later date, while no investment in new talent is forthcoming. Within the *open domain* framework, producers and composers alike have share musical and literary works, and in some instance original ownership is irrelevant. This is the reality of music making in the *creative echo chamber model*, which has eluded both industry operatives and creative industries legislative interventions. If experience has shown anything, it is that copyright protection and enforcement do not support innovation and creativity. Unfortunately, Jamaican copyright laws have blatantly ignored the cultural specificity of the Jamaican music making experience. As Toynbee points out, 'copyright law doesn't mesh with the practice of popular music' (204, 127). There has been no effort to align local best practices with the appropriateness of international copyright regimes so as to serve the mutual interest of Jamaica and its international partners. Instead, since 1993 amendments have been enacted which suit the international copyright regime, but puts Jamaican creators at a serious disadvantage. Additionally, the status quo of the copyright industry, where original creators benefit the least from their creative output, is perpetuated. This point is exemplified by Carolina Rossini and Yana Welinder who argue:

> The incorporation of international copyright obligations into national law does not focus on whether the protection is "economically, culturally, or socially desirable." Rather, it presents new lobbying opportunities for the entertainment industry that can result in broader copyright regimes than required by the international obligations, which in turn could be used back home to demand matching legislation.[16]

Literary Property and the Author

Another point of contestation in North Atlantic copyright philosophy is the existence of the author. Many cultural theorists including Ronald Barthes, (1977, 142–48), Michel Foucault (1984, 101–120) and Martha Woodmansee (2003, 425–48) have all questioned the validity of the genius author. They have all emphasised, as Mark Rose (1993) puts it, 'the notion of the author as a relatively recent formation and, as a cultural formation, it is inseparable from the commodification of literature' (1). They all argue that there was no unified notion of an author until the eighteenth century and that any trace of authorship was manifested through a collaborative and communal system of information. Barthes in the *Death of the Author in Image Music Text* (1977) states:

> We know now that a text is not a line of words releasing a single 'theological' meaning (the message of the Author-God) but a multi-dimensional space in which a variety of writings, none of them original, blend and clash (77, 146).

Therefore, Barthes suggests that copyright couldn't account for the issue that all works are derived from pre-existing cultures, ideas and texts. J. Boyle (1996) also supports this proposition:

> Contemporary intellectual property law is constructed around the notion of the author, the individual, solitary and original creator, and it is for this figure that its protections are reserved. The 'author' in the modern sense is the sole creator of unique works of art, the originality of which warrants their protection under laws of intellectual property – particularly those of 'copyright' and 'author's rights'. The notion, however, is neither natural nor inevitable (195).

The dilemma arises as to why authors should be given any monopolistic right under copyright when all thoughts are borrowed and 'original works' are not independent of previous thought and writing. The counter to such a position argues that the reassembly of melodies and lyrics constitutes a new work and hence qualifies as an original. This, however, brings into question notions of the genius composer who creates work that is entirely original. The open domain environment which has created version and dub, and is also responsible for communal/social authorship, more akin to African traditions, has impacted on transnational trends which have questioned Euro-American notions of the genius authorship and property rights invested in creative works by the Anglo-American copyright industry. The issue of originality continues to face Jamaican composers and dancehall artists in particular. The ongoing practice of using copyrighted melodies and lyrics in their composition has created a major bottleneck for international companies who have to spend an enormous amount of time clearing the copyright on a song. It is not unusual for one song to have more than three copyrighted portions to clear. This results in delays and increased costs for the record companies and has become a serious deterrent for many record executives who are looking for instant sales and 'quick' success.

The Internet and Copyright

The internet presents some new challenges to the hegemony of copyright control on the free flow of ideas, creativity and the expression of these ideas. This technology has allowed the line of distributions to be altered, in significant ways, in favour of the creators of so-called original works. The creators of content are now directly connected to the consumers of that content, thus breaking the cycle of the middleman (the printer/publisher/distributor) which was the foundation of the copyright law legislation. With the growing cry for a loosening of the copyright control and democratisation of cultural production, the internet presents a site for the playing out of a new dispensation as it relates to ownership of the output of cultural production. The outcry and subsequent legal actions from copyright owners about technologies including file-sharing websites such as Napster, Limewire, Mega Upload, and Pirate Bay are areas sites of contestation on the usefulness of copyright control on the music business. Social networking platforms such YouTube, Facebook, LoudUp, ReverbNation, OurStage, SoundCloud and Shazam continue to disrupt the music ecosystem. In the process, intellectual property rights are being challenged in various ways as copyright protected music is constantly copied and shared without charge and without the authorization of the rights owners. This unauthorized use creates the potential for infringement liability. Despite the provison of a 'safe harbor' clause generally (where a website is protected from liability if infringing content is removed after receiving notice), policing these mattters can be prohibitably expensive and time consuming.

The current move toward streaming by the music industry through services such as Spotify, Last FM, Rdio, Pandora, Apple Music and TIDAL, have further disrupted models of income flows. Predictably, several of these services are not available in the Caribbean due to licensing and other legal and trade issues. The launch of Radial, a streaming service geared towards the Caribbean, provides an opportunity for exposure to Caribbean genres that are not generally played on the other services. 'Radial treats each country's music as the market and pushes that not only to the local market but also to the very large diaspora.'[17] Streaming services such as Spotify have left many international artists complaining about the inconsequential pay-outs by these services. This reality has led to harsh criticism from many American songwriters most notably pop superstar Taylor Swift, who pulled pulling her catalogue from Spotify. Swift's contention was that Spotify allows its subscribers the use of millions of songs while changing a nominal fee of US$5–10 per month. In an interview with online giant Yahoo, Swift declared, 'I'm not willing to contribute my life's work to an experiment that I don't feel fairly compensates the writers, producers, artists, and creators of this music.'[18]

Conclusion

Some scholars and entertainment practitioners have suggested the dissolution of copyright due to its monopolistic control and the inability to effectively police infringement due to the easy access that technology has facilitated. The development of the Creative Commons option pioneered by Harvard academic, Lawrence Lessig and others, offers a viable alternative to the monopolistic and restrictive nature of copyright 'that enables the sharing and use of creativity and knowledge through free legal tools.' However this option is not an attempt to replace copyright as it states on their website, 'Creative Commons licenses are not an alternative to copyright. They work alongside copyright and enable you to modify your copyright terms to best suit your needs.'[19] In 2004 the US Congress reviewed The Digital Consumers Rights Acts (DMCRA), 2003, intended to liberalise what consumers could do with digital music. This was a measure intended to strike a balance with the Digital Millennium Copyright Act (DMCA) passed in 1998 by the United States Congress. The anti circumvention provisions were deemed too onerous and impinged on fair use due to prohibitions on the circumvention of technology to facilitate fair use. Again, the classic struggle to balance the rights of consumers and that of copyright holders had arisen. Miriam Nisbet from the American Library Association, speaking before a hearing of the subcommittee of energy and commerce looking at the proposed law, argued that the existing laws forbidding duplication was very expensive for libraries in light of their goal of facilitation of free flow of information.[20]

Is this a proposition that would serve small nation states, like Jamaica, who have not been at the forefront of copyright control over cultural production? How would this affect the great expectations of state agencies like Jamaica Trade and Invest (JAMPRO) and JIPO that have been promulgating the economic windfall that the proper exploitation of intellectual property will afford? According to a report from the International Intellectual Property Alliance (IIPA), the copyright industries of the United States earned US$1.25 trillion in 2002. This accounted for 12 per cent of Gross Domestic Product (GDP) and employed 4 per cent of US workers (US$5.48 million). In 2013 IP generated over $1.1 trillion dollars of economic output accounting for 6.71% of the entire economy and the core copyright industries employed nearly 5.5 million workers, accounting for over 4% of the entire US workforce, and nearly 5% of total private employment in the US. Creative workers earned on average 34% higher wages than other US workers.[21]

It is certainly hard to argue with the impact of copyright as an economic juggernaut. However, not enough attention is placed on how copyright helps to constitute and reinforce media and cultural hegemony. Small nation states such as Jamaica are certainly at a disadvantage if it is accepted that the richer and more powerful developed states like the United States, with the TRIPS/WTO agreement, have shifted the discourse of copyright from the sphere of cultural production to the realm of politics and economics.

In recounting the genesis of copyright in this brief historical review, several ideas bear consideration and reflection. Copyright is, as Mark Rose (1993) puts it, 'a specifically modern formation produced by printing technology, marketplace economies and the classical liberal culture of possessive individualism' (142). Secondly, the concept of the genius author who creates something out of nothing and therefore, deserves to have a monopoly on the economic exploitation of his/her creation. Then, there is the French and German tradition of copyright being not only for economic aggrandizement but protection of an author's uniquely personal expression in creating a work, hence evoking his/her moral rights to that work. These ideas have become the sites for many contestations and scholars have spent the last 35 years attacking these ideas as being unstable, irrational and 'transitory social constructs which grew out of a very specific set of economic and social conditions' (Hunter 2001, 12).

Under the modern copyright regime the principle of fair use or fair dealing provides that the public is entitled to use, without cost, portions of copyrighted material for purposes of commentary and criticism. Any such use however, must credit the original author. In recent years, the courts have had to grapple with the question of just what is fair use and determine when it amounts to infringement upon the rights of copyright holders. This decision is made on a case-by-case basis and some creators might be left feeling dissatisfied with decisions. Herein lies the dilemma, which Hunter calls the 'neo-classical economic paradox' (12). While on the one hand economists recommend that the authors be given the incentive of a copyright monopoly, on the other, they argue that markets, including the 'marketplace of ideas', operate best under 'perfect information' conditions, where access to information is inexpensive and available to all.

Any analysis of the development of copyright will denote one critical fact, that copyright laws were never an issue of protecting all creators' works. In fact, copyright law has its genesis in censorship. During the Reformation era in the sixteenth century, the church and government used its power to grant the authors the exclusive right to print/copy their books to the exclusion of many other books. Copyright laws came into being for the protection of the rich, privileged and educated class in Europe who wanted to ensure control of the economic gains from the production and distribution of books and other creative outputs. It is fair to suggest that the early processes of copyright were designed to protect the publisher and distributor and disregarded the centrality of the original creator of the work.

From these observations it is reasonable to deduce that copyright is indeed a legislative monopoly which was a direct response to the development of printing. The need for copyright was defended as protection for authors and creators of original works. The argument was that whatever emanated from a man's creative endeavours, he had the right to protection of that creation and by extension, an economic right to exploit his creation to his benefit. Copyright laws, however, also represented a tool for censorship and were antithetical to the notion of freedom of speech and creativity. Copyright continues to be a legislative monopoly, insensitive to the rights of the real creators of cultural production. As Jessica Litman (1990) suggests, 'cultural production is typically a matter of appropriation and transformation rather than creation' (1000). How will the copyright doctrine play out in Jamaica in the foreseeable future? The Kingston *creative crucible* has been a site of exploitation, sharing, sampling, piracy, communal authorship and music making practices that are incongruous to copyright. It remains to be seen whether compliance to requirements of globalization will reap the necessary economic benefits, which copyright supporters are hoping for.

NOTES

1. Jason Toynbee, *Making Popular Music Musicians, Creativity and Institutions* (London: Arnold, 2000).
2. J. Spitzer and R. Walters, *Making Sense of American Song*, http://historymatters.gmu.edu.
3. Under the copyright system, owners of copyright earned income in the form of a royalty based on the usage of the copyrighted material by end-users such as radio, restaurants and concert promoters. The payments usually go through several different agencies, including the rights management societies and publishers, with each agency taking a percentage of the revenue before it reaches the copyright owner. This takes a considerable amount of time to reach the original creators of the work, hence the delayed remunerations.
4. In the early years of copyright legislation, music had to be registered to be eligible for protection under copyright laws. This changed in later updates of the law.
5. This phrase is borrowed from Robert Kelly.
6. JAMRAS gave way to The Jamaica Music Society (JAMMS) in 2006 but not before winning a lawsuit against the big media conglomerate Radio Jamaica Limited (RJR), who was ordered to start paying producers royalties.
7. JAPAS, after some legal issues with their counterpart in France, went into hibernation due to ill health of its chairman. It was decided in 2009 to officially hand over the administration of performers' rights to the Jamaican Music Society (JAMMS) putting all neighbouring rights under the one collecting agency.
8. According to data published in USTR's April 29, 2005, Special 301 Report, industry sources believe that China's inadequate IPR enforcement is resulting in infringement levels of approximately 90 per cent or above for virtually every form of intellectual property.
9. The Cultural Industries In Caricom Trade and Development Challenges Report prepared for the Caribbean Regional Negotiating Machinery November 2006 (Revised December 2007) Keith Nurse et. al.
10. Several countries including France, Canada, Australia have passed quota content laws to ensure the development of their national music industries.

11. Special thanks to Dean McKellar who provided the data.
12. http://www.theguardian.com/music/2011/sep/15/copyright-extension-cliffs-law-beatles
13. http://www.theguardian.com/music/2011/sep/15/copyright-extension-cliffs-law-beatles
14. http://jamaica-gleaner.com/article/news/20150823/protecting-poetry-music-and-all-amendments-copyright-act-critical-component
15. Report: The Australia-US Free Trade Agreement - An Assessment Dr. Philipa Dee APSEG, Australian National University p. 23 (box) and 33 (2004). http://www.aph.gov.au/Parliamentary_Business/Committees/Senate_Committees?url=freetrade_ctte/rel_links/index.htm
16. https://www.eff.org/deeplinks/2012/08/all-nations-lose-tpps-expansion-copyright-terms
17. http://www.infodev.org/articles/radial-streaming-music-developing-world
18. http://www.rollingstone.com/music/news/taylor-swift-scott-borchetta-spotify-20141108
19. http://creativecommons.org/about
20. According to The Electronic Frontier Foundation "The anti-circumvention" provisions of the Digital Millennium Copyright Act ("DMCA"), codified in section 1201 of the Copyright Act, have not been used as Congress envisioned. The law was ostensibly intended to stop copyright infringers from defeating anti-piracy protections added to copyrighted works. In practice, the anti-circumvention provisions have been used to stifle a wide array of legitimate activities. As a result, the DMCA has become a serious threat to several important public policy priorities." https://www.eff.org/wp/unintended-consequences-16-years-under-dmca
21. Copyright Industries in the U.S. Economy: The 2014 Report.

Tek-no-li-gy Processing: Reshaping the Soundscape

> *This continuum represents a technosphere that is a domain of imaginary possibilities and constraints which lies between performance on one side and the more or less remote reception of sound on the other. The technosphere is thus premised on the idea of a performative gap or dislocation, but also a belief on the part of musicians that this might be bridged.*
>
> Jason Toynbee

The adaptation and appropriation of technology, namely the invention of the sound system, the jukebox as a tool of mediation and the precursor to the karaoke machine, and the development of the studio and turntable as instruments in the production process in unconventional and radical ways, have been at the root of the unorthodox modes of production, composition, marketing and aesthetic value that has been the hallmark of popular music production in Kingston. Also linked to this are other facets of the production of culture perspective namely, law and industry structure and occupational careers.

The importance of technology to the popular music industry cannot be overstated. Scholars have noted the fact that in tandem with technological innovations and inventions, industries have experienced major advances through a mass production modality that has resulted in massive increases in profits for the industry. Dominic Power and Allen Scott (2004) state:

> Over much of the twentieth century, the leading edges of economic development and growth were largely identifiable with sectors characterized by varying degrees of mass production, as expressed in large-scale machine systems and a persistent drive to produce standardization and cost cutting. Throughout the mass-production era, the dominant sectors evolved through a succession of technological and organizational changes focused above all on process routinization and the search for internal economies of scales (4).

The evolution and development of the global popular music industry has been significantly impacted by several innovations in technology that have facilitated the reorganisation of the sector to maximise the added value that emerges with every advance in technology. The phonograph, the microphone, speakers, vinyl records, the jukebox, the long playing thirty-three-and-a-third-rpm record, the cassette, compact disc, mini disc, MIDI, synthesizers, sequencers, drum machine and the MP3 player are some of the technologies that have driven the music industry to develop new business models that have led to significant increases in profit. Invariably, there was initial resistance, but, ultimately, the technology has assisted the industry in creating new product formats and expressions that have resulted in seismic shifts in its bottom line. The Jamaican experience has also been technology led, and it is for this reason that this chapter highlights some of the main technologies that have influenced our systems of production.

Recording technology, sound transmission and audio storage formats are critical to the music industry, globally. Jamaica, however, provides a unique experience in the innovative manipulation of these technologies. I focus on the jukebox as the genesis of popular sound technology and the recording studio as an instrument and architect of sound. I also propose an alternative perspective on the use of technology in the Jamaican context and suggest that the experience in *the creative echo chamber* provides a unique shift in technology application and aesthetics. It is my contention that technologies related to the recorded music industry, like the jukebox, amplifiers, turntables, speakers and the recording studio, were inverted in our creative milieu to provide alternative uses for these specific technologies that I call the *Tek-no-li-gy Process* (taking new knowledge). Simply put, the symbol creators *within the creative echo chamber* extracted new knowledge and methodologies out of existing Western technologies that were not the original intent of the technologies. This was achieved through the process of hybridisation, innate inventive capacity, the creative intellect and the creative imagination based on a non-Western cosmology and ontology with an Afrocentric pedigree.

The production of culture perspective has become an important part of most research which has at its core production within the sociology of culture (Wikström 2006, 23). Richard Peterson (1982, 143), in his seminal articles, posits that cultural production is shaped by the social, legal and economic milieux in which they are produced. Peterson suggests, as an analytical tool for examining the milieux, a set of facets or constraints 'which alone, or in combination, often constrain or facilitate the evolution of culture' (143). One of these facets or constraints is technology. Technology and cultural production are inextricably intertwined; there is no mass-mediated popular music without technology. From Thomas Edison's primitive phonograph to the sophistication of the iPod, technology has been changing the shape and form of cultural text. Technology has affected the production, marketing and distribution of most cultural texts with its concomitant developments and this certainly has been the case in the development of Jamaican popular music.

The theoretical framework of technological culture will provide a very useful analytical tool for the role of technology within the context of the making of popular music and will complement the production of culture perspective which focuses on technology as one the constraints which affect the way in which culture is produced. Jennifer Slack and J. Wise (2007) identify the difficulty of separating technology from culture and vice versa, stating, 'from the perspective of culture as a whole way of life, technologies are integral to culture, not separate from it' (4). They suggest that what is needed 'is a model and a vocabulary that brings technology fully into the concept of culture to begin with, they propose technological culture' (5). Wise (1997, 101), in an earlier work, suggests that perceptions about technology fall into two major perspectives, namely a mechanistic perspective on causality and a non-mechanistic perspective on causality. These perspectives are further divided into subgroups. The two mechanistic perspectives are identified as expressive causality and symptomatic causality and the two non-mechanistic perspectives are expressive causality and articulation and assemblage.

Punching for Recognition of the Jukebox Culture in Jamaica

Jacques Attali (1985) notes that when Western technology made the recording of sound possible, 'a new society emerged, that of mass production, repetition, the nonproject. Usage was no longer the enjoyment of present labours but the consumption of replications' (87–88). The invention of sound reproduction devices such as the phonograph and the jukebox represented 'A radically new social and cultural space demolishing the earlier economic construction of representation' (94). David Hesmondhalgh reminds us that the international movement of cultural text and technologies goes back many centuries, but it was the movement of the post–Second World War era that is significant to the present discussion. Using Jeremy Tunstall's analysis of these waves of international flows, Hesmondhalgh (2007, 74) states that during the post-war period, there was an increase in the flow of cultural goods, internationally, with most of the content in text and technologies coming from the United States, a process he calls internationalisation. This intensification in international flows was a direct response to the need to improve profitability within the cultural industry.[1] The jukebox was first introduced into the Jamaican entertainment scene in the early '50s. Though there are no definitive dates as to exactly when it was first used, all evidence suggests that it became popular in Jamaica during this period. Evidence provided by interviews suggests that most jukeboxes came from the United States of America, consistent with the internationalisation process.

Cyril Ehrlich (1989) said of the jukebox in Britain, 'jukeboxes, which had been common in pre-war America, came late to Britain. In the 1930s, there was merely "an experimental handful" of jukeboxes across Britain, but by 1955, over 500 were licensed' (130). Given its status as a British colony, it is plausible to suggest that Jamaica closely followed the trends impacting its colonial master. The proximity of the United States, combined with its hegemonic influence over Jamaica's popular culture, also significantly affected the timing of the introduction of the jukebox into Jamaican rum bars. Similar to the Delta region of the United States, the jukeboxes in Jamaica were scattered in bars all over Kingston and in town squares of many rural communities. Almost all rum bars/pubs in the corporate area were located in downtown Kingston and frequented by working-class men and women.

The postcolonial realties of the lack of respect for the music of the other are apparent early with the advent of the jukebox in the Kingston context. Like the juke joints of the black American south, rum bars of Kingston were lowbrow establishments where only blacks of the underclass gathered and where no decent person, black or white, was expected to be seen. The high/low cultural dichotomy of American culture at the time necessitated this binary opposition, which had the effect of cultural segregation and occupational exploitation. This is illustrated by Michael Chanan (1995):

> The machine and its music carried low-life connotations...as for the music, the jukebox particularly stimulated 'race' and 'hillbilly' recordings for the black and white markets respectively; and the record companies found distinct advantages in using jazz musicians to help them to cut the costs of production (88).

Referring to early blues records, Courlander (qtd. in Chanan, 51) notes that radio and records introduced a new element into the development of Negro musical traditions which ought to be called 'feedback'. Chanan (1995) states that the process allowed the blues to develop into a new vernacular, what he calls 'the lingua franca of North American music' (51). In the same way, the amplification of mento songs, mainly through the juke-box,[2] allowed for the development of a new vernacular based on the transfer of rural traditions of folk songs to the urban space, which was the crossroads for the many folk and religious traditions of Jamaica. It was also a validation of mento music and its lyrics in the face of the cultural imperialism of Anglo-American pop culture that had dominated the airwaves in Jamaica. Alma Mock Yen (2002) recalls the cultural scene in the 1950s:

> The 1950s cultural scene was lively and fitted neatly into my radio activities. For example, I played a lot of Nat King Cole's songs, which I once described rather grandly on air as: 'set like gems in Nelson Riddle's scintillating orchestral accompaniment...' The 1950s saw 'pop' stars going and coming... Sammy Davis Jnr. danced, sang and played drums at the Carib. Oscar Peterson and his trio, and the incomparable Ella Fitzgerald, queen of 'scat', winner of 13 Grammy awards, did their 'thing' at the Carib. 'Sassy Sarah Vaughan, the divine' and other top-rated American pop artists did shows elsewhere, welcomed resoundingly by local 'fans'. In pop music the strong 'UP-SO ' influence had implications for a local music industry, but in the 1950s no one I knew questioned or cared (72–73).

Local diversity in musical taste at the time was satisfied only by the jukebox, which had the North American and British hits as well as the early mento recordings. Harold Courlander's 'feedback' process was realised through musicians who copied the style of a particular recording which was an interpretation of traditional folk songs brought through ancestral memory, hence reinterpreting the traditional folk songs in a new form to become the standard for another generation. Daniel Neely (2008) supports the observation:

152 | THE CREATIVE ECHO CHAMBER

Fig 6.1 Jukeboxes at a bar in east Kingston © Dennis Howard 2006

Indeed, while the early, recording era might for some represent a 'golden era,' producers were after a particularly marketable sound. I am of the opinion that the range of mento's style represented by early commercial recordings is strikingly limited in comparison to what was likely practiced in those days (41–42).

Sociocultural Hybridity and Imperial Hegemony

Placement of boxes was based on social standing, class and race. The better quality boxes went to the more upscale pubs and bars often frequented by brown, middle-class patrons. Even the type of music available was different. In the average downtown Kingston bar, particularly in western Kingston, Oxford Street, Bond Street or Pink Lane, the music compilation of the boxes would be a mix of mento, ska, gospel, rocksteady, and country which appealed to a working-class taste and fit the 'low-life connotations' associated with the jukebox in the US in the postwar period (Chanan 1995, 88). Most of the upscale joints had a very heavy dose of British pop and

American rhythm and blues with Jamaican music limited to what I referred to earlier as *gentrified reggae*. The jukebox did not escape the hegemonic realities of colonial and postindependent Jamaica. The majority black and poor population was engaged in a struggle to forge a Jamaican identity, consistent with their own reality and worldview. The ruling class, however, imposed on the masses an Anglo-American stylistic aesthetic. In much the same way that early blues and rock and roll were rejected in the United States of America, the Jamaican elite did not accept the people's music. Radio reflected this even more poignantly. Kevin O'Brien Chang and Wayne Chen (1998) note:

> Programming was heavily middle class and did not reflect popular preferences. RJR's most popular musical programmes for 1956 (in Order of decreasing popularity) were: calypso corner; Treasure Isles Times; Geddes Grant Hour of music; Reynolds Hour of Music: Les Paul and Mary Ford; Bing (Crosby) Sings; Sweet and Swing, (Nat) King Cole's Count; Hits of the Day; Music by Montavani. And this was a time when rhythm and blues was the dominant sound of the land! (17–18).

Jukeboxes in the Kingston metropolitan area thus became the central site in everyday life for the expression of working-class sensibilities through all popular music genres. Many popular records that did not enjoy the privilege and benefit of airplay, due to their revolutionary tone, and political messages and mainstream rejection, found a home in jukeboxes. Mento tunes, such as 'Big White Shirt', and 'Night Food'; rocksteady hits such as 'Tougher than Tough'; and reggae classics, such as 'Beat down Babylon' and 'Declaration of Rights', which were either banned or frowned upon in high society, enjoyed free expression and exposure in jukeboxes located in ghetto universities all over Kingston and rural town squares. Along with the sound systems, jukeboxes became the 'voice of the people', a moniker which was adopted by Prince Buster for his popular sound system. Adult entertainment, political protest, nationalism, roots culture and Marcus Garvey's philosophy were talking points around the ubiquitous jukebox. Rex Nettleford (1996), in describing the tone of the music states:

> In the late sixties the reggae songs (musically more akin to the traditional mento than the contemporary revivalist) went back to the Rastafarian themes while maintaining the rudie social comment on poverty and

general distress. The song 'Babylon's Burning' reflects a definite Rastafarian view of the wider society and its likely fate as retribution for its wickedness (98–99).

The jukebox, like the sound system, was the arena for the contestation of colonial and postcolonial oppression and identity formation.

While Jamaica is known for its popular music, many outsiders are astounded by the variety of popular genres. Primarily due to our colonial past and the Anglo-US hegemonic structures which persisted, Euro-American genres, R&B, tin pan alley, soul, funk pop, country and western and gospel were very popular in the country, not only among the ruling class but ordinary Jamaicans developed a serious love for the imported music. In the twentieth century, the music of the North Atlantic dominated the Jamaican cultural space. Jacques Attali (1985) correctly notes, 'Mass music is thus a powerful factor in consumer integration, interclass levelling, cultural homogenization, and the disappearance of distinctive cultures' (111). With the growing popularity of Jamaican music forms, there emerged a high/low dichotomy with Jamaican music at the lowest level of the pyramid. Ordinary Jamaicans rejected this cultural hierarchy to some extent, but for the most part, the music of the North Atlantic was dominant. This was reflected in the jukebox compilation which was, and still is, a potpourri of popular genres. One could find songs to suit any taste in popular music. As mentioned before, mento music survived due to the fact that the jukebox, ska, rocksteady, reggae, dub and dancehall were supplemented by choice selections of country and western, gospel, rock 'n' roll and pop and rock. Notable favourites include the 1975 country and western and crossover pop hit, 'Please Mr. Please' by Olivia Newton John. This particular song had a jukebox reference which said 'Please Mr. Please don't' play B17', referring to the selection number of the jukebox. Most jukeboxes that had the song, placed it at selection B17.[3] Risqué mento tunes such 'Sixpence' and 'Baggy Beef' were staples for the jukebox compilation. American and British recording stars like Tom Jones, Englebert Humperdinck, Mahalia Jackson, Pat Boone, Little Richard and Fats Domino representing pop, R&B, gospel and rock and roll were always a part of the jukebox compilation. This allowed for a high level of cultural appropriation and hybridity and allowed the regular Jamaican to develop a very cosmopolitan musical taste and appreciation. This hybridity is the fusion of Jamaican music and the music of the West, which has been at the foundation of popular music production from the 1940s onwards. Our music has been a consequence of symbiotic influences derived from American rhythm and blues, jazz, salsa, bolero and country and western. It is a symbiotic relationship because it has been established that some of these so-called American original music have significant Caribbean connections. Herbie Miller (2003) notes:

> Not only were the sounds, social habits and language of some of jazz's earliest contributors informed by a Caribbean aesthetic, but so too was rhythm and blues. Louis Jordan, arguably that genres most dynamic performer, hit the rhythm and blues chart with calypso spiced songs like *Mo and Joe*, as he did again working with jazz singer Ella Fitzgerald with *Stone Cold Dead in the Market* and *I Put the Peas in the Pot to Cook*. Pianist 'Professor Longhair' (whose real name is Roy Byrd) was dexterous at integrating his blues inflected music with a diasporic intelligence and described his own playing variously as 'a combination of offbeat Spanish beats and calypso downbeats', and a mixture of rumba, mambo, and calypso (22).

Homi K. Bhabba (qtd. in Taylor 2007) states:

> [H]ybridity to me is the 'third space' that enables other positions to emerge. This third space displaces the histories that constitute it, and sets up new structures of authority, new political initiatives, which are inadequately understood through received wisdom. The process of cultural hybridity gives rise to something different, something new and unrecognisable, a new area of meaning and representation (145).

Jamaican music has always had hybrid tendencies which have been strengthened through the interaction of its symbol creators with the influences of so many outside genres. Within the Jamaican hegemonic machinery, however, these have been placed at a lower level than their Anglo-American counterparts. Timothy Taylor in his critiques of Bhabba suggests that Bhabba did not consider the 'oppositional and destabilizing' effects of hybridisation, and believes that Bhabba missed the fact that the colonial powers and its mimic men might view the hybrid forms of music, e.g., ska and reggae, as inferior versions of what is considered the dominant culture, which is that of the West. Taylor (2007) continues:

> Interpretations aren't made solely by those in power, of course, but hegemons have ways of ensuring that their interpretations prevail, at least in those institutions that they control, such as the major record labels, the radio market, and large retailers and, to some extent, the less responsible music journalists (146).

Certainly, the situation in Jamaica provided a sociocultural space where the Euro-American aesthetic was the dominant cultural force. The jukebox compilation represented the discursive dynamics of centre/periphery negotiations, class prejudice, national identity, creative synthesis, resistance, self-deprivation, hegemonic and counterhegemonic ripples and cultural dialectics that were played out during popular music-making in that period when the jukebox was an integral part of the value chain of the music industry.

In the mid-1960s, James Howard, my father, operated a bar on Charles Street. The jukebox in the bar was famous for having the widest variety of rhythm and blues, rocksteady, ska and pop. His bar became a music 'Mecca', in essence a mini *web of creativity*, for many top sound men including Bunny Goodison, owner the of Soul Shack sound system. Goodison and his cohorts, including Jackie Bell, a famous footballer, would meet each Sunday at the bar to play music from the jukebox and engage in major discussions on the music. This continued, over a few years, until my father moved the business to Rose Lane in 1974. Again, the sharing of ideas on music and the mediated orality around the phonograph was achieved through the jukebox.

Many young talents used the jukebox to hone their singing skills by imitating American and British stars such as Fats Domino, Tom Jones, Jim Reeves and the Impressions. A practice Paulo Freire refers to as the effects of 'cultural invasion.' Freire (1978) argues that:

> The invaders penetrate the cultural context of another group, and ignoring the potential of the latter, they impose their own view of the world upon those they invade and inhibit the creativity of the invaded by curbing their expressions (121).

Freire's observations are particularly relevant to the music scene in Kingston and is similar to Nettleford's (1996) analysis that 'most things African, including Africa's black offspring have come to be denigrated or relegated to the periphery of all that is considered central to human development'

(27). The dominant cultural ideology in Jamaica, during most of the period of cultural production, was Euro-American in orientation through devices such as Freire's cultural invasion. Young Kingstonians and other young Jamaicans often sang in front of jukeboxes along with the records of American and British artists of all genres until they had perfected the styles of these Euro-American artists. In a sense, what took place around the jukebox was a partial expression of Freire's concept of 'cultural invasion' as young Jamaicans felt they had to master the pop aesthetics of the United States and Britain to be relevant and to have a voice. Despite the counterhegemonic forces that were challenging the hegemonic philosophy of Anglo-American superiority, there was also a mixing of cultures. Along the way, these singers developed their own styles resulting in what I have referred to as phonographic synthesis

There is a synchronic connection between the jukebox and the creation of dub with its attendant techniques. When versions became popular in the late 1960s, that is, the instrumental B side of a record, aspiring artists who could not afford to get auditions at the various studios and talent shows practised their craft by using the instrumental versions in jukeboxes. This was jukebox karaoke (without the visual cues) long before the Japanese had invented the technology.[4] Sly Dunbar (2006) recounted spending all his money on the jukebox just so that he could learn the drumming style of his hero Lloyd Knibb of the Skatalites and the distinctive Motown drum sounds. The practice of 'jukebox karaoke', as explained by Dunbar, suggests a mode of production which paralleled the other modes in the record industry. Jason Toynbee calls this practice phonographic orality. Musicians learnt their craft by listening to records and reading music or through formal training. In the case of Jamaica, as elsewhere, learning from records sometimes took precedence over formal training. Access to the jukebox was critical for Dunbar as it had many songs which were not available elsewhere. Also, access to records was limited to the sound system and the radio. The latter was not as accessible to many young musicians. Commenting on jazz and the blues, some cultural writers (Jones 1970) and (Toynbee 2000) have noted that the circulation of records in African American communities facilitated the 'crystallization' of jazz and blues styles. Tonybee notes, 'as sound technology developed, so, too, did phonographic orality with the result that it quickly became the dominant way of making popular music' (126). This trend quickly developed in Jamaica, facilitated by the jukebox.

Jukeboxes were better suited for this when compared to the sound system. First, jukeboxes were located in bars and grocery stores, which allowed for a more intimate mediation. Second, the songs could be repeated as many times as needed which allowed for repetition and transference. The jukebox, as a sound technology and its unique applications in *the creative echo chamber*, prepared the way for what was to come with the sound system revolution that changed popular music forever. It made people comfortable with the notion of talk over the rhythm track and led to the emergence of the DJ with the developments associated with the studio techniques. This was the point in music development in Jamaica where the machine became one with man, losing its technological mystique and intimidation. The relationship was not only between the listener, the music and the object of entertainment; but also between the machine and the underclass of Kingston, through 'a complex set of connections' (Slack and Wise 2007, 109) and relationships within the cultural space of *the creative echo chamber*, a defining moment when the medium became central to the message.

Another decisive advantage the jukebox had over the sound system was its silence (a description I have borrowed from Winston 'Niney' Holness), that is, it never spoke back. Patrons could play the same song, repeatedly. With jukebox technology, according to Attali (1985), 'music becomes a monologue' (88), 'a concrete example of commodities speaking in place of people' (111). Hence, victims of unrequited love could soothe their sorrows while listening to their favourite love song ad nauseam. Songs such as Ernie Smith's 'I Can't Take It', with lyrics such as 'tears on my pillow, pain in my heart, you on my mind', were regularly played. Other popular targets were The Wailers' 'Small Axe', 'if you are a big tree, I am a small axe ready to cut you down' (oppression, the rich versus the poor), Prince Buster's 'Black Head Chiney' (racism and interracial issues) and 'Neither One of Us' by Gladys Knight and the Pips (heartbreak).

In summary, the jukebox and the rum bar provided a space for ordinary Jamaicans to work out the emotional anxieties of urban life. The technology not only aided in the entrenchment of indigenous Jamaican music forms and cultural hybridity but also functioned as a release valve for the pressures of everyday life. By embracing a non-mechanistic perspective of causality, it is clear that the jukebox was an integral part of the process of music making in the creative echo chamber. The jukebox was interlinked with the environment, in this case the open domain, the inner city areas and the creative zones of Kingston which had the highest concentration of jukeboxes. The jukebox was critical for the Jamaican soundscape and architecture because it dominated other mass mediations in sound technology[5] and made possible all the later developments in that particular Jamaican nexus of technology, music, pleasure, audience and sound. Clement Dodd is on record stating that when he first saw the jukebox in the United States on one of his farm work details, he got the idea for the amplification of sound on a larger scale in Jamaica (Reynolds 2006). In fact, Dodd's first experiment was the use of a speaker to amplify the sound of the radio at his mother's business place, Nanny's Corner, on Love Lane.

The jukebox and other early attempts at amplification were critical to the development of the fetishisation of sound technology that has become the hallmark of the Kingston music scene and has fascinated music lovers and music scholars, who have asked why such a gift of sound had its roots in *the creative echo chamber*. Peter Dalton and Steve Barrows (2004) also recognised the role of the jukebox; they observe:

> Once vinyl 7' 45s started to be made at the end of the 1950s, jukeboxes – not as powerful as a custom-built sound system, but also noted for heavy duty bass – began to contribute markedly to local sales, taking the music beyond the dancehall' (30).

This connection between the jukebox and the sound system is key. It reiterates the critical position they enjoyed in the value chain of the echo chamber, but equally important is the fact that it makes clear the importance of sound and sound technology to the recording process in the Kingston music scene. The emphasis on heavy duty bass is critical in the recording (45 records) and reception (sound system/jukebox) process. These technologies are appropriated, tek-no-li-gyzied and fetishised in an ongoing power struggle between the imperialist tendencies of transnational corporations, who control the flow of technology globally, and small nation states such as Jamaica. This is the beginning of a specific Jamaican/Caribbean technosphere, a distinct space of dislocation and of transcendence. The jukebox as a sound technology was reconstructed in *the creative echo chamber* through the articulation of distinct relations, connections, and the intermingling of creative and economic factors which Slack and Wise call articulation *assemblages*. In the 1950s, these assemblages laid the framework for those 'conditions of possibility' that are responsible for Jamaica's distinctive sound culture, responsible for the sound system, dub, remix culture, deejaying and genre developments globally. Gilles Deleuze and Félix Guattari state that, 'the rationality, the efficiency of an assemblage does not exist without the passions that the assemblage brings into play, without the desires that constitutes it as much as it constitutes them' (qtd. in Miller 2007, 349).

Jukeboxes and sound systems were the main technological devices which aided in the dissemination and promotion of Jamaican music. While most sound systems concentrated on Jamaican music, the jukebox facilitated the exposure of several external genres of music, significantly contributing to a cultural hybridity, which ultimately found its way into Jamaican music and, to some extent, enriching it. Jukeboxes were also critical to rum bar culture in the 1960s, 1970s and 1980s and were an extension of the webs of creativity in the creative echo chamber. Working-class Jamaicans found a place of commune, expression, creative synthesis, performance, camaraderie and resistance to North Atlantic hegemony through the once ubiquitous jukebox.

From Ghetto Laboratories in the Creative Echo Chamber to the Technosphere

I will now look, in more detail, on the role of the creative intellect, imagination, and Afro-centred cosmology in the creation of cultural icons such as King Tubby and Lee 'Scratch' Perry, studio production techniques, versions and genres. The sociocultural and political milieu in *the creative echo chamber* which fermented these innovations will also be interrogated. The contribution of Jamaican music to world culture has been elucidated and analysed in previous chapters. However, despite this major feat, only a handful of scholars have attempted to examine the influence of Jamaican production techniques on the global music industry (Toop 2007; Veal 2000; Hebdige 2000; Alleyne 2000). It is my contention that innovations within the Jamaican music space, born out of a combination of creativity and economic and technological expedience, have greatly influenced global pop music production techniques.

Version Galore

Contrary to conventional belief, the phenomenon of 'versions' and dub, which began in the late 1960s, did not emerge out of the studio production culture. Dub mushroomed out of the creativity of another Jamaican innovation – the sound system. Similar to most great discoveries, dub was, arguably, accidentally discovered. Ruddy Redwood, a popular businessman and sound system operator from Spanish Town, St Catherine, has been credited with the discovery of the instrumental version, which was the progenitor of dub (Barrow and Dalton 2004, 216; Bradley 2000, 312). Prior to the advent of the instrumental version, producers had the sometimes challenging task of finding a B-side song for each 45-rpm record they produced. This was standard practice at the time; however, in the case of Jamaica, this was particularly costly due to the undercapitalised nature of the small recording business. The version concept dispensed with the need to record a track for the B-side, using instead the rhythm track of the same song to fill that side. This was described as the B-side instrumental; the version. This development also allowed selectors to talk on the track without interference from the vocals. There were several variables at play here. Firstly, the technology, or, more accurately, the lack of superior technology, allowed for a chance occurrence which created a new form of expression, while simultaneously creating a more economical avenue to produce 45-rpm records. Acceptance of this new rhythm-driven format by dance attendees was due to the following factors. Reggae is heavily based on drum and bass and this resonated well with the mainly black population. The experiment was a success among the dance crowd given the percussive elements and the low frequency register of the electronic bass which drew on the African ancestral memory of black, working-class people who had a long history of identifying with the drums and the percussive and poly-rhythmic elements it translated. Invoking Paul Gilroy's concept of the Black Atlantic, echoes of African rhythms were transported via slave ships, cargo ships and banana boats and are retained throughout the centuries and manifested through the creative imagination, aptly described as 'noises in the blood' by Carolyn Cooper.

The instrumental version reinterpretation is another manifestation of the vibrating drums of a reconstructed ancestral Africa combined with the technological tools of modernity along a trajectory labelled by Erik Davis as the *Black Electronic*, thus extending Gilroy's concept of the Black Atlantic along a techno-spatial dimension. Dance attendees accepted versions and producers saw an opportunity to reduce their production cost. This economic relief should not be undervalued, though some scholars have paid scant regard to the economic dimension. The popularity of the version phenomenon is, to a great extent, based on the fact that producers were now able to realise maximum value from their rhythm tracks by using one rhythm on a 45-rpm record, instead of two.

So, one can argue that the economic factor is a critical element in the enduring value and longevity of the version innovation (Veal 2007, 54). In support of this stance, Louis Chude-Sokei (1997) describes version/dub as 'a product of financial necessity' (11–12), while Toynbee (2000) also notes, 'technologies must serve profit-making strategies and have a broader cultural fit if they are to succeed' (99). The version was only able to survive due to the open domain environment where enforcement of the 1913 Copyright Act of Jamaica was never a priority. Our industry operated under a social authorship system, which did not regard original work as private property. Cater Van Pelt (2006) accurately asserts:

> Copyright laws are designed to reward those who 'originate' expressions, such that those creators can receive payment for their work and thus have as incentive to continue to create. Versions and no-attribution confuse this process, although…the origins of most versions are traceable to an original. Copyright in an original composition should entitle the author to royalty when subsequently versions are made, although, until recent years there was little more than vigilantism to enforce these rights in Jamaica (63).

The King at the Control

In late 1960s, the remix practice of versions was taken a step further by the innovative and very skilled engineer, Osbourne 'King Tubby' Ruddock. King Tubby was once the top mastering engineer at Treasure Isle studio. He began experimenting with versions at his own small studio, by using tape delay, echo and frequency manipulation. Tubby also began to strip the rhythm track down to drums, bass and piano dropping in and out between different instruments during the mixing. This technique recreated the particular recording; in essence, he invented the remix process. These simulacra were radical departures from established norms of recordings and sound aesthetics. These methods of mixing were groundbreaking and his signature sound, which I will call *Hometown Space Odyssey*, became popular among many producers who sought out Tubby to give them the *Hometown Sound*. Michael Veal (2007) describes the phenomenon:

> [T]hese new mixes stripped tracks even further, decreasing the emphasis on the horns, guitars, and keyboard instruments, while increasing the emphasis on the electric bass line and drum set, which now provided the main musical interest. A typical drum & bass mix would focus on the propulsive motion of those two instruments throughout, with the chordal instruments only occasionally filtering through. This treatment of the chordal instruments reflects what would become two central strategies of dub mixing fragmentation and incompletion (57).

I am calling these methods of mixing/remixing the *Ruddock Techniques*, which embarked on an odyssey with the art of noise, experimenting with regeneration and reinterpretation of the 'implements of sound'. The *Hometown Space Odyssey* took musical sound out of its limited variety of timbre, breaking out of this 'limited circle of sounds and conquer the infinite variety of noise-sounds' (Russolo 2007, 11). These techniques became the blueprint for engineers/producers like Lee 'Scratch' Perry, Keith Hudson, Errol Thompson, Herman Chin Loy and Horace Swaby (Augustus Pablo). These innovators subsequently added their own interpretations to this new studio compositional and recording tool. Perry took the *Hometown Space Odyssey* further when he introduced a layered sonic motif to dub by using everyday sounds, harmonies, lead vocals and toasting (Barrow and Dalton 2004, 225) to create a 'full blast of sounds', which I will dub the Black Ark Miracle. Perry's techniques, which I will call the Perry Methodology, allowed for the manipulation of musical notes and rhythmic patterns which were distorted, delayed, contorted and sustained to create this new soundscape in reggae, introducing a sonic dimension not previously explored in the music. Perry also started using this technique in the production of his vocal songs, which were the A-sides, and not the B-side remixes.

Again, Veal (2007) describes the transition pioneered by Perry:

As much as drum and bass cleared a space for inventive rhythm section composing and vocal improvisation, so did it also clear a space for the increasing creative mixing skills of engineers. In fact, if drum and bass can be considered a distillation of the reggae structure to its most basic elements, the next stage in the evolution of the reggae remix would reanimate riddims not by reintroducing chords and melodies but rather by a system of atmospheric remixing techniques that emphasized timbre, spatiality, and texture as primary musical values (61).

Perry (2007) invokes spirituality and a cosmic dimension in his description of the critical elements in the creation of dub:

> The bass is a line, and people need a good line to listen, the drum is a heart beat which is true, therefore, you need a good drummer that can be positive, imitate a perfect heart beat like you are making a man. Therefore, I see the music as if we are making man, God making man and I see the music as a man, I see the music as the high priest Melchesidec so when I go to the studio, I go to make Melchesidec over with a perfect heart beat, so we need a perfect drummer to make a perfect heart beat for the man we want to make alive. We need a perfect bass player to play a perfect bass line because the bass line goes around like this, that's the brain, the brain cells. So that is the way I see the line of Solomon is the bass and the heart, the heart beat we present, the heart beat of fire which some people say is not Jesus Christ but I call my heart Jesus Christ.

Here, Perry continues the theme of the heavy bass line, which typifies the soundscape of both the jukebox and the sound system. He introduces the pulsating heartbeat and suggests the unification of man and machine through the bass line when he states he is trying to 'make man'. His ontological focus is more than creative; it's spiritual and ancestral. Perry is alluding to a methodology of science of self where the music is made not in the machine but in the mind of man long before it reaches the machine, God-inspired and perfect, becoming one brain, body and soul. His exposure to the Revival Church becomes evident when he equates dub's cerebral connotations with the religious practice of repossession, of being in the spirit, dancing in the head. As Clinton Hutton puts it, repossession is the first form of creative performance,[6] creating the aesthetics of a full blast of sound and iconographic fragmentation. Perry (2007) takes the discourse into the mythical dimension in his description of the sound. He dubs it:

> Mystic magic miracle, you hear the sounds from the stones, the stones are magic, rock stones are magic, when you hear the stones from the magic clap the genie who creates energy whatever the genie creates he does not do like this (snapping fingers) he does like this (clapping hands) and it manifests by the clapping. So you call this thunder claps before the rain drops so they work together so they are magic miracle, they make things happen, they make the impossible become possible.

Perry is probably harking back to his rural roots when he worked in a quarry as a youth. When he refers to the 'stones' he draws on the rural environment alluding to raindrops in a magical space where a magical genie whose lifeline is maintained, magically, by the rhythmic motions of hand clapping, again invoking the steady heartbeat, the drum and bass ethos of dub. Again, alluding to the revival roots of mysticism and the magical energy of nature in creating and expressing a cosmology of spiritual/mythological African ancestry, 'A tale of catching vibrations and tuning into spiritual trance' (Davis 2007, 4).

A Likkle a Dis an a Likkle a Dat (The Remix Culture)

The studio innovations of version, dub, the Ruddock Techniques and Perry Methodology heralded the remix culture which is the enduring facet of genres such as disco (now known as dance music), hip hop, techno, house, trance, trip hop, drum and bass, jungle and electronica. Dub became the first remix when King Tubby remixed instrumental versions of now classic reggae singles, to create the kaleidoscopic soundtrack of sonic booms, polyrhythmic drum patterns, echoes, low frequency vibrations, psychedelic tripping and ambient sounds reminiscent of the African heartland and the concrete jungles of Trench Town and Kingston 13; as Lee Perry puts it, 'making the impossible possible'. In brief, dub aesthetics, through the Ruddock Technique and the Perry Methodology, introduced the human ear to frequencies and sound waves which were, hitherto, latent in some cases thus allowing for a different experience with musical notes, aural interpretations and space, affording the studio space a new methodology of mixing/remixing which is now used by practically all producers of popular genres of music worldwide. Mike Alleyne (2002) states:

> Dub was not simply about the song but about the use of sound, and the vast imaginary soundscapes, which were created on extremely

limited equipment, which, by today's standards, would be considered truly primitive. This, though, is once again indicative of the inventiveness of dub's pioneers and of the extent to which the technology served the ideas rather than imposing itself on creativity (8).

Dub studio techniques, in a real way, can be considered the first truly original Jamaican technique and compositional tool which was consistent with the social and communal authorship of the open domain in *the creative echo chamber* by way of technological inspiration. While tape recordings, mixing boards, drum kits and razor blades are synonymous with recording globally, the Tek-no-li-gy process engaged the recording process in radically novel methodologies of song construction, aural text and occupational reordering. By way of non-Western cosmological reinterpretation, it is the only form of music expression that borrowed nothing from another genre of music, in terms of methodologies and techniques.

It was also the first music form to shift the focus from traditional symbol creators like singers and musicians. In dub, the star was the engineer/producer and his mixing board, an instrument which, essentially, predates the turntable in terms of importance and status; long before Brian Eno and Adrian Sherwood embraced the concept of the studio as an instrument. This occupational change was significant to the *multi simultaneity production model*. First, version reduced the need for studio musicians, as there was no need to record new rhythms from the B-side of the records, hence, fewer tracks were made per session. With the emergence of Tubby, engineers became creative primaries in the production process in a major way. This shift in occupational career was significant in that it allowed entry to many new players who were now interested in being on the technical rather than the performance side. New players included Lloyd 'Jammy' James, Philip Smart, Overton 'Scientist' Brown, Peter Chemist, and Bunny Tom Tom. These new 'scientists', along with the pioneers Errol Thompson and Clive Chin, played a pivotal role in reshaping the reggae aesthetics beyond its traditional norms and codes. They engaged the musical tapestry of popular culture in what I call *aural code shifting*.

In terms of the significance of dub methodologies I would have to agree with Louis Chude-Sokei's (1997) assessment that:

> [D]ub has emerged triumphant for its metaphysical and historical textures and, perhaps most important, as an example of how cold, alienating Western technologies can be domesticated by those for whom it was not intended. For it is through dub that the mixing board becomes an instrument and sound becomes isolated within the context of music as the focus of production. It is through dub that the fundamental dynamics of human thought-sound, silence and echo become fore-grounded through technology. And it is through dub that memory becomes the explicit focus of ritual (12).

Appropriation and adaptation in North America started when disco producers in the 1970s adopted the instrumental version concept when they moved to extend disco songs for dance purposes. These early adaptations were based more on lengthening and reconstruction than on sonic reinterpretations, but the influence of dub and version is indisputable (Brewster and Broughton 2000, 121; Alleyne 2000, 9). The shift was heralded by a new breed of DJ turned producer/remixer in the US. Trailblazers such as Francois Kevorkian, Larry Levan, Shep Pettibone and Arthur Russell introduced dub-influenced production to the US market. Kevorkian has acknowledged that dub and other Jamaican studio techniques (the Osbourne Technique and Perry Methodology) have been major influences on him. Kevorkian and Levan both encountered producers Sly and Robbie and engineer and producer, Steven Stanley, at the famous Compass Point Studio in Nassau. They introduced them to the dub aesthetic. The subsequent work of these remixers was steeped in dub methodology and technique that had been passed on to them by their Jamaican counterpart. 'Today's remixers still use principles developed by Jamaica's visionaries, and almost every dance track has some sort of 'dub' mix to fuel the dance floor' (Brewster and Broughton 2000, 121).

Dub aesthetic began to emerge in the work of songwriter/producers/musicians, Nile Rodgers and Bernard Edwards in the work of disco groups such as Chic, Sister Sledge and Diana Ross. The emphasis of drum bass and guitar reminiscent of reggae is clearly evident in their work. Edwards' bass-lines were thumping and prominent in the mix and had a thunderous low frequency resonance. Tony Thompson's drum licks, although classic 4/4, had energy similar to reggae because of his abundant emphasis on snare and tom toms. While Rodgers guitar riffs were also prominent in all their productions, it never overpowered the mix but 'exudes distinctive kinetic and tonal characteristics and a rare stylistic economy' (Alleyne 2007, 4) possessing the same syntax and energy of the ubiquitous ska lick of reggae.

The Black Ark Miracle and the Hometown Space Odyssey soundscape of Perry and Ruddock can be heard in many of the works of Rodgers and Edwards, including 'Good Time' by Chic and 'I'm Coming Out' by Diana Ross. While I will make no claims of direct influence or cooptation on the part of Rodgers and Edwards, the sound of the Chic production bears an uncanny similarity with the dub aesthetics, so it would not be a stretch to imagine some interaction between these producers and this post-modern Jamaican soundscape. It was not unusual for Western music producers to be influenced by esoteric aural architectures (Connell and Gibson 2003, 144–59; Taylor 2007, 123–39; Guilbault 1996, 4–8). Mike Alleyne (2007) concurs with my observations while explaining Rodgers's production methodology:

> It's a percussive mechanical realisation achieved through technology which Rodgers harness and successfully integrates into the fabric of the song. In a sense, his sonic sensibility might be broadly compared to the mixers of dub reggae production, arguably the masters of post-modern ultra-futuristic spatial reconfiguration in popular music (4).

It is not by accident that the first rap hit single, 'Rapper's Delight', sampled the rhythm of Chic's 'Good Time'. Jamaican Clive 'Kool Herc' Campbell, universally credited for creating hip hop's technological foundation, with his break beat phenomenon and huge sound system famous for his heavy and thunderous bass enclosures, had set the trend for heavy bass-line which became the hallmark of early hip hop (Toop 2001). This was the birth of the deejaying culture and the new urban youth culture in the United States took some of its major influences from the Jamaican sound system, dub and studio techniques. David Toop (2001) points out that:

> Whatever the disagreements over lineage in the rap hall of fame or the history of hip hop, there is one thing on which all are agreed. 'Rap is nothing new', says Paul Winley. Rap's forebears stretch back through disco, street funk, radio DJs, Bo Diddley, the bebop singers, Cab Calloway, Pigmeat Markham, the tap dancers and comics, the last poets, Gil Scott-Heron, Muhammad Ali, acapella and doo wop groups, ring games, skip rope rhymes, prison and army songs toasts, signifying and the dozens all the way to the griots of Nigeria and Gambia (19).

What cannot be questioned, however, is the fact that hip-hop and dance music owe their production techniques to the studio and deejaying to the Jamaican sound system culture and the dub aesthetics pioneered by King Tubby, Scratch Perry, Sylvan Morris and Errol Thompson among others. The radically subversive dub version of D Train's 'Keep On' by Francois Kevorkian is a fine example of the dub aesthetics at work in the US market; other dubs include 'The Music Got Me' by Visual and 'Addicted 2 Luv' by Bas Noir, both remixed by Tony Humphries; and 'Don't let Me Wait' and 'This is Something Special' both by the Peech Boys, remixed by Larry Levan. The 1976 disco record 'Spring Rain' by Silvetti within its full orchestration and beautiful harmonies had, at two minutes 40 seconds in the record, a drum and bass dub interlude. Shep Pettibone's instrumental remix of Aurra's 'Baby Love' is sheer hometown space odyssey magic. These were the earliest indications of appropriation of the Osbourne Technique and Perry Methodology by North American producers.

The Tom Tom Club Mash up: A Case Study

It was, again, at Compass Point studio that one of the most influential international pop hits, 'Genius of Love', heavily influenced by Jamaican studio techniques, was produced. In the early 1980s, the rhythm section of the group Talking Heads – Chris Franz and Tina Weymouth – teamed up with Steven Stanley as the Tom Tom Club to create one of the most influential and enduring dance hits.[7] The 'Genius of Love', engineered and co-produced by Stanley, utilised techniques he had perfected while working first at Aquarius studio in Kingston. Stanley utilised many of the Osbourne/ Perry mixing techniques and production aesthetics. Echo, delays and the trademark mixing in and out of particular instruments at different intervals are clearly evident. Steven Stanley (2007) explains the process behind the song:

> Chris Franz said he wanted it to sound like more bounce to the ounce, while he was there trying to play the drum, trying to play that double beat on the bass drum, it was giving hell because he play rock and roll more straight forward so the funk beat is kind of mixed up. So I tell after a while he can't get it. I tell him don't worry play straight, so when he finish now I put a delay 150 milli second on every first foot drum, so it go 'du dup' you know I finger it.

This is the fusion of two aesthetics through technological manipulation, only possible through transcending space and questioning the authenticity of genre construction underscoring the primacy of the absence of originality in post-modern philosophies. Stanley related that the bass line was created by him and was played by engineer Kendal Stubbs, an accomplished funk musician. Stanley also used a technique he had developed in which he arranged the mix sonically. By using the dub aesthetics, Stanley prearranged where instruments came and went and with the use of effects, created the aural space and the psychedelic tonality associated with dub and the remix process. Stanley continued:

> I arrange the song that way. Remember, I was co-producer so they use to trust me to do thing because I have this energy, they tell me do that do that like a force say do that do that so whatever you hear it's not really me pulling it out. That's how I arrange it. Is me arrange the thing like that, like pulling out the guitar here, and doesn't play anywhere else, if it play anywhere else I erase it. So because I am coming from the Jamaican background, that's why I get that inspiration inside of me so it came like that naturally. So, whatever you hear because it was inside of me to mix it that way, but when it was mixing time it was easy because everything already arrange in place only like the guitar I put on little delay to make it more exciting

Again, Stanley spoke about a spirit within him which told him what to do; it was as if he was possessed by external forces. Again, this signifies the importance given to the innate gifts of an ancestral past where the echo of a spiritual recreation of ancestral and symbolic Africa reverberates in the psyche of our symbol creators. Stanley credits as his main influences, King Tubby for spatial wizardry; Boris Gardener bassist, singer and engineer for his precision in frequency tonality; and producer/musician Willie Lindo for his arrangement of instruments in mixing. Stanley fine-tuned the process by determining the exact points at which he wanted a particular instrument or effect in the mix. He did not rely on feel and spontaneity, which was the methodology of pioneering dub masters. Employing a variation of the process of bouncing, pioneered by technical innovator Les Paul in the 1950s, which was also used effectively by Perry at his Black Ark studio, he re-recorded instruments to get the desired effect and impact, by utilising Perry's and Osbourne's innovations. Stanley was able to achieve the dub aesthetic long before the final mix.

Replacing the organic post-modern construction, which was the hallmark of the Perry and Osbourne methodologies, was a new skill set which insisted on aural precision and a more predictable outcome. This precision is, to my mind, illusionary, reminiscent of Perry's trickster persona because Stanley still mixed the wild abandon of Perry and Osbourne when executing his preproduction technique. When prompted to name this technique, he facetiously called it 'Set it Before You Tek It' (set it before you take it). I would suggest a more sophisticated nomenclature for this technique; Stanley's innovation in mixing can be described as *preset dub bouncing*.

Stanley's utterance can be viewed in several ways. First, his nonchalant reference to his innovation is an indication of a deeper sociopolitical manifestation that is ever present in postcolonial societies like Jamaica. There is an old Jamaican saying which states 'anything too black nuh good' which translates to anything that is done by Jamaicans cannot be looked at with any degree of importance and sophistication. This indoctrination of racial and geo-political inferiority has made us believe that this is indeed a reality, inducing Bob Marley to rhetorically ask, 'Can anything good come out of Trench Town?'[8] Hence, Stanley does not see his production innovations as anything worthy of valorisation. Second, his comments underscores the fact that, as Stanley notes, the techniques are almost within the spirit and psyche of the Jamaican musicians and engineers calling on ancestral memory and what Hanna Appel (2004) calls the 'disembodied connectedness'(74) of the African Diaspora. There has never been any effort to formalise the techniques pioneered by Osbourne, Perry, and Thompson et al., which have facilitated appropriation without adequate recognition.

As noted by Chude-Sokei (1997), 'dub has become appropriated in the west as a radical statement of "Third World technological sophistication"' (4). The phrase 'Third World technological sophistication' is somewhat problematic at first glance, because apart from its reference to locality and othering, it can also suggest a hierarchical system of cultural production which differentiates between Anglo-American technological advances and innovations of the subaltern. With the highest achievement being the preserve of white male innovators of the North Atlantic, while for the rest of the non-white world innovations are labelled 'Third World' not only as an indication of geography or spatial specificity but it also brings to the conversation issues of authenticity, location and value. Jason Toynbee's (2007) observations are instructive in underscoring this interpretation:

> A third approach is oriented towards the far side of the technosphere. The aim here is to construct a sonic environment, a virtual dimensionality which never existed 'originally'. In historical terms this is the last strategy to develop. It was first discerned at the beginning of the 1950s with the advent of techniques such as tape echo. It reached an advanced stage with Phil Spector's Wall of Sound in the early 1960s. Today, it is the dominant approach. All popular music now takes on the aspect of a virtual sonic environment – although it can perhaps be heard to most extravagant effect in dance music (70).

Toynbee makes the unfortunate omission[9] of the works of Osbourne, Perry and Thompson, manifested through dub, and jumps all the way to dance music, which owes its existence in significant measures to dub and its production techniques; reinforcing the observations (Chude-Sokei 1997, 12; Alleyne 2002, 4), in this case, methodologies created by the reggae aesthetic being appropriated, but discounted as influential in the global popular music production process.

However, there is an alternative interpretation of the term 'Third World technological sophistication'; it is decidedly a fact that this is how dub was/is fetishised and how reggae is still seen/heard in some quarters of academia and the Euro-American music industry. That it comes from a place seen/heard as 'below' the West is crucial to its appreciation in North America and in Europe/Japan, a form of 'techno-primitivism' that many academics and cultural arbiters are prone to. So Chude-Sokei's use of the term 'Third World technological sophistication' was to mark that hierarchy, not to erase it (Chude-Sokei 2010).

Outro

Technology is one of the constraints which determines the ways in which cultural artefacts are created in the production of culture perspective. Clearly, the jukebox along with the recording studio and the sound system had a profound effect on how popular music developed within *the creative echo chamber*. The technique of dub bouncing combined with the techniques pioneered by Perry and Osbourne provide an exciting set of tools which are being used by producers and engineers of innumerable pop genres including techno, house, hip hop, dance, trance, reggaeton and ambient. Producers such as Fat Boy Slim, Moby, Rza from Wu Tang Clan, Guadi, Todd Terry and Kanye West are but a few of the big names who have been influenced by these techniques. The process of tek-no-li-gy, where Western technologies through the creative intellect and imagination, were appropriated, deconstructed and reformatted to suit the purpose of sound construction on counterhegemonic grounds has been a very powerful phenomenon in the production of word sound and power in *the creative echo chamber*. Reinforcing the non-mechanistic perspective of causality, the concept of articulation and assemblage are useful tools to engage in this discourse to explain the importance of the jukebox and the studio techniques of dub. The concept assumes that technology cannot be viewed as autonomous and is 'integrally connected to the context within which it is developed and used' (Slack and Wise 2007, 112). It also states that culture is made up of these connections and it is through these connections that technologies emerge as part of them and 'as effective within them' (112).

From a production of culture perspective, technology is viewed as one of several moments within the production cycle that determine how cultural artefacts are created, in the *creative echo chamber*. Along with the other facets of the perspective, technology certainly has had a profound effect on the way and the types of cultural artefact output created in Jamaica. In the process of creating a new soundscape, Jamaican symbol creators have reshaped the way the world has interpreted and composed music and has redefined the philosophy of copyright and the notion of the genius author in the process. Through counterhegemonic devices and the use of the creative intellect and imagination within a postcolonial environment, these technologies were used as democratising tools for freedom and identity formation through the soundscapes they invented and reinvented; reshaping meaning and context in the process. This reinvention of authenticity and the amplification of possibilities have been appropriated by the Anglo-American cultural industries and, in some cases, to the detriment of its creators and innovators. As Timothy Taylor notes, 'the marketing of hybridity frequently triumphs over the third space'. The jukebox and the recording studios of *the creative echo chamber* are tools of listening and time capture of notes, chords, chord progressions, rhythmic patterns, 'fragmentation', 'incompletion' and riddim, the heartbeat of the beat street aesthetic. They were critical components in the production of popular music during almost all the periods of cultural production[10] assisting in creating the music in all its interpretations from European notions of tonality, and in the Jamaican case, the alternative focus on rhythmic vibrations, hybridised harmonies/melodies and ambient echoes of the (re) presentation of the African heartland.

NOTES

1. Jamaica did not escape this internationalisation process and as part of the British Empire, Jamaica participated in receiving these international cultural flows which included cultural goods such as records and the jukebox. Hence, 'Britain reaped the benefits of empire even after its empire went into decline' (Hesmondhalgh 2005, 74).
2. In the 1950s, ordinary folks could not afford a phonograph so the jukebox was their main source of entertainment.
3. Many models of jukebox did not have a selection system that facilitated the B17 selection.
4. A Japanese musician named Daisuke Inoue invented the karaoke machine, but Roberto Del Rosario, a Filipino inventor who called his sing along machine Minus One, owns the patent for the invention. Inoue did not patent his invention 'The 8 juke', which he did in 1971; ten years after, Rosario patented his invention in 1983 and 1986. The original machine did not have a screen for lyrics, it was a box with amplifier, microphone and an 8-track player, hence the similarity with the use of the jukebox to sing-along in Jamaica. http://www.theage.com.au/articles/2003/01/13/1041990224535.html
5. Radio and rediffusion boxes were early sound technologies but did not have the reach of the jukebox as most ordinary Jamaicans could not afford radios, and before transistorisation and electrification. For most rural parishes, the only connection to the popular music scene in Kingston was through the jukebox.
6. 'From Douens to El Tucuche: The Amazing Art of LeRoy Clarke.' The ICS graduate seminar series March 26, 2010.
7. Stanley noted that the group originally wanted to work with Lee 'Scratch' Perry but negotiations broke down due to misunderstanding over service fees.
8. Lyrics taken from the song 'Trench Town' from the posthumously released album, *Confrontation*. Trench Town is the inner city shanty town where many of the pioneers of reggae, including Marley, lived and honed their musical skills.
9. An omission he makes up for in subsequent works on reggae's impact on the

international recording industry. See 'One Step Forward? Translating Jamaican Popular Music in the Core'. The Society For Caribbean Annual Conference paper Vol. 7 2006 ISSN 1471-2024; also see 'Copyright and the Conditions of Creativity: Social Authorship in Reggae Music and Open Source software,' CRESC Working Paper Series, working paper No. 60.

10. The importance of the jukebox declined significantly after the neoinnovation period with only a few jukeboxes surviving. The introduction of component stereo sets in bars and the proliferation of sound systems as well as the reluctance to retool contributed to the demise of the jukebox as a significant technological tool.

Mastering our Fate: Jah Jah Children Them a Moving Up

> *If you don't have a earthly possession how can you be strong?*
>
> Black Uhuru

> *I trust that you will so live today as to realize that you are masters of your own destiny, masters of your fate; if there is anything you want in this world it is for you to strike out with confidence and faith in self and reach for it.*
>
> Marcus Garvey

Music for Days and Extra Days

Popular music production in Jamaica has been a significant indication of the productivity and creativity of a colonised people whose lives are affected, on a daily basis, by an unequal relationship with advanced societies of the West, namely, the UK and the USA. Several schools of thought can be employed to analyse the interaction of the Jamaican music industry and these developed countries. Theodor Adorno's pessimistic view of what he called the *culture industry* has painted a picture of the massification of culture to suit the needs of the huge corporations who own and control the music industry. Adorno (1991) suggests that the system has been developed on certain formulaic principles which have stymied true creativity in favour of packed and stylised versions of culture, controlled by the industry itself, creating products which are determined by the industry to fit certain profiles.

Another position places certain types of popular music, for example black music, in the position of being manipulated and controlled by big corporate interests. Simon Frith (1996) notes, that whenever corporate interests are involved in the process of black music production 'commercial mediation replaced direct emotional experience' (18). According to Frith, the emotional qualities of black music, born out of marginalisation and racism, are subjugated in the interest of the star system and are marketed as novelty and gimmick (18). While acknowledging the critical contributions of Kingston to global music, Dominic Power and Daniel Hallencreutz (2002) have noted that the problems which have plagued the Jamaican music industry are first the many, small, fragmented firms which have no structural linkages. Second, there is a lack of a proper copyright system, advanced technology and other institutional structures that are necessary to maximise profit-making within the global music industry which is controlled by only a few transnational conglomerates.

Zjelka Kozul-Wright and Lloyd Stanbury (1998, 33–34) have argued a similar position to Power and Hallencreutz (2002), noting also that the industry should adopt a national system of innovation based on agglomeration practices. The development of the industry in isolation from the mainstream Jamaican economy has created a disconnect between the national system of innovation and the industry. Due to the lack of commitment from the private sector (whose reticence has been historical) they see the engagement of the government in 'formulating and clearly stating a definitive policy on entertainment and in particular, the music sector' (33) as a possible solution. They believe that all stakeholders, music industry practitioners, academia and the private sector should cooperate with the government in designing and implementing strategies 'to reduce the existing barriers to enterprise development and greater participation in the global music market' (34).

The analyses of Kozul-Wright and Stanbury, as well as Power and Hallencreutz, have all missed a very crucial issue – the global relationship between the conglomerates, who control over 80 per cent of music production and distribution, and small countries, which provide creativity and innovation in popular music. The relationship has always been unequal and is informed by such issues as cultural imperialism, globalisation, racism, centre/periphery dynamics, exploitation, appropriation, self-deprivation, resistance, hybridity, innovation, tek-no-li-gy, transnationalism and identity struggles.

To divorce the conversation from these critical issues is a major analytical flaw. The prevailing approach to popular music research on Jamaican music has privileged an analysis which critiques the absence of traditional institutional frameworks of copyright, rights management, record industry structure, advance technology, management regime and distribution and marketing. Jamaican music and its potential has never been dependent on having the right institutional framework, a strong intellectual property regime and management, technological advances and a trained cadre of music industry professionals. The fact is that despite having none or little of the above, as we have shown in this work, Kingston has been a major player in the global music industry and its contribution to popular music has no parallel, when the size of the city and the country is considered. The unique nature of popular music production in what I call a *habitus of nonlinear creativity,* which flourishes under conditions and motivations that are inconsistent with popular music production in the Anglo-American recorded music industry, has led to the description of the city of Kingston as the cradle of popular music production in the Caribbean, as *the creative echo chamber,* consisting of webs of creativity throughout the city where spatial agglomeration took place which facilitated high levels of innovation through transference of artistic and technological knowledge. An amazing array of innovations in songwriting, genre development, studio production techniques, studio engineering techniques, pop iconography, business models and performance style have all come out of *the creative echo chamber* in a comparatively short period. Despite this success, there are still some serious structural deficiencies inherent in the Jamaican music industry which are heightened during relationships and negotiations between the creative echo chamber and the Anglo-American recorded music industry.

Cultural Production Periods

The making of popular music in Kingston has been marked by six distinctive periods of production – Folk Culture, Appropriation, Innovation, Internationalisation, Neoinnovation and Global Interaction. A periodisation of popular music production is critical to the historiography of popular music production in Kingston but is also important in tracking the development and progress of the recorded music industry and the fact that this production was achieved through parochial social relationships. Periodisation also gives structure to any analysis of the industry and allows for a clinical dissection of the music-making process which omits reference to periods that are based on issues such as genre creation, artist emergence and chart appearances. These factors sometimes confused the process instead of highlighting and clarifying the history of cultural production in *the creative echo chamber.* We have seen how, during the different periods, the production process has evolved and how various socio-economic, cultural, political and creative factors have influenced the making of popular music. We have also seen from the start that popular music production has operated on complex, multi-tiered levels and that popular music-making was done for many different audiences, motivations, intentions and environmental conditions. This has led to a unique production process involving the production of music for the cultural industries which have been at the heart of debates on globalisation, cultural imperialism, multiculturalism, exploitation, appropriation and cultural dilution. The involvement of the transnational conglomerates, which have been in control of the recording industry since the 1950s, have been hugely ignored in any research project on Jamaican music, its origins and production. The major record companies that are controlled by these conglomerates have had a significant influence on the development of the industry and the production of some of the output of *The Kingston Creative Echo Chamber*.

On the other hand, we have seen the explosion of creativity based on both art for arts sake and a burst of microcapitalism by the working class of Kingston. This creativity, based on mix of economic and non-economic motivations, has been the foundation of success of Jamaican popular music internationally. The creative city of Kingston, with Orange Street as its first hub, was the foundation of the rich legacy of Jamaican music that has endured to place Jamaica as one of the major contributors to world culture. This has been the big dilemma of the Jamaican music business – Bob Marley's catalogue is foreign owned; some of the greatest music produced in Jamaica is licensed to various overseas distributors who, it is believed by some commentators, have exploited these treasures to their benefit, leaving the original creators to die as paupers. While it is abundantly clear, Roger Wallis (2004) notes that:

> The music industry's history is inextricably linked to the dynamic relationship between the big and the small (the small group of multinational conglomerates which control almost 80–90% of the global music business, and the plethora of smaller enterprises which function as talent incubators all around the world). The majority of artist and composers suffer a negotiating disadvantage in this relationship, partly through lack of knowledge/good advisers, and partly because the lure of becoming a star tends to cloud wisdom and common sense (17).

Jamaica has managed to create a disproportional number of musical genres and superstar musicians that have impacted the global music industry in significant ways. This was not achieved by following international best practices in the international recorded music business. In fact, we have seen that most attempts at mimicking the Anglo-American modes have had less than spectacular results. Success was achieved by charting an alternative direction, based on the power of the creative imagination through which music-making was achieved by an unorthodox organisational structure in an open domain environment based on different motivations in music making and expression. Innovative processes such as *tek-no-li-gy*, a unique device of inverting Western technology by use of the creative imagination to attain culturally specific goals, have been significant in the popular music production in Kingston and have been manifested in the creation of the sound system, the remix culture, mash ups, the engineer as producer/auteur, the deejay, turntablism and version which have changed significantly popular music, globally. Dub and its techniques have revolutionised the production process and, presently, the techniques developed by Tubby, Perry and Thompson are at the heart of popular music production in all universal genres of music, including rock pop, hip hop, R&B, dancehall reggae, drum and bass, country, hyphy, kwaito, grime dub step and reggaeton.

The Jamaican music business emerged out of the inner city of Kingston and a major catalyst for its creation was the invention of sound systems. This revolution in *tek-no-li-gy* that provided entertainment for the inner city poor came out of the racial and social inequities of colonial Jamaica where black, marginalised youth were left out of the system which promoted them as less than human, the scars of which are still with us today. Sound systems and dancehall in the inner city formed webs of creativity and self-expression, a space, an echo chamber, 'the field of cultural production' which they had been denied by imperial edict. Through their own creative intellect and imagination, these pioneers developed several music forms. Creativity took precedence over the business aspects surrounding the music and although there was always a business model and legal framework, these did not always work efficiently or in the best interest of the creators of the music.

Value Chain

The Copyright Act of 1913 did not sufficiently protect copyright owners. It was inadequate due to the fact that the law had not been updated to meet the demands of the times. There was also a serious lack of knowledge on the business side of the music in the early days of the industry. Many creators did not understand the value of their copyright and signed over their rights to others. Jamaican producers/managers knew enough about copyright protection to establish publishing companies to protect themselves. This, however, was an unequal relationship with the composers, in many cases, giving up their copyright through work for hire contracts. In recent decades, with the enactment of a better copyright law (1993) and with the development of a music management culture, Jamaican music creators are poised to benefit in a more significant way than their predecessors. It is hoped that the success of Shaggy, Patra, Sly and Robbie, Cobra, Sean Paul, Shabba Ranks, Inner Circle and Dawn Penn will be the norm in the near future.

Management structures revolved around the producer/studio owner who trained and developed many of the early talents. Not only did they provide training in the recording business but provided an income and an opportunity to develop in the music business. The extent to which they benefited economically has been a sore point among many of the pioneers who have maintained that they were never compensated for their work. Some creators are still locked in lawsuits to claim their 'piece of the pie'.[1] While some claims can be justified, equally, some are without merit. One thing that cannot be disputed is the fact that under this business and management system many of the finest performers, producers, impresarios, engineers and composers came to the fore to contribute significantly to world culture.

The open domain in which the production process evolved is of major significance as this precipitated the development of important areas of the global music industry, for example, sampling and the deejay culture turntablism. It also brought the issue of ownership of copyright and a reinterpretation of 'secular European enlightenment philosophy' of copyright to the forefront.

Future Research Initiatives

A critical area of popular music study and ethnomusicology which has not been sufficiently addressed is the financing and capitalisation of the music industry. While the financial power of the major conglomerates that control the industry is well established, very little has been done to interrogate the source of financing of the independent record companies which have been the engines of innovation and creativity and cultural trends in popular music production. *The Kinston Creative Echo Chamber* is one such phenomenon that needs to be interrogated in terms of the financial backing of the industry; an important area for future study. The association and nexus between political parties and criminal gangs and the music fraternity in Kingston has been the subject of serious debate and scholarly interventions. This is another area that needs to be addressed in a comprehensive way.

In his 2004 study, *Music and the Jamaican Economy*, Michael Witter lamented that 'the participants in the industry admit to the almost endemic secrecy about their operations that in turn condition the quality of estimate of indicators of industry activities' (58). This is still a sore point in academic research and it is hoped that this area will engage future research providing there is cooperation between participants in the industry and researchers, as the level of trust develops.

Recommendations

1. **Venture Capital Fund Public/Private**

    The establishment of a venture capital fund, both public and private, to encourage the development of artists and the music product is of vital importance. This is necessary to ensure the continued development of the music product and the strengthening of international links in the broader recorded music industry.

2. **Standard Regime**

    The development of a recording industry standards tribunal to ensure minimum standards and quality to meet international tastes is an important step forward.

3. **Training**

    Training in music business management and production by tertiary institutions has to be expanded so that the industry can export talent to the international marketplace. Technical production capacity has to be expanded.

4. **Strengthening of Links with International Cultural Industries**

    Collaboration, networking and cooperation with countries such as Trinidad and Tobago, Barbados, the United States, the United Kingdom, Sweden, France and Japan is essential for the expansion of the Jamaican recorded music product. These are markets where Jamaican music has a strong presence. However, there is no formal agreement or arrangement between government agencies and the mainstream music industry in these territories. If this is achieved it would benefit the Jamaican industry immensely.

5. **Formalising Our Indigenous Structure**

   There is need for the industry to recognise the indigenous methods of music-making in the *creative echo chamber* of Kingston. While there are deficiencies in the system, there are clearly areas that are uniquely creative and innovative and have contributed to enhancing the global practice of music production. Instead of relying on Anglo-American practices exclusively while aiming at international success, we must create best practices from our indigenous structure that have developed over the past 50 years.

6. **Marketing Alliance**

   While distribution companies like VP Records still exist, there is need for a concerted effort to develop international marketing alliances which would help to create the buzz necessary for international success. These marketing structures are controlled by the major conglomerates that control the bulk of the music industry. Alliances must be formed with these entities and independent marketing companies to ensure the necessary exposure for the Jamaican music and associated products.

7. **Performing Arts school**

   To ensure a steady stream of professional talent who are industry ready, the establishment of three performing arts high schools, one in each county of the island, is a vital ingredient. This will ensure that young talent gains exposure to high levels of professionalism in their respective craft and develop an appreciation for the business aspects of the entertainment business.

Las Lick

In closing it is fitting to quote Caribbean cultural studies pioneer, the Hon. Rex Nettleford, who states, 'in the field of culture there is no "developing world'" (89). This is a poignant statement which exemplifies and amplifies the contribution of Kingston through the creative webs in Jamaica, to the development and sustenance of the global recording music industry. The Jamaican music industry is a unique and phenomenal machinery which, despite its acute inadequacies and weak institutional framework (especially when viewed through North Atlantic lenses), has made an indelible mark on global culture. As Nettleford (1995) notes, 'the Eurocentricity of mainstream Caribbean life for all this time is the problematique of cultural development' (84). I contend that this Eurocentric orientation, combined with North Atlantic geopolitics, is at the root of our economic underdevelopment. Jamaican music output, despite the odds, has made significant strides both culturally and financially to the development of the nation state. Kingston has contributed more genres, artistic innovation, production techniques, technological innovation and business models than any other space of comparable size. This was achieved through the several devices enunciated in this work in significant detail. While other studies (Witter 2006, 56–57; Kozul-Wright and Stanbury 1998, 31–33), have detailed various strategies for the maximisation of revenues from the music industries, these recommendations have ignored critical considerations which are integral to the continuation of the industry. My recommendation is a radical departure from Eurocentric solutions to a Creole reality. While it is clear that some institutional frameworks have to be overhauled, it is also clear that these should take place within the unique sociocultural space which is occupied by the industry which has generated so much innovation and creativity and alternative business models within a heterogeneous, syncretic, creolised, Western, and non-Western construct. As Antonio Benítez-Rojo (1996), reflecting on Caribbean culture, points out, 'traditional culture refers to an interplay of supersyncretic signifiers whose principal centres are localised in preindustrial Europe, in sub-Saharan regions of Africa, and in certain coastal zones of southern Asia' (21).

The continued development of the cultural industries with the music at the centre will be an important component of the way forward if true economic development is to be realised.

NOTE

1. Jimmy Cliff, 'Piece of the Pie,' *Power and the Glory*, Columbia Records, 1988.

References

Adorno, Theodor. 1991. *The Culture Industry*. London and New York: Routledge.
———, and Max Horkheimer. 1993. *The Culture Industry: Enlightenment as Mass Deception from Dialectic of Enlightenment*. New York: Continuum.
Alasuutari, Pertti. 1995. *Researching Culture: Qualitative Method and Cultural Studies*. London: Sage Publications.
Albarran, Alan B. 1996. *Media Economics*. Ames: Iowa State University Press.
Alleyne, Mervyn. 1988. *Roots of Jamaican Culture*. London: Pluto.
Alleyne, Mike. 1998. 'Babylon Makes the Rules': The Politics of Reggae Crossover. *Social & Economic Studies* 47, no. 1:65–77.
———. 2001. White Reggae: Cultural Dilution in the Record Industry. *Popular Music & Society* 24, no. 1:15–30.
———. 2002. Echoes of Dub: Spatiality, Assimilation & Invisibility. An IASPM Conference Proceedings. In *Looking Back, Looking Ahead: Popular Music Studies 20 Years Later*. Ed. K. Karki, R. Leydon and H. Terho, 469–75. Turku/Copenhagen: IASPM Norden.
———. 2003. Positive Vibration? Capitalist Textual Hegemony and Bob Marley. *Bob Marley: The Man & His Music*. Ed. Eleanor Wint and Carolyn Cooper, 12–22. Kingston: Arawak Publications.
———. 2007. Nile Rodgers: Navigating Production Space. *Journal on the Art of Record Production*. http://www.artofrecordproduction.com.
———. 2009. Globalisation and Commercialisation of Caribbean Music. *World Music Roots and Routes*. Ed. Tuulikki Pietila, 76–101. Studies across Disciplines in the Humanities and Social Sciences 6. Helsinki: Helsinki Collegiums for Advanced Studies.
Andy, Bob. 2001. Personal interview.
Appel, Hannah. 2004. Dance Hall: Hip-Hop and Musical Cross-Currents. *Glendora Review: African Quarterly on the Arts* 3, no. 3 and 4:71–79.
Ashcroft, B., G. Griffiths and H. Tiffin. 1989. *The Empire Writes Back*. London and New York: Routledge.
Attali, Jacques. 1985. *Noise: The Political Economy of Music*. Trans. Brian Massumi. Minneapolis, Minnesota: University of Minnesota Press.
Babbie, Earl. 2004. *The Practice of Social Research*. 10th ed. Chapman University: Thompson Wadsworth.
Barker, Chris. 2003. *Cultural Studies: Theory and Practice*. 2nd ed. London: Sage Publications.

Baker Jr, Houston, et al., ed. 1996. *Black British Cultural Studies: A Reader*. Chicago: University of Chicago Press.
Barrow, Steve, and Peter Dalton. 2004. *The Rough Guide to Reggae*. London: Rough Guides Ltd.
Barthes, Roland. 1977. *The Death of the Author in Image Music Text*. New York: Hill and Wang.
Basch, Linda, et al. 1994. *Nations Unbound: Transnational Projects, Postcolonial Predicaments and Deterritorialized Nation-States*. New York: Gordon and Breach Science Publishers.
Benítez-Rojo, Antonio. 1996. *The Repeating Island: The Caribbean and the Postmodern Perspective*. 2nd ed. Trans. James E. Maraniss. Durham and London: Duke University Press.
Bernard, H. Russell. 1988. *Research Methods in Cultural Anthropology*. Newbury Park, London and New Delhi: SAGE Publications.
Bettig, Roland V. 1996. *Copyrighting Culture: The Political Economy of Intellectual Property*. Colorado: Westview Press.
Blackwell, Chris. 1991. Personal interview.
Bourdieu, Pierre. 1993. *The Field of Cultural Production: Essays on Art and Literature*. Ed. and Intro. Randal Johnson. United States: Columbia University Press.
Boyle, J. Shamans. 1996. *Software, and Spleens: Law and the construction of the Information Society*. Cambridge, MA: Harvard University Press.
Bradley, Lloyd. 2006. *Bass Culture: When Reggae was King*. London: Viking Penguin Group.
Bradshaw, Sonny. 2006. Personal interview.
Brathwaite, Kamau. 1971. *The Development of Creole Society in Jamaica 1770–1820*. Oxford: Oxford University Press; 2005 reissued Kingston: Ian Randle Publishers.
Brewster, Bill, and Frank Broughton. 2000. *Last Night A DJ Saved My Life: The History of the Disc Jockey*. New York: Grove Press.
Brodber, Erna. 1975. A Study of Yards in the City of Kingston. Institute of Social and Economic Research (ISER), University of the West Indies, Working Papers, No. 9, Kingston: University of the West Indies.
Brynes, William J. 2009. *Management and the Arts*. 4th ed. Amsterdam, Boston, Heidelberg, London, New York, Oxford, Paris: Focal Press.
Burning Spear. 1974. Foggy Road. Studio One, 45 rpm.
Bynoe, Yvonne. 2005. *Money, Power, and Respect: A Critique of the Business of Rap Music in Rhythm and Business*. Ed. Norman Kelly. New York: Akashic Books.
Campbell, Frankie. 2009. Personal interview.

Caves, Richard E. 2000. Creative *Industries: Contracts between Art and Commerce.* Cambridge, Massachusetts, and London England: Harvard University Press.

Chang, Heewon. 2008. *Auto-ethnography as Method.* Walnut Creek, CA: Left Coast Press.

Chang, Kevin O'Brien and Wayne Chen. 1998. *Reggae Routes: The Story of Jamaican Music.* Kingston: Ian Randle Publishers.

Chanan, Michael. 1995. *Repeated Takes: A Short History of Recording and its Effects on Music.* London: Verso New Left Books.

Chevannes, Barry. 2001. Ambiguity and the Search for Knowledge. Inaugural Lecture. An Open-ended Adventure of Imagination. The University of the West Indies, Mona Campus, Kingston, 22 March. Kingston: UWI Press.

———. 2006. *Betwixt and Between: Explorations in an African-Caribbean Mindscape.* Kingston: Ian Randle Publishers.

Chude-Sokei, Louis. 1997. 'Dr. Satan's Echo Chamber: Reggae, Technology and the Diaspora Process.' Bob Marley Lecture. The Institute of Caribbean Studies, Reggae Studies Unit, The University of the West Indies, Mona, November 19.

———. 2010. Personal interview.

Clarke, Sebastian. 1980. *Jah Music: The Evolution of the Popular Jamaican Song.* London: Heinemann Educational Books.

Clayton, Martin, Trevor Herbert and Richard Middleton, eds. 2003. *The Cultural Study of Music: A Critical Introduction.* New York and London: Routledge.

Cliff, Jimmy. 1988. 'Piece of the Pie.' Columbia Records, 45 rpm.

Cole, Stranger. 20008. Personal interview.

Connell, John, and Chris Gibson. 2003. *Sound Tracks: Popular Music, Identity and Place.* London and New York: Routledge.

Coombe, Rosemary J. 1998. *The Cultural Life of Intellectual Properties: Authorship, Appropriation, and the Law.* Durham and London: Duke University Press.

Cooper, Carolyn. 1993. *Noises in the Blood: Orality, Gender and the 'Vulgar' Body of Jamaican Popular Culture.* London: Macmillian Press.

———. 2004. *Sound Clash: Jamaican Dancehall Culture at Large.* New York: Palgrave Macmillan.

Cox, Christoph, and Daniel Warner, ed. 2007. *Audio Culture: Readings in Modern Music.* New York and London: Continuum.

Creswell, John W. 2009. *Research Design: Qualitative, Quantitative, and Mixed Methods Approaches.* 3rd ed. Los Angeles, London, New Delhi and Singapore: Sage Publications.

Curtis, Jim. 1987. *Rock Eras Interpretations of Music and Society 1954–1984.* Bowling Green, Ohio: Bowling Green State University Popular Press.

D'Acci, Julie. 2004. *Cultural Studies, Television Studies, and the Crisis in the Humanities in Television after TV: Essays on a Medium in Transition*. Ed. Lynn Spiegel and Jan Olsson, 418. Durham, North Carolina: Duke UP.

Daley, Dianne. 2001. Copyright Law and Administration in Jamaica (1990–2000): A Decade of Positive Development 2001. http://www.fogadaley.com/home.html

Daley, Dianne. 2006. Personal interview.

Davis, Erik. 2007. 'Dub, Scratch, and the Black Star: Lee Perry on the Mix.' *Sound, Theory, Dub, History, DJ Culture, Criticism*. Monday, Dec. 17. Trackback. http://remixtheory.net/?p=276

———. n.d. Roots and Wires: Polyrhythmic Cyberspace and the Black Electronic. http:www.techgnosis.com/cyberconf.html.

Dawes, Kwame. 1999. *Natural Mysticism: Towards A New Reggae Aesthetic*. Great Britain: Peepal Tree.

———. 2002. *Bob Marley: Lyrical Genius*. Great Britain: Sanctuary.

Dodd, Clement. 1995. Personal interview.

du Gay, P., et al. 1997. *Doing Cultural Studies: The Story of the Sony Walkman*. London: Sage Publications.

Dunbar, Sly Lowell. 2006. Personal interview.

Edgar, Andrew, and Peter Sedgwick, ed. 1999. *Cultural Theory: The Key Concepts*. London and New York: Routledge.

Ehrylich, Cyril. 1989. *Harmonious Alliance: A History of the Performing Right Society*. Oxford: Oxford University Press.

Eldridge, Michael. 2002. There Goes the Transnational Neighbourhood: Calypso Buys a Bungalow. *Callaloo* 25, no. 2: 620–38.

Ellis, Alton. 2008. Personal interview.

Ellis, C.S., and A. P. Brochner. 2000. Auto-ethnography, Personal Narrative, and Personal Reflexivity. *Handbook of Qualitative Research*. Ed. N. K. Denzin and U.S. Lincoln. Thousand Oaks, CA: Sage.

Flick, U. 2000. Episodic interviewing. *Qualitative Researching with Text, Image and Sound: A Practical Handbook*. Ed. M. Bauer and G. Gaskell, 75–92. London: Sage Publications.

Florida, Richard. 2002. *The Rise of the Creative Class*. New York: Basic Books.

Forbes, Copeland. 2006. Personal interview.

Foucault, Michel. 1984. *The Foucault Reader*. Ed. Paul Rabinow. New York: Pantheon.

Freire, Paulo. 1978. *Pedagogy of the Oppressed*. Trans. Myra Bergman Ramos. England: Penguin Books.

Frith, Simon. 1981. *Sound Effects: Youth, Leisure, and the Politics of Rock 'N' Roll*. New York: Pantheon Books.

———. 1996. *Performing Rites: On the Value of Popular Music.* Harvard: Harvard University Press.

Frith, Simon, and Andrew Gooden. 1990. *On Record: Rock, Pop, And The Written Word.* London: Routledge.

———, and Lee Marshall, ed. 2004. *Music and Copyright.* 2nd Ed. Edinburgh: Edinburgh University Press.

Frost, Robert. 2007. Re-architecting the Music Business: Mitigating Music Piracy by Cutting out the Record Companies. *First Monday* 12, no. 8–6 Aug. http://www.uic.edu/htbin/cgiwrap/bin/ojs/index.php/fm/article/viewArticle/1975/1850.

Gardener, Boris. 1973. 'Every Nigger is a Star.' Leal, 45 rpm.

Garvey, Amy Jacques. 1986. *The Philosophy & Opinions of Marcus Garvey: Or, Africa for the Africans.* Preface by Tony Martin. The New Marcus Library, No. 9. Dover, MA: The Majority Press.

Geertz, Clifford. n.d. Ethos, World View, and the Analysis of Sacred Symbols. *The Interpretation of Cultures: Selected Essays* (United States: Basic Books, Library of Congress 1977), 127–37.

George, Nelson. 2004. *The Death of Rhythm & Blues.* New York: Penguin Books.

Gibbs, Joe. 2006. Personal Interview.

Gilroy, Paul. 2002. *The Black Atlantic: Modernity and Double Consciousness.* London and New York: Verso.

Golding, P., and G. Murdock. 2000. Culture, Communications and Political Economy. *Mass Media and Society.* 3rd ed. Ed. J. Curran and M. Gurevitch. New York: Oxford University Press.

Goodison, Bunny. 1990/2006. Personal interview.

Gray, Ann. 2003. *Research Practice for Cultural Studies: Ethnographic Methods and Lived Cultures.* London, Thousand Oaks and New Delhi. Sage Publications.

Guilbault, Jocelyne. 1996. *Beyond the World Music Label: An Ethnography of Transnational Musical Practices.* Beitrag zur Konferenz Grounding Music, Mai, Autorin & FPM 1996. http:www2.hu.berlin.de/fpm/text/guilbau.htm.

Guins, Raiford, and Omayra Zaragoza Cruz, ed. 2005. *Popular Culture: A Reader.* London: Sage Publications.

Hall, Peter. 2000. Creative Cities and Economic Development. *Urban Studies* 37, no. 4 (April): 639–49. http://usj.sagepub.com/content/37/4/639.citation.

Hall, Stuart. 1996. Minimal Selves. In *Black British Cultural Studies: A Reader,* edited by Houston A. Baker Jr, Manthia Diawara and Ruth H. Lindeborg, 114–19. Chicago: University of Chicago Press.

———. 1997. The Television Discourse – Encoding and Decoding. In *Studying Culture: An Introductory Reader.* 2nd ed. edited by Ann Gray and Jim McGuigan, 28–34. London: Arnold.

Harrington, Lee, and Denise Bielby, ed. 2001. *Popular Culture: Production and Consumption*. Oxford: Wiley Blackwell.

Harriott, Derrick. 2006. Personal interview.

Hebdige, Dick. 1993. *Subculture: The Meaning of Style*. London and New York: Routledge.

———. 2000. *Cut 'N' Mix: Culture, Identity and Caribbean Music*. London and New York: Routledge.

Hegarty, Paul. 2008. *Noise/Music: A History*. New York: Continuum.

Hennion, A. 1983. The Production of Success: An Anti-Musicology of the Pop Song. *Popular Music* 3 (1983): 158–93.

Henry, Paget. 2000. *Caliban's Reason: Introducing Afro-Caribbean Philosophy*. New York and London: Routledge.

Henry, William (Lez). 2006. *What The Deejay Said: A Critique From the Street!* London: Nu-Beyond Ltd.

Henriques, Julian. 2011. *Sonic Bodies: Reggae Sound System, Performance Technique, and Ways of Knowing, The Continuum International Group*. New York.

Hesmondhalgh, David. 2007. *The Cultural Industries*. 2nd ed. London: Sage Publications Ltd.

Hibbert, Toots. 2005. Personal interview.

Hirsch, Paul M. 1970. *The Structure of the Popular Music Industry*. Survey Research Centre, Ann Arbor: University of Michigan

———. 1990. Processing Fads and Fashions: An Organization – Set Analysis of Cultural Industry Systems. *On Record: Rock, Pop, & The Written Word on Record*. Ed. Simon Frith and Andrew Goodwin, 127. London and New York: Routledge.

Holness, Winston. 2002. Personal interview.

Howard, Dennis. 2007. Punching For Recognition: The Juke Box as a Key Instrument in the Development of Popular Jamaican Music. *Pioneering Icons of Jamaican Popular Music* Ed. Clinton Hutton. Special issue of *Caribbean Quarterly* 53, no. 4 (Dec. 2007).

Howard, James. 1990. Personal interview.

Hull, Geoffrey P. 2001. *The Recording Industry*. 2nd ed. New York and London: Routledge.

Hunter, Christopher. 2001. Copyright and Culture. http://www.asc.upenn.edu/usr/chunter/copyright and culture.html.

Hurst, Walter E. 1977. *Copyright: How to Register Your Copyright & Introduction to New & Historical Copyright Law*. Hollywood, California: Seven Arts Press.

Hutton, Clinton. 2007. Forging Identity and Community through Aestheticism and Entertainment: The Sound System and the Rise of the DJ. *Pioneering Icons of Jamaican Popular Music*. Ed. Clinton Hutton. Special issue of *Caribbean Quarterly* 53, no. 4 (December).

IIPA. 2004. New Economic Study Reveals the Copyright Industries Continues to be a Driving Force in the U.S. Economy. <http://www.iipa.com/pressreleases/2004 Oct7 Siwek.pdf>

IFPI. 2000. The Recording Industry in Numbers 2000: The Definitive Source of Global Music Market information. International Federation of the Phonographic Industry. London.

James, C.L.R. 1989. *The Black Jacobins: Toussaint L'Ouverture and the San Domingo Revolution*. 2nd ed. Revised. New York: Vintage Books.

Jaszi, Peter. 1991. Towards a Theory of Copyright: The Metamorphoses of 'Authorship.' *Duke Law Journal*, 455–502.

Jenson, J. 1984. 'An Interpretive Approach to Cultural Production.' *Interpreting Television*. Ed. W. Rowland and R. Watkins. London: Sage.

Johnson, Richard, et al. 2004. *The Practice of Cultural Studies*. London, Thousand Oaks and New Dehli: Sage Publications.

Jones, Leroi. 1970. *Black Music*. New York: Apollo Editions.

———. 2002. *Blues People: Negro Music in White America*. New York: Perennial.

Katz, David. 2000. *People Funny Boy: The Genius of Lee 'Scratch' Perry*. Edinburgh: Payback Press.

———. 2003. *Solid Foundation: An Oral History of Reggae*. London: Bloomsbury.

Kellner, Doulgas. n.d. Cultural Studies, Multiculturalism, and Media Culture. http://www.gseis.ucla.edu/faculty/kellner/essays/culturalstudiesmulticulturalism.pdf.

Kelly, Norman. 2005. Notes on the Political Economy of Black Music in Rhythm and Business. *The Political Economy of Black Music*. Ed. Norman Kelly. New York: Akashic Books.

Kozul-Wright, Zjelka, and Lloyd Stanbury. 1998. Becoming a Globally Competitive Player: The Case of the Music Industry in Jamaica. *UNCTAD Discussion Papers* 138.

Krasilovsky, M., William and Sidney Shemel. 2003. *This Business of Music: The Definitive Guide to the Music Industry*. 9th ed. New York: Watson-Guptill Publications.

Kumler, Emily. 2004. Consumers' Digital Rights Debated. *PC World*. http://www.pcworld.com/resource/article/O.aid.11612.00asp

Laing, Dave. 2004. Copyright, Politics and the International Music Industry. In *Music and Copyright*. 2nd ed., edited by Simon Frith and Lee Marshall, 70. Edinburgh: Edinburgh University Press.

Laing, Tony. 2003. Personal interview.

Landry, Charles. 2000. *The Creative City: A Toolkit for Urban Innovators*. London: Earthscan.

Lehman, Bruce. 2002. Modernizing Jamaica's Property System: A Report and Recommendation. http://www.iipi.org/reports/Jamaica Report.pdf

Leslie, Colin. 2006. Personal interview.

Leyshon, Andrew. 2001. Time-space and Digital Compression: Software Formats, Musical Networks, and the Reorganisation of the Music Industry. *Environment and Planning A* 33:49–77.

Lewin, Olive. 1974. Folk Music Research in Jamaica. In *the Black Communication: Dimensions of Research and Instructions*. Ed. J. Daniels. New York: Speech Communication Association.

Llewllyn, Meic. 1998. Beyond The Transatlantic Model: A Look at Popular Music as if Small Societies Mattered. *Critical Musicology Journal*. http://www.leeds.a A Virtual Journalc.uk/music/Info/CMJ/Articles/1998/02/01.html.

Litman, Jessica. 1999. The Public Domain. *Emory Law Journal* 39 (1990). Yma Sumac, in P. Hayward, ed., Widening the Hoirzons, 965–1,023. *Exoticism in Post-War Popular Music*. John Libbey, Sidney, 45–71. 1999.

Litter. 2003. Personal interview.

Luigi, Russolo. 2007. *The Art of Noises: Futurist Manifesto in Audio Culture: Readings in Modern Music*. Ed. Christoph Cox and Daniel Warner. New York and London: Continuum.

Manley, Michael. 1982. *Jamaica: Struggle in the Periphery*. London: Third World Media.

Mann, Larisa. 2000. Intellectual Property and the Jamaican Music Industry. MA Diss. London School of Economics.

Manuel, Peter, Kenneth Bilby and Michael Largey. 2006. *Caribbean Currents: Caribbean Music from Rumba to Reggae*. Kingston: Ian Randle Publishers.

Manuel, Peter, and Wayne Marshall. 2006. The Riddim Method: Aesthetics, Practice, and Ownership in Jamaican Dancehall. In *Popular Music*, 447–70. Cambridge University Press.

Marginalised, James. 2008. The Circuit of Culture – A Brief Study Case. United Kingdom. November 7. http://www.ebooks4free.net/ebooks/Circuit.htm

Markowitz, Robin. n.d. Canonizing the Popular. http:www.culturalstudies.net/canon.html.

McMillan, John. 2005. Trench Town Rock: The Creation of Jamaica's Music Industry. http://facultygsb.stanford.edu/mcmillan/personal_page/documents/Jamaicamusicpaper.pdf. Stanford: Stanford University Graduate School of Business.

Middleton, Richard. 1996. Over and Over, Notes Towards a Politics: Survey the Ground, Charting Some Routes. The Open University.

Miller, Herbie. 2003. In Search of the Lost Riddim: Caribbean Culture, Jazz and Socio-Political Activism across the Atlantic World. MA Diss. New York University.

———. 2006. Personal interview.

Miller, Paul D. 2007. Algorithms: Erasures and the Art of Memory. In *Audio Culture: Readings in Modern Music*. Ed. Christoph Cox and Daniel Warner. New York and London: Continuum.

Ministry of Justice. 1911. Copyright Act 1911 (Copyright, Act Consolidation), 16 December.

Mock Yen, Alma. 2002. *Rewind: My Recollections of Radio and Broadcasting in Jamaica*. Kingston: Arawak Publications.

Morley, David, and Kuan-Hsing Chen, ed. 1996. *Stuart Hall: Critical Dialogues in Cultural Studies*. London and New York: Routledge.

Morse, David. 1971. *Motown and the Arrival of Black Music*. New York: Macmillan.

Neely, Daniel T. 2007. Calling All Singers, Musicians and Speechmakers: Mento Aesthetics and Jamaica's Early Recording Industry. In *Pioneering Icons of Jamaican Popular Music*. Ed. Clinton Hutton. Special issue of *Caribbean Quarterly* 53, no. 4 (2007).

———. 2008. Mento, Jamaica's Original Music: Development, Tourism and the Nationalist Frame. PhD Diss. New York University.

Negus, Keith. 1996. *Popular Music in Theory: An Introduction*. Connecticut: Wesleyan University Press.

Nettl, Bruno. 2005. *The Study of Ethnomusicology: Thirty-one Issues and Concepts*. Urbana and Chicago: University of Illinois Press.

Nettleford, Rex M. 1972. *Mirror Mirror: Identity Race and Protest in Jamaica*. New York: William Marrow & Company, Inc.

———. 1978. *Caribbean Cultural Identity: The Case of Jamaica*. Jamaica: Institute of Jamaica. 2003 re-issued Kingston: Ian Randle Publishers.

———. 1995. *Inward Stretch Outward Reach: A Voice From the Caribbean*. New York: Caribbean Diaspora Press.

———. 1996. Black Classicism and the Eurocentric Ideal: A Case for Integrative Inquiry into Black Expressive Arts. *Lennox Avenue – A Journal of Inter-artistic Inquiry* 2.

Okpewho, Isidore, Carole Boyce Davies and Ali A. Marui, ed. 2001. *The African Diaspora: African Origins and New World Identities*. Bloomington and Indianapolis: Indian University Press.

Oliver, Paul. 1998. *The Story of the Blues*. Boston: North-Eastern University Press.

Pallas-Loren, Lydia. 2006. The Purpose of Copyright. *Outer Space Quarterly*. http://www.open-spaces.com/article-v2n1-loren.php.

Passman, Donald S. 2008. *All You Need to Know About The Music Business*. 6th ed. London: Penguin Books.

Patterson, Orlando. 1994. Global Culture and the American Cosmos. The Andy Warhol Foundation for the Visual Arts Paper Series on the Arts and Society.
Payne, Michael, ed. 1997. *A Dictionary of Cultural and Critical Theory*. United Kingdom: Blackwell Publishing.
Perry, Lee. 2007. Personal interview.
Peterson, Richard A. *The Production of Culture*. Beverly Hills: Sage Publications, 1976.
———. 1982. Five Constraints on the Production of Culture: Law, Technology, Market, Organizational Structure and Occupational Careers. *Journal of Popular Culture* 16:143–53.
———. 1985. Six Constraints on the Production of Literary Works. *Poetics* 14:45–67.
———. 1997. *Popular Music is Plural*, Popular Music and Society 21, Issue 1 (Spring): 53–58.
———, and David G. Berger. 1990. Cycles in Symbol Production: The Case of Popular Music. In *On Record: Rock, Pop, & The Written Word*, edited by Simon Frith and Andrew Goodwin, 140. London and New York: Routledge.
Porter, M.E. 1985. *Competitive Advantage: Creating and Sustaining Superior Performance*. New York: Free Press.
Power, Dominic, and Daniel Hallencreutz. 2002. Profiting from Creativity the Music Industry in Stockholm, Sweden, and Kingston, Jamaica. *Environment and Planning A* 34 (May 2002): 1833–54, 23.
Power, Dominic, and Allen Scott. 2004. *Cultural Industries and the Production of Culture: Routledge Studies in International Business and the World Economy*. Taylor and Francis.
Pratt, Andy C. 2002. The Cultural Economy: A Call for Spatialized 'Production of Culture' Perspectives. *International Journal of Cultural Studies* 34 (May): 1833–54, 23. London: London School and Planning A.
Quinn Patton, Michael. 2002. *Qualitative Research & Evaluation Methods*. London: Sage Publication.
Reed-Danahay, D. E., ed. 1997. *Auto-Ethnography: Rewriting the Self and the Social*. Oxford: Berg.
Reynolds, Julian. 2006. Personal interview.
Roberts, Michael. 2005. Papa's Got a Brand New-Bag: Big Music's Post-Fordist Regime and the Role of Independent Music Labels. In *Rhythm and Business: The Political Economy of Black Music*, edited by Norman Kelly. New York: Akashic Books.
Rose, Mark. 1993. *Authors and Owners: The Invention of Copyright*. London: Harvard University Press.

Rossman, G., and Rallis, S.F. 1998. *Learning in the Field: An Introduction to Qualitative Research.* Thousand Oaks, CA: Sage.

Ryan, J. 1985. *The Production of Culture in the Music Industry.* New York: University Press.

Samuelson, Pamela. n.d. WIRED: The Copyright Grab. Washington DC: Wired Digital, Inc. 4.01: 1994-2003. http://www.wired.com/wired/archive/4.01/white.paper_pr.html.

Sardar, Ziauddin, and Borin Van Loon. 2004. *Introducing Cultural Studies.* United Kingdom: Icon Books.

Scott, Brendan. 2001. Copyright in a Fictionless World: Towards a Rhetoric of Responsibility. http://firstmonday.org/issues/issue6 9/scott/index.html.

Shank, B. 1994. *Dissident Identities: The Rock 'n' Roll Scene in Austin, Texas.* Hanover, NH: Wesleyan University Press.

Skjerdal, Terje Steinulfsson. 1998. Structures vs Interaction, Political Economy vs Cultural Studies. http://www.oocities.com/capitohill/2152/pol_ec.htm.

Slack, Jennifer Daryl, and J. Macgregor Wise. 2007. *Culture and Technology: A Primer.* New York: Peter Lang.

Snead, James. 1981. On Repetition in Black Culture. *American Literature Forum* 15, no. 4:146–54. St Louis; St Louis University Press.

Spitzer, J., and R. Walters. 2003. Making Sense of American Song (2003). http://historymatters.gmu.edu/mse/songs/.

Stanley, Steven. 2007. Personal interview.

Stokes, Martin, ed. 1997. *Ethnicity, Identity and Music: The Musical Construction of Place.* Oxford and New York: Berg Publishers.

Stolzoff, Norman C. 2000. *Wake the Town and Tell the People: Dancehall Culture in Jamaica.* Durham, North Carolina: Duke University Press.

Storey, John. 2001. *Cultural Theory and Popular Culture: An Introduction.* England: Pearson Education.

Taylor, Don. 1994. *Marley and Me.* Kingston: LMH Publishing.

Taylor, Timothy D. 2007. *Beyond Exoticism: Western Music and the World.* Durham and London: Duke University Press.

Toop, David. 2000. *Rap Attack 3: African Rap to Global Hip Hop.* London: Serpent's Tail.

———. 2001. *Ocean of Sound: Aether Talk, Ambient Sound and Imaginary Worlds.* London: Serpent's Tail.

———. 2007. Replicant: On Dub in Audio Culture. *Readings in Modern Music.* Ed. Christoph Cox and Daniel Warner. New York and London: Continuum.

Toots and The Maytals. 1969. Sweet and Dandy. Beverley Record, 45 rpm.

Tosh, Peter. 1981. Reggaemylitis. EMI/Rolling Stones, 45 rpm.

Towse, Ruth. 2004. *Copyright and Economics in Music and Copyright*. 2nd ed. Ed. Simon Frith and Lee Marshall. Edinburgh: Edinburgh University Press.

Toynbee, Jason. 2000. *Making Popular Music: Musicians, Creativity and Institutions*. London: Arnold.

———. 2004. *Musicians in Music and Copyright*. 2nd ed. Ed. Simon Frith and Lee Marshall. Edinburgh: Edinburgh University Press.

———. 2006. One Step Forward? Translating Jamaican Popular Music in the Core. *The Society for Caribbean Studies Annual Conference Papers* 7. Ed. Sandra Courtman. http:www.scsonline.freeserv.co.uk/olvol7.html>.

———. 2007. *Bob Marley: Herald of a Postcolonial World*. UK: Polity Press.

———. 2008. Copyright and the Conditions of Creativity: Social Authorship in Reggae Music and Open Source Software. CRESC Working Paper Series. Working Paper No. 60. CREWC, Open University. November. http://www.cresc.ac.uk.

Tuomola, A. 2004. Disintermediation and Re-intermediation of the Sound Recording Value Chain: Two Case Studies. *Journal of Media Business Studies* 1, no. 1:27–46.

Vaidhyanathan, Siva. 2001. *Copyrights and Copywrongs: The Rise of Intellectual Property and How It Threatens Creativity*. New York and London: New York University Press.

Van Der Merwe, Peter. 1989. *Origins of the Popular Style: The Antecedents of Twentieth Century Popular Music*. Oxford: Oxford University Press.

Van Pelt, Carter. 2006. Towards Conventional Copyright System: The Jamaican Experience with Rights Management and a New Law. MA Diss.

Veal, Michael E. 2007. *Dub: Soundscapes and Shattered Songs in Jamaican Reggae*. Middleton, CT: Wesleyan University Press.

Vignolle, J. 1980. Mixing Genres and Reaching the Public: The Production of Pop Music. *Social Science Information* 19, no.1:79–105.

Wallis, Roger. 2004. Copyright and the Composer In *Music and Copyright*. 2nd ed. edited by Simon Frith and Lee Marshall, 103–22. Edinburgh: Edinburgh University Press.

Wallis, Roger, and Krister Malm. 1990. Patterns of Change. In *On Record: Rock, Pop, & The Written Word*. edited by Simon Frith and Andrew Goodwin, 160. London and New York: Routledge.

West, Kanye. 2005. Touch The Sky. Roc-A-Fella Records, Island Def Jam, 45 rpm.

Whitburn, Joel. 1996. *The Billboard Book of Top 40 Hits: Fascinating Trivia and Complete Chart Data about the Artists and Their Songs 1955 to the Present*. 6th ed. United States: Billboard.

White, Timothy. 1984. *Catch a Fire: The Life of Bob Marley Illustrated*. Great Britain: Corgi Books.

Wikström, Patrik. 2006. Reluctantly Virtual: Modelling Copyright Industry Dynamics. Doctoral diss. Karlstad University.
Williams, Raymond. 1983. *Culture & Society: 1780–1950*. New York: Columbia University Press.
Wise, J. Macgregor. 1997. *Exploring Technology and Social Space*. Thousand Oaks CA: Sage Publication.
Witter, Earl. 2006. Personal interview.
Witter, Michael. 2004. Music and the Jamaican Economy. Prepared for UNCTAD/WIPO.
Woodmansee, Martha. 1984. The Genius and the Copyright: Economic and Legal Conditions of the Emergence of the 'Author'. *Eighteenth-Century Studies* 17, Issue 4 (Summer): 425–48. http:www.compilerpress.atfreeweb.com/nno%20 Woodmansee%.
Yin, Robert. 2003. *Case Study Research: Design and Method*. 3rd ed. London Sage Publication.

MAGAZINES
Reggae Directory Publications 4, no. 2, June 1992
Reggae Directory Publications 5, Fall 1994
Reggae Times 3 no: 8, Summer 2002
Reggae Times 2 no. 9, Christmas 1999

Index

Adami: and royalties for Jamaican musicians, 134
Adorno, Theodor: analysis of the culture industry, 42, 176
Affiliated Artistes Union: and copyright advocacy, 129, 130
Africa: foundation of the Black Atlantic, xxii, xxiv
Albarran, Allan: and music industry revenue, 80
A-list musicians: in the Kingston music business, 92
All You Need to Know about the Music Business, 16
Alleyne, Mike: analysis of the *Catch a Fire* album, 56–57; on the cultural dilution of reggae, 66–68; and collectivity in Jamaican society, xxvii; on dub, 165–66
American Library Association: and duplication of information, 137
American Society of Composers Authors and Publishers (ASCAP): and royalties for Jamaican music, 134
Anglo-American music industry: interaction with Jamaican music, 42, 97–98, 102–104, 116–17
Anglo-American culture: distributor's preference for, 100; and popular music, 52
Apprenticeship structure: in the creative process, xxviii
Appropriation (1957–60): period of cultural production, 10, 41, 43–47, 167
Aquarius: recording studio, 30, 59
Arista: and cross-over reggae, 105

Artiste & repertoire agent (A&E): role of the, 20
Artistes: free movement of, 99
Assemblages: in Jamaica's music, 160
Atlantic Record: and Lt. Stitchie, 65
Attali, Jacques: on technology and mass production, 149–50, 154
Authors and Owners: and copyright, 31–32
Author: copyright and the, 126–27, 137–45; literary property and the, 139–41
Auto-ethnography: research methodology, xviii–xxiv

Bandele, Lassana, xviii
Barthes, Ronald: and the concept of the author, 139–40
Beckford, Theophilus: and development of ska, 48
Beat Street: Orange Street as the, 72
Beat Street mode: of production, 97–99, 102–106
Beatles, The: and adoption of reggae, 52
Belafonte, Harry: and calypso in the USA, 41
Bennett, Mikey, 105
Berne Convention for the Protection of Literary and Artistic Works, 130, 133
Bettig, Roland: and copyright, 31
Bhabba, Homi K.: on hybridity, 155
Bilby, Kenneth: on Jamaican music technology, 18
Big Youth, 87
Biographies: on Jamaican musicians, 15–16
Black Atlantic: Caribbean cultural interaction with the, xxviii, xxiv, 47,

51–52; Gilroy and the concept of the, 161–62
Black electronic: concept of the, 162
Black music: exploitation of, xxx–xxxi, 176–77
Blackwell, Chris: and Jimmy Cliff, 54; and crossover reggae acts, 61, 96, 97
Boney M: and reggae, 60
Bop Girl Goes Calypso, 41
Boothe, Ken, xvii
Bradshaw, Sonny: and copyright advocacy, 129–30; and the PRS, 114
Branson, Richard: reggae acts signed by, 60
Britain. See British pop market and United Kingdom
British Broadcasting Corporation (BBC): and airplay of reggae, 104
British pop market: and 'My Boy Lollipop', 50; reggae and the, 52, 60–61
Broadcast Music Incorporated (BMI): and royalties for Jamaican musicians, 134
US collecting agency, 21
Brodber, Erna: and collectivity in Jamaican society, xxvii
Brown, Overton 'Scientist', 166
Bunny and Scully: and early Jamaican music, 44
Business management training: need for, 174
Butterfly: Marley and Streisand's, 57–58
Burning Spear: compositional style of, 119–21

Campbell, Cecil 'Prince Buster'. See Prince Buster
Chang, Heewon: on auto-ethnography, xix, xx
Calypso: album by Belafonte, 41
Calypso: in Hollywood, 1; influence on Jamaican music, xxii, xxxii, 41
Calypso Joe, 41

Campbell, Live 'Kool Herc': on the influence of the sound system and studio techniques, 168
Capitol Records: Lord Flea's contract with, 41
Caribbean: intellectual interaction with the USA and Black Europe, xxiii
Caribbean Currents: Caribbean Music from Rhumba to Reggae, 18
Caribbean Diaspora: and Jamaican music, 49–50
Caribbean music: the creative process in, xxii–xxix; Jamaican music and the influence of, xxii–xxiii, 76, 147; repetition in, xxv–xxvi
Catch A Fire: versatility and range of Marley's, 56–57, 96, 97
Caves, Richard: and musicians in the value chain, 92
Censorship: and copyright legislation, 142–45
Circular income flow: Witter's, 25–27, 89
Circularity: concept of, xxv
Chang, Kevin O'Brien: on the Jamaican music business, 17
Channel One, xviii, 87, 94
Chen, Wayne: on Jamaican music business, 17
Chic: and the influence of dub, 159, 160
Chin, Clive, 158
Chin, Vincent: and the development of the recording industry, 94
Chude-Sokei, Louis: on dub, 166–67, 171, 172
Clapton, Eric: and the Kingston music scene, 58
Clarke, Augustus, 105; on record touting, 90
Class: and the jukebox culture, 152–53, 156
Cliff, Jimmy: international success of, 53–54; and Island Records, 50; and ownership rights, 128

Collecting agencies: in the music industry, 21, 131–32
Colonialism: and Jamaican's musical preference, 145; music as resistance to, 74–76
Columbia Records: and cross-over reggae, 105
Commercial Records: and cross-over reggae, 105
Communal authorship: and copyright, 140, 145; in the Kingston music scene, xxvii–xxix, 117–23
Communality: and the creative process, xxvii–xxix, 123, 124, 136
Compact disc (CD): emergence of the, 11
Compass Point studio: and the influence of Jamaican studio techniques, 169–72
Composer: concept of the genius, 140
Conglomerates. See Entertainment conglomerates.
Conservative Connoisseur Limited, 73; and copyright issues, 3
Consumers' rights: vs copyright holders' rights, 141–42
Consumption orthodoxy: theory, 91
Contractual arrangements: in the music industry, 4, 8, 81–83, 88, 113
Convention for the Protection of Producers of Phonograms Against Unauthorized Duplication, 130
Coombe, Rosemary L.: and copyright, 31
Cooper, Carolyn: analysis of Jamaican popular music, 33–34, 121–22
Copyright: definition of, 110, 134; earnings from, 132, 133, 145n; and the internet, 141–42; in the Jamaican music business, 176, 180–81; ownership, 112–13
Copyright Act (1913), 4, 8, 123, 127, 180

Copyright Act (1993), 8, 111, 129–30; amendment of the, 131, 132
Copyright Act of Britain (1911), 111
Copyright legislation: and the music industry, xxx, xxxii, 3, 4–5, 22, 31–32, 123–45
Copyright Office of Trinidad and Tobago (COTT), 21
Copyright protected works: revenue from, 23, 26–27, 79–80, 84
Copyright Unit: establishment of the, 130
Copyrighting Culture: The Political Economy of Intellectual Property, 31
Copyrighting culture, 110–46
Count Ossie and the Mystic Revelation of Rastafari: influence of, 108n; and the feedback process, 151
Courlander, Harold:
Covers: in the Jamaican music business, 115–17, 124
Cowan, Tommy: and copyright, 3
Coxsone Downbeat, xvi, 44
Creative cauldron: Kingston as, xxii, xxiv, xxii, xxiv, xxviii, 72–76, 117–23, 155–69, 180
Creative city: concept of the, 30, 73–74; Kingston as the, xv, xxii–xxiv, xxii, xxiv, 72–76, 155–69
Creative echo chamber: communal authorship in the, xxvii–xxix, 117–23; copyright dynamics in the, 1141–17; Kingston as the, 72, 75–76, 92–106, 108n, 178; technology appropriation in the, 148–69; theoretical research mechanism, xxi–xxii, xxiv
Creative field: in the music network value chain, 24
Creative imagination: and the appropriation of technology, 148; in the Kinston echo chamber, 160, 179; in the music industry, 176; Nettleford's thesis of the, xviii, 48

Creative managers: and copyright, 113; in the music industry, 12, 85
Creative process: collectivity in the, xxvii; in the Kingston music industry, 129, 178–80
Cross-over reggae acts, 58–61, 65–66, 67, 68, 95–96, 104–106. See also Gentrified reggae
Crystallisation: in early Jamaican music, 116, 117
Cuban music: Jamaican music and the influence of, xxxii
Cultural industries: concept of, 176; organisational structure of the, 84–85; strengthening links with international, 182; UNESCO and the role of the, 14
Cultural artefacts: long playing records as, xix
Cultural dilution: of reggae, 60–61, 66–68, 95–96
Cultural hierarchy: in Jamaican musical preferences, 154–55. See also Class
Cultural Imperialism: and popular music, 52; radio and, 90–91
Cultural invasion: in the Kingston Echo Chamber, 156–57
Cultural Life of Intellectual Properties: Authorship, Appropriation and the Law, 31
Cultural production: concept of, xxx–xxxi, 140–141; in Kingston, xxv; ownership of, 142; periods of, 9–11, 37–68, 84–92, 178–80; and technology, xxx, 5–7, 11, 22, 28–29, 139, 149–50, 166, 173, 180
Cultural studies perspective: of music research, 32

Daley, Diane: and copyright advocacy, 130
Daley, Lloyd: and sound system movement, 46
Dancehall: emergence of, 11, 62–65, 98

Deejays: emergence of, 62
Dekker, Desmond: overseas success of, 51, 97, 104
Diaspora: Caribbean music and the, xxiv, 49
Digital Consumers Rights Act (2003, USA), 142
Digital technology: and cultural dilution, 67; and dancehall, 64–65; emergence of, 11, 22
Disintermediation: concept of, 22–23, 108n
Distribution challenges: 100
Distributors: role of, 20, 100. See also Promoters
Dodd, Clement 'Sir Coxsone: and the contracting of artistes, 81–82, 92; and the copying of riddims, 124; and copyright protection, 126; and dancehall, 63; and the recording industry, 94, 108n; and ska, 48; and the sound system, 43–44, 46
Dowe, Brent, xvii
Dub: creation of, xxiv, 7, 29, 40, 157, 161–62; and the remix culture, 165–69, 171, 180
Dub plates: revenues from, 26; and the value chain, 93–94
Dunbar, Sly: and the jukebox, 157
Dunkley, Errol, 67
Dumbarton Avenue: as a creative hub, 74
Durie, Alec: recording of mento music, 40
Dynamic Recording Studio, xviii, 30
Dynamic Sounds, 94, 95, 104; and the Rolling Stones, 58
Dynamics: recording studio, 30

Economic model: value chain, 80
Eccles, Clancy, 87
Edwards, Bernard: and the dub aesthetic, 167–68
Edwards, Vin: and the sound system culture, 46

Ellis, Alton: and the music business, 82, 108n
Engineer: dub and the studio, 166
Entertainment conglomerates: influence of transnational, 178, 181–82; and intellectual property, 133
Epic Records: Shabba Ranks's deal with, 65
Exodus: album of the year, 15
Exploitation: of reggae music, 2; of musicians, 123–26

Fabulous Five, 105
Fair use: copyright and the concept of, 142, 144
Feedback loop: in the music industry, 79, 88–89, 102, 106, 151–52
Feeder sound systems, 46, 101
Federal Records, 95; and Ernie Smith, 104; revolutionary techniques of, 30, 94; and Tomorrow's Children, 105
Ffrench, Robert, 87
Flack, Roberta: adaptation of reggae, 58–59
'Foggy Road': compositional structure of, 119–20
Folk Culture (pre-1950s–1956): period of cultural production, 10, 39–42
Foote, Keith: tour of Germany, 60
Foreign markets: and intellectual property rights, 132
Fox Hi Fi, xvi
France: reggae in, 59
Franklin, Aretha: adaptation of reggae by, 55
Free movement: of artistes, 99
Freelancers: in Jamaican music industry, 4
Freire, Paulo: on cultural invasion, 156–57
Frith, Simon: on exploitation of black musicians, 126; and international influences on popular music, 43
Front Line: Branson record label, 60

Frost, Robert: definition of disintermediation, 22

Gainsborough, Serge: and reggae in France, 59
Gardiner, Boris: early releases by, 104
Geneva Convention, 130
Genius author: concept of the, 139–40
Genius composer: concept of the, 140
'Genius of Love': and the influence of Jamaican studio techniques, 169
Genre blending: concept of, 67
Gentrified reggae, 105; and the jukebox culture, 153
Geospatiality: concept of, xxii–xxiii
Ghettoes. See Inner cities
Gibbs, Joe: and copyright infringement, 133
Gilroy, Paul: and the Black Atlantic concept, 47, 50
GG Records: and the recording industry, 94, 95
Global interaction (2001–present): period of cultural production, 11, 66–69
Goat Head Soup: adaptation of reggae in Rolling Stone's, 58
Goldman, Vivien: on Marley, 15
Goodison, Bunny: and the jukebox culture, 156
Gopthal, Lee: and cross-over reggae acts, 61
Gordon, Barry, xviii
Greensleeves Records: and reggae music, 95
Gross, John M.: *This Business of Music*, 16
Grove Music, 30
Guibalt, Jocelyn: and transnationalism, 68–69

Haitian music: Jamaican music and the influence of, xxiii
Half Way Tree: as a creative centre, 74

Hall and Oates: adaptation of reggae, 59
Hallencreutz, Daniel: and Kingston as a creative city, 30
'Hard Road to Travel': and Cliff's success, 50–51
Harder They Come, The: international success of, 54
Harriott, Derrick, xvii, 87
Harry J All Stars: and cross–over reggae, 105
Hesmondhalgh, David: perspective on cultural production, 37–38, 85, 150
Hinze, Chris: and reggae, 59
Hip hop: influence of the Jamaican music culture on, 168–69
Hirsch, Paul: and the popular music industry model, 19–21
History: of Jamaican music, 1–2, 9–11, 37–67
Hebdige: on the use of repetition in Caribbean music, xxv–xxvi; and the sound system, 88–89
Henriques, Julian: on the use of repetition in Caribbean music, xxvi
Hollywood: and calypso, 42
Holness, Winston 'Niney', 87; and cross-over reggae, 105; and paying of advances, 81–82
Hometown Space Odyssey: Tubby and the, 163, 168, 169
Hookim brothers: and the recording industry, 87, 94
Howard, Dennis: professional journey of, xv–xx
Howard, James: music career of, xv–xvi, 156
Hugh Roy, xvii
Hussey, Dermott: on Marley, 16
Hull, Geoffrey: *The Recording Industry*, 28; on recording industry income streams, 79–80; and system theory, 78, 82

Humphries, Tony: on the influence of dub, 169
Hutton, Clinton: and Kingston as a creative centre, 75
Hybridisation: and appropriation of technology, 148; and cultural production, 154–55, 173–74
Hypercreativity: concept of, xxv, xxvii

I Can See Clearly Now: incorporation of reggae in, 55
Identity: music and cultural, 28, 57
Identity Race and Protest: and identity crisis in the Caribbean Creole culture, 28
Independent record companies: and the Anglo-American music industry, 97; and radical music, 94–95
Idler's Rest, 73
Income streams: in the recording industry, 79. *See also* Revenue
Indigenous structure: need to formalise Jamaica's, 183
Industry structure: Jamaican music, xxx, 3–4
Inner Circle: and ownership rights, 128, 173
Inner cities: cultural output of Jamaican, 29–30; and dancehall, 62–65
Innovation (1961–69): period of cultural production, 10, 48–52
Institute of Caribbean Studies (ICS): Howard and the, xviii
Intellectual property rights: and the music industry, 3, 4–5, 21–22, 130, 131
International Convention on the Protection of Producers, Performers and broadcasting Organization, 130
International Intellectual Property Alliance (IIPA): and copyright advocacy in the USA, 132
International Intellectual Property Organization: recommendations by the, 131–32

Index | **205**

International outreach: of dancehall, 65–66, 67; of Jamaican music, 57–58, 168–69, 180
Internationalisation (1970–1980): period of cultural production, 10, 52–61, 96
Internet: copyright and the, 141–42
Inward Reach Outward Stretch: A Voice from the Caribbean: and marginalisation of the Caribbean, 48
Irie FM: Howard and, xviii
Isaacs, Gregory, xvii
Island Records: and cross-over reggae, 105, 109n; Cliff and, 50–51, 54; Marley and, 56; reggae acts, 60, 61, 66, 95, 97
'Israelites': overseas success of, 97, 104

Jamaica Association of Authors and Publishers (JACAP), 21, 131
Jamaica Broadcasting Corporation (JBC): Howard and the, xvii
Jamaica Federation of Musicians (JFM), 4; and copyright advocacy, 129
Jamaica Intellectual Property Rights Office (JIPO): establishment of the, 132
Jamaican Copyright Licensing Agency (JAMCOPY): establishment of the, 131
Jamaican music: business, 1–4; dynamics of, xvi, 94–106; early songs in, 45; exploitation and, xxx; international artists and the, 57–61; revenues from, 4, 9, 80; scholarship on, xv–xvi, 18–35; and world popular culture, xv. *See also* Black music
Jamaican music system: contractual arrangements in the, 4, 8, 81–83, 113–14; fragmentation of the, 176–77; copyright protection in, 111–14, 134–45; organisational structure of, 11–12, 84–88, 178–80, 181; roots of the, 2–4; value chain dynamics in the, 18–35, 72–106. *See also* Industry structure
Jamaican Musical Rights Administration (JMRAS), 131
Jamaica Performers Administration Society (JPAS), 131, 133
Jamaica Recording and Publishing Company (Jamrec), 126
James, Lloyd 'Jammy', 166
Jagger, Mick: and the Kingston music scene, 58
Jazz Hut, The, xvii
Johnson, Cluett: and ska, 48
Jones, Simon: on the sound system, 91
Jukebox: and class, 152–53, 156; and cultural production, 174; culture in the echo chamber, 149–60; and dub, 157; genesis of the, 150; Jamaican music and the, 6, 17, 18; and phonographic orality, 157–58; promotion by, 100; revenues from the, 26; vs the sound system, 156–59
Jukebox karaoke, 157

Kevorkian, Francois: and the influence of Jamaican studio techniques, 167, 169
Khouri, Ken: recording of mento music, 39–41; and development of the recording industry, 94, 104
King Tubby. *See* Ruddock, Osbourne
Kingston: copyright protection in, 111–14; as the creative city, xv, xvi– xiv, 58, 72–76, 94–106, 108n, 178–80; the dancehall scene in, 2–35; international artists in, 59–60; jukebox culture in, 149–60; and the remix culture, 165–69; a singles-driven market, 104
Kingston Echo Chamber. *See* Kingston
Kingston music industry value chain, 80–91

KLAS FM: Howard and, xx
Kong, Leslie: and early Jamaican music, 47, 51, 97
Kojak, 87
Kozul-Wright: and the Kingston music industry, 96
Krasilovsky, M.W: *This Business of Music*, 16

Laing, Tony: and copyright legislation, 3, 73
Lawes, Henry "Junjo": father of dancehall, 62–63, 64, 105
Lazarus, Ken: early songs by, 105
Lee, Bunny, 105; and copyright ownership, 126
Lee, Byron, 87; and copyright ownership, 126; and ska, 104
Legislation. *See* Copyright legislation
Levan, Larry: and the influence of the Jamaica studio system, 161
Lewin, Charles, xvii–xviii
Leyshon, Andrew: and the musical network value chain, 23–25
Listening: in music research, xx
Literary property: and the author, 139–40
Literature: on Jamaican music, 14–35
'Live Loving': and dancehall, 63
Live performances: revenue from, 84
'Lollipop Girl': and the sound clash, 44–45
Lord Flea: and calypso in Hollywood, 1, 42; and early mento recordings, 40, 41

Magnetic tape: technology in the music industry, 6
Manuel, Peter: and riddim method of production, 98
Manley, Prime Minister Michael: and the non-aligned movement, 61–62
Mann, Herbie: and the Kingston music scene, 58

Mann, Larissa: and copyright in Jamaica, 31–32
Market: music industry and the, xxx, 40; reggae and the international, 55
Marketing alliance: need to establish a, 183
Marley, Bob: biographies, 15; catalogue, 179; and Eric Clapton, 58; global influence of, xv, 56–57; global earnings, 9; and Nash, 55–56; songwriters skills, 58–59; and Streisand, 57–58
Marshall, Wayne: and riddim method of production, 98
Mass production: creativity and, 176–77; technology and, 139, 149–50
Matador, Lloyd, 105
Mechanical rights societies: the role of, 22, 110
Media channels: role of, 20–21
Mento: and the jukebox culture, 153; radio and, 17; recordings, 10, 39–42
Microphone: technology in the music industry, 6
Middleton, Richard: on art of iteration, xxiv
Miller, Herbie: on Caribbean influence of Jamaican music, 155
Minott, Sugar: the father of dancehall, 62, 63
Mirror Mirror: Identity race and Protest: on ska, 51
Mixing Lab: recording studio, 31
Morgan, Derrick: singer producer, 87; and free movement of artistes, 99
Morris, Sylvan: and the dub version, 169
Motta, Stanley: and development of the recording industry, 94; recording of mento, 39–40
Motown: Jamaican music and the influence of, 117
Multiple-simultaneity mode of production, 94–106, 123, 128–29, 166

Multinational conglomerates; control of the music industry by, 28–29. *See also* Entertainment conglomerates

Music: and global cultural interconnection, 43

Music business: development of the Jamaican, xv, 94–106, 178–80; technology appropriation in the, 147–69; value chains, 80–85. *See also* Kingston and Jamaican music and Recording industry

Music Mountain: recording studio, 31

Music research, xx

Musical networks value chain, 23–25

Musicians: in the value chain, 92–93. *See also* A-List musicians and B-list musicians

'My Boy Lollipop': and international exposure of ska, 50, 96

Nash, Johnny: adaptation of reggae, 55–56

National Task Force on Collective Administration of Copyright: establishment of the, 131

Neighbouring rights: definition of, 110–11; in the Kingston music industry, 113–14

Neoinnovation (1981–2000): period of cultural production, 11, 61–65

Nettleford, Rex: and the creative imagination, xviii, 48, 184; and ska, 51

Noises in the Blood: Orality, Gender and the "Vulgar" Body of Jamaican Popular Culture: analysis of Jamaican music, 33

Non-linear mode of production, 97

North Atlantic: interaction with Jamaican music, 55

North Parade: music businesses on, 73

Ocean of Sound by, 29

Occupational categories: in the Kingston music industry, 87–88

Omnibus Trade and Competitiveness Act (1988, USA): passing of the, 132

One Love Concerts, 2

'OO7 Shanty Town': overseas success, 51, 97, 104

Open domain: copyright in the, 127; music production in the, 97–100, 123–27, 140, 180, 181; and the version, 162

Orange Street: the Beat Street, 72, 73–74, 75, 106, 106n, 179

Owners and executives: in the music industry, 12, 85, 181; and copyright, 113

Ownership: copyright and, 126–27, 181

Pama Records: and reggae music, 95

Paragons, xvii

Parkes, Arkland 'Drumbago': and development of ska, 48

Participant observation, xvi–xxi

'Pass the Dutchie': and copyright issues, 128–29

Passman, Donald: *All You Need to Know about the Music Business*, 16

Patra, 181

Patterson, Orlando: and regional cultural interaction, xxiii

Paul, Sean, 181

Peech Boys: influence of dub culture on the, 168

Pen, Dawn, 181

Performing arts schools: need for, 183

Performing rights societies: role of, 22, 110–11

Performing Rights Society (PRS), 3, 111, 114

Perry, Lee 'Scratch', xvii, 87; and recording technology, 7, 163–65, 170–71

Perry methodology, 163–65, 170–71, 180

Personnel: music industry, 12–13

Peterson, Richard: and the production of culture concept, 148–49
Pettibone, Shep: and the influence of Jamaican studio techniques, 167, 169
Phonograpic synthesis: concept of, 118
Phonographic orality: concept of, 157
Piracy. See Covers
Planno, Mortimer: influence of, 108n
'Poor Mi Israelite': overseas success of, 51
Popular culture: Bob Marley and world, xv
Popular music industry model, 19–21
Porter, Michael; on value chain analysis, 18–19, 77–78
Pottinger, Sonia: record producer, 72
Power, Dominic: and Kingston as a creative city, 30
Primary creative personnel: in the music industry, 12, 85
Prince Buster, xvi, xvii, 87, 105; and the jukebox technology, 18; and ska, 48; and sound the system, 43–44
Producer/owner: in the music business, 181
Production of culture. See Cultural production
Production houses: emergence of, 3; and copyright issues, 124–27
Profiting from Creativity – The Music Industry in Stockholm, Sweden and Stockholm, 30
Promoters: role of, 20
Publisher: role of the, 21; in the traditional value chain, 22

Race: and Jamaican music production, xxix–xxx
Radio: influence of AM, 43; in the music industry, 6, 21–22, 90–91, 103. See also Media channels
Ranglin, Ernest: and ska, 48, 50
Rap: influence of the sound system culture on, 168–69

Rastafarians: influence of, 108n
Record company: role of the, 20, 22, 24
Record touting, 90
Recorded material: revenue from, 79–80, 83–84
Recording Industry, The, 28
Recording industry: copyright in the, 110–46; Kingston, 30, 40; structure of the, 28–29, 94–106; value chain analysis in the, 77–91
Recording studios: emergence of, 3; and technical innovation, 7–8
Records: farm workers and the importation of, 43; the music industry, 5. See also Vinyl records
Redwood, Ruddy: and discovery of the instrumental version, 161
Reggae: cultural dilution of, 60–61, 66–68; development of, 10, 48, 51–52; internationalisation of, 51–61, 62
Reggae covers: by international singers, 57–59
Reggae festival: concept, 2
Reggae revenues: global, 2, 9
Reggae Sunsplash, 2
Reggaemylitis, xx
Reggaeton: development of, 67–6
Reid, Arthur 'Duke': and the music business, xvi, xvii, 92; and the sound system, 44
Re-intermediation: concept of, 22–23, 108n
Remix culture, 165–69, 171, 180
Repetition: in music, xxiv–xxv
Reproduction stage: of music production, 85
Research: ideas for future, 181–82; on Jamaican music, 7, 8–9, 14–35
Research methodology, xvi–xxi. See also Auto-ethnography and Participant observation
Resistance: music as, 75–76
Revenues: from copyright protected work, 23, 26–27, 79–80; from the

Kingston music industry value chain, 80–85
Riddim method: copying of, 124–26; of music production, 98–99, 122–23
Rights owners: and copyright, 110, 113. See also Mechanical rights agencies and Performance rights agencies.
Riley, Winston: and copyright ownership, 126
Rodgers, Nile: and the dub aesthetic, 167–68
Rocksteady: development of, 10, 48, 51
'Rock Steady': by Aretha Franklin 55
Rolling Stones: adaptation of reggae, 58
Rose, Mark: and the concept of the author, 135; and copyright, 31–32
Ross, Diana: and the influence of dub, 167, 168
Royalties, 22, 138n
Ruddock, Osbourne 'King Tubby': and the version, 162–63, 165–69; recording technique, 7,
Ruddock technique: sound technique, 7, 163, 165–69, 170–71, 172, 180
Russell, Arthur: and the influence of Jamaican studio techniques, 167
Rhythms: revenues from, 81–83
Rhythm & Blues: influence on Jamaican music, 10, 43
Ryan, Bill: on the organisational structure of cultural industries, 84–85

Scholarship: on Jamaican music, xv–xvi, 7, 8–9, 17–18
Scott, Brendan: and the musical network value chain, 23–25
Seaga, Prime Minister Edward: neoliberal agenda, 61; promotion of ska, 104
Shabba Ranks, 65, 181
Shaggy, 87, 180
Shang-hi Solophonic, xvii, 102
Shemel, Sidney: *This Business of Music*, 16

Shervington, Pluto: early songs by, 105
Shot Gun: adaptation of reggae, 59
Simon, Paul: reggae recordings by, 54–55
Singer producers: in the Kingston music industry, 87
Singjaying: phenomenon, 62
Ska: early international exposure of, 1, 96; development of, 10, 48, 50, 104
Skatalites: middle-class rejection of the, 104
Sly and Robbie, 181
Smaditization: early musicians and concept of, 124
Small, Millie: and international exposure of ska, 50
Smart, Philip, 166
Smith, Ernie: early releases, 104
Smith, Simeon, 105
Snead, James: on culture, xxiv
Software: copyright and, 141–42
'Someone Loves You Honey': copyright infringement and, 133
Sonic Sounds: and the recording industry, 94, 108n
Song: value chain and the, 90. See also Voicing
Songwriting formula: North American, 42
Sound Clash: analysis of dancehall music, 33
Sound clash: and the sound system culture, 93
Sound reproduction technology: and creative echo chamber, 149–50, 159
Sound system: and development of dancehall, 62, 63; early development of the, 43–47, 97; revenues from the, 26; and rap, 168–69; and the riddim method of production, 98–99; vs the juke box, 156–58; technology in the music industry, 6, 43, 102, 180; in the value chain, 88–91, 93, 106

Specials: in the recording industry, 81, 93
Spedidam: and royalties for Jamaican musicians, 134
Spreader sound systems, 47, 102
Stranger Cole: and early music industry, 99
Stanbury, Lloyd: and the Kingston music industry, 96
Standard regime: need for a, 182
Stanley, Steven: and the influence of Jamaican studio techniques, 167, 169–72
'Star-bwoy identity: and creative worker, 123, 129
Steely and Cleavie, 105
Stitchie: Atlantic record deal, 65
Stolzoff, xx: analysis of dancehall music, 34
Streisand, Barbara: adaptation of reggae, 57–58
Studio engineer: dub an the role of the, 166, 173
Studio One: and the recording industry, 94, 95, 105; Sugar Minott and, 63
Stranger Cole, xvii
'Sweet and Dandy': composition style in, 118–19
Swinging Calypso, 41
Symbol creators: and the appropriation of technology, 148
System theory: and value chain analysis, 78

Talking Heads: influence of Jamaican studio techniques on the, 169
Taylor, Don: on Marley, 16
Taylor, Timothy: on hybridisation, 155–56
Technical craft workers: in the music industry, 12, 85
Technological culture: theoretical framework of, 149
Technology: appropriation of, 147–74; and cultural dilution, 67; cultural production, 149; and mass production, 147, 173; in the music industry, xxx, 5–7, 11, 22, 28–29; and versioning, 161–62. See *also* Digital technology
Tek-no-li-gy process, 166, 173, 180
Third World, 105; and ownership rights, 128
Third World technological sophistication: concept of, 171, 172
This Business of Music, 16
Thompson, Errol, xvii–xviii, 7, 166, 169, 172, 180
Thompson, Tony: and the influence of reggae, 167–68
'Till the End of Time': and early Jamaican music, 44–45
Tin Pan Alley, 10
Tipper Tone, xvi
Tomorrow's Children: and cross-over reggae, 105
Tom Tom, Bunny, 166
Tom Tom Club: case study, 169–72
Tonybee, Jason: on sound system, 91; on Marley, 15–16; on phonographic orality, 157
Toop, David: *Ocean of Sound* by, 29
Toots and the Maytals: compositional style of, 118, 121
Trade Related Aspects of Intellectual Property Rights (TRIPS), 130
Traditional music industry value chain, 21–23, 79–80
Training: need for business management, 182
Transnationalism: concept of, 68
Treasure Isles: innovative techniques of, 105
Trojan Records: and cross-over reggae acts, 61, 95, 105
Tubby, King: See Ruddock, Osbourne
Tuff Gong: and the recording industry, 31, 94

United Kingdom (UK): Caribbean diaspora and Jamaican music, 49–50; reggae bands in the, 53
UK Copyright Act (1911), 4, 22
United Nations Educational, Scientific and Cultural Organization (UNESCO): and the cultural industries, 14
United States of America (USA): calypso in the, 41; Caribbean cultural interaction with the, xxiii, 54–55; intellectual property protection in the, 132–33; jukebox culture in the, 150–51
Urban youth culture: influence of the Jamaican music culture on, 168

Value chain dynamics, 18–27, 92–106, 172–73
Van Der Merwe, Peter: on repetition in Caribbean music, xx
Van Pelt, Carter: and copyright in Jamaica, 31–32
Venture capital fund: necessity for a, 182
Version: creation of, xxiv, 122, 124, 157, 161–62; Tubby and the, 163
Virgin Records: and cross-over reggae, 105; and reggae acts, 95
Visualisaton: as a research tool, xxvi
Voicing: revenue from, 81–83
Volcano Hi Power: sound system, 63

Wake the Town and Tell the People: Dancehall Culture in Jamaica, 34–35
Wailers, xvii, 87; international success of,

Wallis, Roger: and conglomerates in music business, 179; and the traditional music industry value chain, 21–23, 79–80
West Atlantic cosmos: Patterson and the, xxiii
Whitney, Malika Lee: on Marley, 16
Wikström, Patrik: and popular music research, 15
Williams, Winston, xviii
Willis: and the sound system, 91
Witter, Earl: and copyright advocacy, 130
Witter, Michael: and access to information, 182; circular income flow, 25–27, 89; perspective on cultural production, 38–39
Wonder, Stevie: adaptation of reggae, 58–59
Wonderful World Beautiful People: overseas success of, 53
Woodmansee, Martha: and the concept of the author, 139
Work for hire: principle, 111–12, 181
World Intellectual Property Organization (WIPO), 4; and copyright in Jamaica, 130
World Trade Organization: and intellectual property, 130

Yellowman: and dancehall, 63–64
Young, Desmond: and copyright advocacy, 129–30
Youthman Promotion: Sugar Minott and, 63

www.ingramcontent.com/pod-product-compliance
Lightning Source LLC
Chambersburg PA
CBHW072030170426
43200CB00025B/2395